Biz Stone

BLOGGING
Genius Strategies for Instant Web Content

201 West 103rd Street, Indianapolis, Indiana 46290
An Imprint of Pearson Education

Boston • Indianapolis • London • Munich • New York • San Francisco

New Riders
www.newriders.com

Publisher
David Dwyer

Associate Publisher
Stephanie Wall

Production Manager
Gina Kanouse

Acquisitions Editors
Kate Small
Elise Walter

Development Editor
Laura Loveall

Senior Marketing Manager
Tammy Detrich

Publicity Manager
Susan Nixon

Senior Project Editor
Lori Lyons

Copy Editor
Kathy Murray

Senior Indexer
Cheryl Lenser

Manufacturing Coordinator
Jim Conway

Book/Cover Designer
Alan Clements

Cover Photographer
Photo of Biz Stone by Steve Snider

Proofreader
Julia Prosser

Composition
Amy Parker

This book is dedicated to Marc Ginsburg,
for the role he played in introducing me
to the world of weblogs.

BLOGGING
Genius Strategies for Instant Web Content

Contents At a Glance

Table of Contents

About the Author

Biz Stone is a designer and writer with a keen interest in personal publishing. Upon discovering the blog format in 1999, Biz embraced it and went to work cultivating the medium first as a creative consultant to various blog providers and associated projects—such as Xanga.com, Blogger.com, WebCrimson.com, BlogBuddy, and others—and then as a freelance writer promoting the growing blog phenomenon. For daily updates and more about Biz, check out his blog, bizstone.com.

About the Technical Reviewers

These reviewers contributed their considerable hands-on expertise to the entire development process for *Blogging: Genius Strategies for Instant Web Content*. As the book was being written, these dedicated professionals reviewed all the material for technical content, organization, and flow. Their feedback was critical to ensuring that *Blogging: Genius Strategies for Instant Web Content* fits our readers' need for the highest-quality technical information.

Monsur Hossain graduated from the University of Illinois in 1998, after which he programmed warehouse and website software for Amazon.com. He is currently a programmer for the blog community Xanga.com and the web content management system WebCrimson.com. His latest endeavor is Bloglet.com, an email subscription service for blogs. In his free time, Monsur enjoys catching up on the newest music and movies, banging on his guitar, challenging his roommate to chess, and just reading a good book. Monsur resides in New York City and keeps his own blog at www.monsur.org/; he can be reached by email at monsur@bloglet.com.

Matthew Langham was born in England but has been living in Germany since 1976. He has been working in the IT business since the mid-1980s. Matthew wrote his first book on the Internet in 1993 and has since published several articles on the Net and related themes. His last claim to fame was co-authoring a New Riders book on the open-source project, *Cocoon: Building XML Applications* (2002, ISBN: 0735712352). He currently leads the open-source group at S&N AG, a software company in Paderborn, Germany. Matthew is particularly interested in the corporate use of weblogging for knowledge management and communications. He also thinks Biz "rocks Natick."

Acknowledgments

First, a special thanks to Molly Holzschlag for assigning me my first paid writing gig and for being such a supportive, encouraging, and generous editor.

This book wouldn't exist without the vision and talent of Kate Small. Kate, thank you! It's important to know, as well, that Laura Loveall is largely responsible for anything good in this book—the rest is all me. In addition, my tech editors Monsur and Matthew really know their stuff (you should thank them as much as I do). As always, a general thanks to Livia McRee for not going insane. If you had to be around me as much as she is, you'd know that's quite an accomplishment.

Thanks to New Riders Publishing and thanks, as well, to everyone who reads my blog!

Tell Us What You Think

As the reader of this book, you are the most important critic and commentator. We value your opinion and want to know what we're doing right, what we could do better, what areas you'd like to see us publish in, and any other words of wisdom you're willing to pass our way.

As the Associate Publisher for New Riders Publishing, I welcome your comments. You can fax, email, or write me directly to let me know what you did or didn't like about this book—as well as what we can do to make our books stronger.

Please note that I cannot help you with technical problems related to the topic of this book, and that due to the high volume of mail I receive, I might not be able to reply to every message.

When you write, please be sure to include this book's title and author as well as your name and phone or fax number. I will carefully review your comments and share them with the author and editors who worked on the book.

Fax:	317-581-4663
Email:	stephanie.wall@newriders.com
Mail:	Stephanie Wall
	Associate Publisher
	New Riders Publishing
	201 West 103rd Street
	Indianapolis, IN 46290 USA

Introduction

The challenge of getting published by traditional media is daunting. A proposal or finished work must somehow make it through what seems like a labyrinth before it arrives in the hands of a person who has the vision and power to get it into the machine that is publishing.

Think of all the great writers and artists—maybe you're one of them—struggling to be heard. Beyond that, there are talented people who would write more if they had a forum. There are also people who are experts in certain areas, and all that potentially valuable content stays trapped within them because they don't have an outlet. They don't have access to the "machine."

Actually, they do. Blogging is the easiest way to bring yourself to the Web and make your voice heard. I began blogging simply because it was so easy. All I had to do was type in a box and click a button, and my text was published to the Web and incorporated into a community of people waiting to read it. If my words had evaporated into a void, that would have been the end of it.

But they didn't. They were ingested, perused, and linked to. Commented on, emailed about, and repeated. All this was very exciting. It was as if I were a published author. My interest in publishing to my blog snapped to attention—I had an audience. Out of the woodwork came opinions, editorials, and thoughts on things I hadn't realized I even had thoughts about. My blog was helping me shape my character, and I found myself publishing several times a day to a responsive audience—not a wide audience mind you, but responsive nonetheless.

Today's Web has become fertile soil for personal publishing. Not only is it easy to get your voice out, but your voice is heard, acknowledged, and in many cases, responded to by interested, intelligent readers who have found your work most likely because they sought it out and are happy to have found it.

Blogging is the new and future platform for instant publishing, but it is not alien technology. After all is said and done, a blog is a web page. The same, but totally different. A blog is alive; it's you—on the web. Blogs are fast, simple, and streamlined web pages that funnel your thoughts and work to the web as quickly as you can type. What makes a web page a blog is the format and the frequency of updates. It's the proliferation of tools and services that make it so easy to create and maintain blogs that has created the phenomenon.

In this book, we'll usually use the term blogs instead of weblogs. But keep in mind that the terms are interchangeable; they are the same. The word *weblog* is a contraction of web log, and the word *blog* somehow became more popular than weblog. So don't be confused!

Who Should Read This Book

This book is an emergency kit for anyone disappointed with their flat, static home page, and it's a hands-on manual for people who are already blogging. If you're new to web building and you can barely work email, don't despair, there are chapters in this book that will get you publishing a sporty new blog in minutes—from your mind to the web in moments: guaranteed. That's what blogging is all about.

On the other hand, if you're a webmaster, web designer, or you're currently an active blogger and you're looking for some projects to tear into, then some of the more advanced chapters are designed just for you. Open to the page that documents how to build a user-commenting system into your blog, look up how to achieve an elegant type treatment for your posts using CSS, or read up on blogs for knowledge management so that you can impress your boss at work. In short, let *Blogging: Genius Strategies for Instant Web Content* be your guide to... well, blogging!

Overview

There are hundreds of thousands of people blogging even as we speak. Some estimates put the number at more than a million. This is up from about a dozen in 1999. So it's safe to say there's something to this blog thing.

With this book, I've created a guide to the world of blogs, starting with the newbie and steadily growing more advanced. The chapters of this book are separated into four main parts.

All the chapters in Part I, "Basic Blogging," are intended for readers who have little or no experience with blogging. Chapter 1, "The Blog Phenomenon," provides some background information on why blogging grew so rapidly into a phenomenon and who was behind it. Chapter 2, "Quick Start to Creating Your First Blog," walks you through setting up a blog of your own and assumes that you know nothing (about blogging that is). Chapter 3, "Overview of the Major Blog Providers," breaks down some of the features of the bigger players in the blogging space. I chose these providers because they have staying power and a large user base. I wrote Chapter 4, "A Blogger's Guide to Simple HTML," based on my own experience and the questions of friends I have introduced blogging to. This chapter gives you the "inside scoop" on how to achieve many of the tools of the trade everyone takes for granted, such as linking and displaying images. After you've glimpsed what you can do, you'll want to know more; so the following chapter, Chapter 5, "Blog Design 101," brings you up to speed and gives you inspiration for your own blog design.

All the chapters in the next part of the book, Part II, "So, You Already Know How to Blog!" are intended for more experienced bloggers. We start out with Chapter 6, "Blogging with Style," an introduction to the art and craft of excellent presentation of text and how to achieve it on your blog. The next chapter is very American, Chapter 7, "Blogging for Dollars." I'll tell you how to pave your blog with gold. After the excitement of that, you'll want to hunker down and learn about "Working with Blogger Archives," a way to make older entries readily available—this is extensively covered in Chapter 8. The intricacies of "Group Blogging" will be revealed to you in Chapter 9, and that will flow effortlessly into Chapter 10, "Corporate Blogging," where we'll talk about the amazing potential of blogs as knowledge management. At which point you'll want to add some dynamic features like the ability to search, fear not: Chapter 11, "Adding Dynamic Features," is there for you. Next, you'll be ready for Chapter 12, which involves finding your voice, learning the do's and don'ts of writing on the Web, building tiny helper programs, and other tips for "Better Blogging." And let's not forget Chapter 13, "Increasing Traffic on Your Blog," because after all, you will want people to read your work.

After we get into Part III, "Power Blogging," the advanced bloggers will start having their field day. Learn how to syndicate your blog for a broader reach in Chapter 14, "Syndicating Your Blog," group multiple blogs onto one page in Chapter 15, "Sideblogs, Email Blogging, and Blogging Alternative Interfaces," and grow beyond just a blog and into site-wide content management in Chapter 16 "Beyond the Blog". Then we'll learn about building blog-related applications with XML-RPC in Chapter 17, "Building a Blog-Related Application: Bloglet," and finish up the whole book with a bunch of blog goodies in Chapter 18, "Blog Goodies." As you'll see in this chapter, you can even post to your blog with AOL Instant Messenger and email. There are also ways to syndicate your blog so that the information you put into it is broadcast to an even wider audience.

But that's not all! Appendix A, "Blog Web Links," in Part IV, "Appendix," is yours if you act now! The appendix is chock-full of everything that I couldn't fit into the other chapters but is still fantastic stuff that you can't blog without.

Take this book with you on your journey, use it to inspire you, use it when you forget how to include an image in your post, or keep it handy just for the appendix. Many of the chapters stem from questions bloggers inevitably ask. Other chapters are celebrations of blog design or simply suggestions for better blogging. In any case, let this book be your companion as you set out to dig deep into blogging. (Pay no attention to the subliminal messages I have hidden within this book.)

Conventions

Computer books often have individual solutions for presenting information. The sophisticated reader of this particular book will notice that we have developed an individual layout all our own—a certain "style," if you will, to guide you through the realm of blogging.

One of the most important layout conventions is the way that the code is being treated. A lot of the code falls under a numbered listing, like this:

Listing 1.1   Example of a Code Listing

```
javascript:alert('You\'re%20a%20wonderful%20person%20and%20I%20know%
20you%20will%20succeed%20at%20anything%20you%20try!');alert('I%20rea
lly%20mean%20it.');alert('Would%20I%20tell%20you%20that%20if%20it%20
weren\'t%20true?')
```

These code listings are available for download from this book's companion web site, which is located at http://www.blogging.biz. (You can also get to that link when you locate this book at http://www.newriders.com.)

You'll also see that there are two different types of asides. Here are examples of both:

Genius Tip

Example of a Genius Tip
You, too, will be able to claim you are a genius! Being a genius is fun because you're so busy thinking that you don't have to worry about things like clean underwear or showing up to work on time.

> ### You'll See These, Too
>
> Sometimes you and I will need to have a little conversation "off the record." That's when these sidebars come in handy. Be sure to read the sidebars because there may be nuggets of wisdom contained therewithin that transcend the ordinary. Sidebars are not Genius Tips by any stretch of the imagination, but they get the job done nevertheless.

This book also follows a few typographical conventions:

- A new term is set in *italic* the first time it is introduced.

- Program text, functions, variables, and other "computer language" are set in a fixed-pitch font—for example, `<$BlogItemAuthorNickname$>`.

So now you know the secret insider-code that will get you through this book without a hitch. Or do you? Surprises may lurk ahead, but one thing is for sure: You'll be blogging like a champ before you can even put this bad boy down. Now, turn the page!

Part I

Basic Blogging

Chapter 1

The Blog Phenomenon

Maybe you've heard of blogs, and maybe you haven't yet—but you will. I discovered blogging through a web site called Blogger when it launched in 1999, and I have been hooked ever since. I fell in love with this automated method of independent publishing the day I created my first blog. Now, more than two years later, I am still blogging away like a maniac.

Today, blogs are taking over the web at warp speed. Where did they come from? Why are they here? Are blogs merely a means to some devious alien end for humanity? Perhaps. In this chapter, we'll dig into the history and chronology of the blogging revolution, discuss what a blog actually is, tour some good examples of blogs, and find out why they're so popular.

A Guy Named Tim—The Invention of the WWW

Tim Berners-Lee graduated from the Queen's College at Oxford University, England in 1976. He built his first computer with a soldering iron and an old television. Then Tim spent two years with an equipment manufacturer, working on bar code technology. In 1978, Tim wrote some typesetting software.[1]

---

1. *Tim Berners-Lee Bio on the World Wide Web Consortium web site. Available on the Internet:* http://www.w3.org/People/Berners-Lee/

After a few years as an independent consultant, Tim went to work as an engineer at a particle physics laboratory in Switzerland. While there, Tim proposed a global hypertext project. It was designed to allow people to work together by combining their knowledge in a "web" of hypertext documents. This work was started in October 1990, and the program "WorldWideWeb" was first made available on the "Internet" in the summer of 1991. I was mowing lawns that summer.

What was this Tim guy up to? That's right, you guessed it: Tim invented the web. Let's all give him a big round of applause. Good job, Tim! We always knew you could do it. And your mother wanted you to be a doctor? Good thing you didn't listen to her. My mom keeps telling me I should work at the supermarket so I can get 20% off groceries. How will I invent things if I'm too tired from bagging groceries? I'm not doing it. She can't make me.

Figure 1.1 shows a glimpse of what the web looked like in 1992.

Figure 1.1

The Web circa 1992.

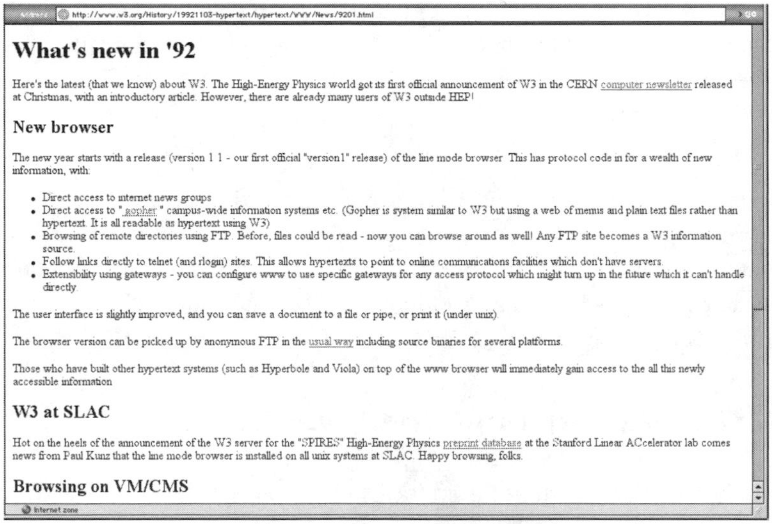
http://www.w3.org/History/19921103-hypertext/hypertext/WWW/News/9201.html

What's new in '92

Here's the latest (that we know) about W3. The High-Energy Physics world got its first official announcement of W3 in the CERN computer newsletter released at Christmas, with an introductory article. However, there are already many users of W3 outside HEP!

New browser

The new year starts with a release (version 1.1 - our first official "version1" release) of the line mode browser. This has protocol code in for a wealth of new information, with:

- Direct access to internet news groups
- Direct access to "gopher" campus-wide information systems etc. (Gopher is system similar to W3 but using a web of menus and plain text files rather than hypertext. It is all readable as hypertext using W3)
- Browsing of remote directories using FTP. Before, files could be read - now you can browse around as well! Any FTP site becomes a W3 information source.
- Follow links directly to telnet (and rlogin) sites. This allows hypertexts to point to online communications facilities which don't have servers.
- Extensibility using gateways - you can configure www to use specific gateways for any access protocol which might turn up in the future which it can't handle directly.

The user interface is slightly improved, and you can save a document to a file or pipe, or print it (under unix).

The browser version can be picked up by anonymous FTP in the usual way including source binaries for several platforms.

Those who have built other hypertext systems (such as Hyperbole and Viola) on top of the www browser will immediately gain access to the all this newly accessible information.

W3 at SLAC

Hot on the heels of the announcement of the W3 server for the "SPIRES" High-Energy Physics preprint database at the Stanford Linear ACcelerator lab comes news from Paul Kunz that the line mode browser is installed on all unix systems at SLAC. Happy browsing, folks.

Browsing on VM/CMS

Internet zone

Through 1991 and 1993, Tim continued working on the design of the web, coordinating feedback from users across the Internet. I continued mowing lawns. Another thing Tim starting doing—and this is of particular interest to you—was link to new sites as they came online.

What was Tim doing? Anyone? Anyone? He was blogging! This was the first blog. So you see, the blog has been around since the beginning of the web; that is how basic the concept is. Today's blogs, and the activity of blogging, have taken on more meaning, but the concept of it all is still very simple and rooted in the beginning and intentions of the web itself.

The Home Page Explosion

In 1996, GeoCities opened up web publishing to the masses (see Figure 1.2). Anyone who wanted to dabble with HTML or play around with an early What-You-See-Is-What-You-Get (WYSIWYG) web editor could do so without the barrier of acquiring and maintaining a dedicated web server.

Figure 1.2

GeoCities opened the floodgates.

People began pioneering the web in the mid '90s as personal home pages were created in droves with thoughts, opinions, and life experiences. They were learning how to build their own sites, experimenting with design, and sharing their voices with the world. It was good stuff.

But there was a problem. After the initial creative burst and FTP upload, most home pages just sat out there like a big, lumpy matzo ball getting dry in the wind. The page would just languish, never to be updated again. Nobody would visit it because they had already seen it—it wasn't changing, so why visit again? The web became littered with freshman attempts at web design and the occasionally funny, but still hideous, "Welcome to my homepage, I KISS YOU!" genre of site.

Tim's invention was growing, but it seemed to be growing out instead of up. Kind of like my friend Marc in fifth grade. But Marc is now very tall and fit, so I can say that without upsetting him. Right, Marc? Marc?

Then there was the whole dot-commerce scramble. Tim's invention became swollen with e-stores, bloated with search engines, and puffed up with mega-portals offering streams of relentless, commercialized content, and "free services." People were trying to pave the web and build a mall. Ultimately, that bubble burst and reality came down hard all around us. But not before some talented people developed some real products and services that were actually good ideas.

Early Blogging before Blogger™

One of the innovations to survive and actually flourish was the concept of a blog as offered to the public in August of 1999 by a small web company called Pyra Labs with a product called Blogger. But before we get to that, let's begin at the beginning.

Legend has it that the term *weblog* was coined by a guy named Jorn Barger in December of 1997. In 1998, there were only a few blogs like those that are flourishing today. So how did it all get started?

Well, Jesse James Garret, a blog author, started a list of people maintaining blog sites like his and later sent that list to another blogger, Cameron Barret. Cameron posted that list on his site and continued to cultivate it. *Cultivate* is a good word here because this little garden started to grow. I started experimenting with blogs at the end of 1999, when there were already multitudes of bloggers. But before that, in November of 1998, it was easy to keep track of all the blogs in existence and even read most them on a daily basis.

Blogging became a small-but-popular publishing format among a certain web crowd. Another early blogger, Peter Merholz, came up with the term *wee-blog*, and it was contracted a little later to *weblog* and then to just plain *blog*. The word *blog* got more publicity and became the preferred term. (I'll be using the term *blog* throughout the book.)

More and more people starting launching their own blogs, and the numbers started racking up. The lists of blogs grew longer every day. Early in 1999, Brigette Eaton published *Eaton Web Portal*, an exhaustive list of bloggers along with a clear and simple definition of a blog: "a site with dated entries." Her definition was accepted, and even more people started creating blogs. Figure 1.3 shows Brigette's current blog.

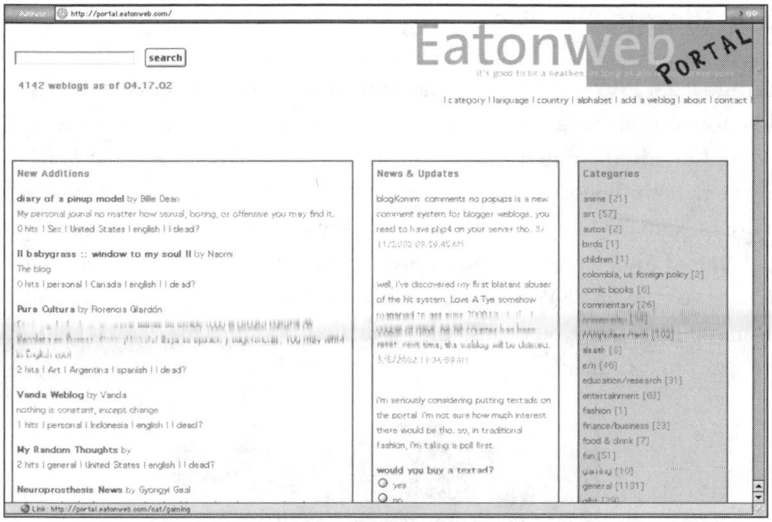

Figure 1.3

EatonWeb Portal today.

The original bloggers were HTML-savvy people who probably worked days in some web-related capacity and would spend their evenings surfing the web and working on their sites. Their blogs were closer to the media-filter variety. That is, they were a combination of annotated links to news articles and interesting sites with the occasional personal thought or maybe an essay. This was to be a model for future bloggers, or at least a jumping-off point.

The typical blogger at this point served as a guide to the Internet, bringing his or her readers to unexplored sites on the web or news articles on a subject of particular interest. The links would, of course, include commentary. Early bloggers often had an area of expertise and would follow a topic or several topics with their blog, making the blog a valuable resource to anyone else in that field. A blog became an easy way to make a name for yourself on the web, not just because you could build a web page, but because you tracked down information of particular interest to you and your audience.

These early bloggers were good at what they did, and this helped to promote the concept of blogs even more. Blogs were practically designed for short, pithy commentary and links, so it was important to be succinct when posting. This had two beneficial results: good, clean writing and great web reading.

At this point, blogs were popular only with a certain crowd—they were not yet a phenomenon. But that was soon to change.

After Blogger™—Blogging for the Masses

On August 23, 1999 a site called Pitas launched. It was a very easy-to-use online tool for building your own blog. Now it was much easier to create a blog, and hundreds of more sites appeared very quickly. In August of the same year, both Blogger and GrokSoup, two more build-your-own blog providers, launched and the popularity of the blog format soared (see Figure 1.4). I started my blog with Blogger around this time. Soon after, software industry veteran Dave Winer and crew announced Edit This Page, yet another personal publishing system, and blogs starting popping up everywhere. They were growing off the charts.

Figure 1.4

Blogger in 1999 before its modern design.

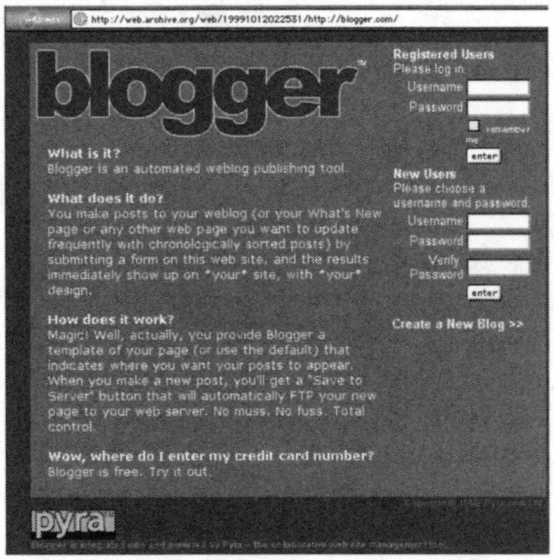

Although all these services helped to promote and grow blogging as a medium, it was Blogger that really propelled the popularity of blogs. Ironically, Evan Williams and his team at Pyra Labs never intended Blogger to be a big product. It was just a side project.

> "We started a company with some notions about better ways to manage information, both for personal and team-based project work. We were developing, basically, Web-based groupware. That morphed into group-ware specifically designed for Web teams, for which we thought Blogger would be one simple piece. Of course, it was the simple thing that proceeded to envelop everything else. After a while, we realized that the blog thing was interesting enough to pursue in itself."
>
> *—Evan Williams, CEO and co-founder of Blogger.com*

The introduction of Blogger had a huge impact. Its simple interface and big empty box for entering a post made creating and posting to a blog so easy that the format of the blog began to take on a more free-form style. People began blogging random thoughts, musings, and things that happened on the subway several times a day. Bloggers took to linking to each other rather than remote corners of the web or news articles, and a strong community began to develop.

There were still a number of serious media-filter type of blogs, but now there was also a growing crowd of diarists filling up the web and strengthening the community. Around this time, Blogger and blogs in general started to get some press. This only made the format more popular. *New Yorker Magazine*, *The New York Times*, *Wired Magazine*, and other traditional print media covered the blog explosion.

In February of 2001, Blogger had a very public break up. Everyone except Evan Williams, the CEO, had to leave the company. Rather than crumble, this garnered even more media attention and new signups continued to flow in.

So, What Is a Blog?

Although the basic concept has been around since the primordial days of the web, today's blogs and the community that binds them are a relatively recent phenomenon. Sites like Blogger.com make it easy for writers to manage and update a site from a web browser. The blog is very much a writer's medium.

Blogs are usually made up of brief, frequently updated posts that are arranged chronologically. The text most often flows vertically down the page, and modules or boxes aligned in columns down the sides of the page very often provide information about the author—favorite links, recently read books, recently seen movies, currently playing albums, and so forth.

Some blogs serve as microportals, publishing commentary and links to other sites relating to a particular topic; whereas others lean more toward online journals, where the content focuses mainly on the thoughts and experiences of the author and the links more frequently point to that person's other projects, essays, and so on. In any case, a blog usually takes on the character of the person or persons that contribute to it because it is so simple to update. This ease of use leads to frequent posting, which creates a fluid, ongoing "conversation" with an audience that helps to bring out the nature of the person "behind the screen."

Blogs feed off the web, digest it, recycle it, and infuse it with new life. Created by feisty, intelligent, opinionated, subversive people—and sometimes small groups—blogs are the future of personal publishing.

How Blogging Works

The idea behind blogging is simple. Software, either web-based or download-able, allows you to work in a friendly, familiar environment, while behind the scenes, your thoughts, links, and pictures are being uploaded, formatted, placed according to your preset design, and saved to your web page. This means that you can surf around as you normally would, occasionally con-tributing to your blog—right from your browser.

Most blogging applications strive to separate form from function by provid-ing an area for you to paste in your template—that is, your page design. Once you've placed your design HTML in the designated area, you don't need to worry about layout (until you want to change it). Blogging software then takes over, merging your dashed-off text with your stored page design and publishing them together to the web as an updated page. With that ease, is it any wonder there has been such an explosion of blogging? If you're new to blogging, fear not—there are plenty of great already-designed templates for you to choose from.

Posting to a blog is easy; that's why bloggers post so frequently. It's usually just a matter of going to a web site, typing information in a form, and clicking Publish or something similar. Then your post is sent right away to your site. It's almost addictive, which is perhaps another reason why blogging has caught on.

Most blogging applications also feature archives. Nothing you publish is wasted. If you incorporate a search feature into your blog, anything you post over the months, years, or decades to come is searchable by keyword or browseable by date. If you keep a blog long enough, your grandchildren might be able to create an artificial intelligence based on your entries. Nice.

Blog Tour

One way to get to know a little more about blogs is to have a look at a few of them. The following blogs are blogs I read on a regular basis. They are not obscure little-known blogs, although I have many like that bookmarked as well. These blogs have been around awhile and are maintained by people who have helped to shape the medium or are just good examples of a blog in action.

Jason Kottke

http://www.kottke.org

Jason is a freelance web designer and developer based in San Francisco. His blog is very popular and has been around for a long time—his archives go all the way back to March, 1998. At kottke.org, you'll find mini-interviews with web developers and Jason's own comments and insights on media, design, and the web.

Evan Williams

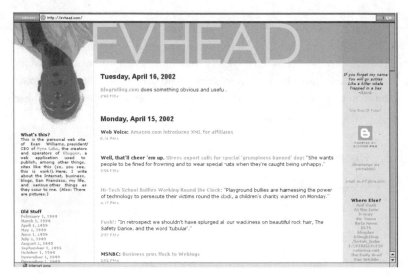

http://www.evhead.com

Evan Williams is the president and CEO of Pyra Labs, the creators and opera-
tors of Blogger. Ev uses his blog to publish what he writes about the Internet,
business, blogs, San Francisco, his life, and various other things. Occasionally
on Ev's site, you will see the odd post like, "testing…testing" or something
similar. It usually means he's planning to launch a new feature to Blogger.

Wil Wheaton

http://www.wilwheaton.net

Wil is an actor you may remember from *Star Trek the Next Generation* or *Stand By Me.* He created his blog so people could get to know the real Wil, not the space-suited, enterprising young ensign, or the sweet, vulnerable little dead body seeker. He taught himself a server-side, HTML-embedded scripting language called PHP so that he could build the site himself, and he spends way too much time blogging. Visit his blog to experience the ups and downs of an actor's life.

Meg Hourian

http://www.megnut.com

Meg Hourian is co-founder of Pyra Labs and co-creator/director of development of Blogger. Her personal site, Megnut, has been around for almost three years, and she's been blogging most of that time. A typical post on Meg's blog might be about the latest book she's reading, a suggestion for improving Amazon.com, or an update on her next speaking engagement.

Molly Holzschlag

http://www.molly.com

Molly is an author, teacher, and speaker with over 20 web development books to her credit. She uses her blog to share web development work as well as personal thoughts. I check in from time to time to find out what she's up to next. It's not unusual to spot a poem on one of Molly's posts.

Biz Stone, Genius

http://www.bizstone.com

I use my blog as a platform to claim genius status. I post something every day. Sometimes it's an idea, sometimes it's an update on a project one of my friends is working on, and occasionally it will be top secret information that I am not at liberty to disclose—but do anyway! I use my blog as my index page and keep other pages such as Essays, Articles, and Web Projects on separate pages. This is common to the blogging set.

MetaFilter

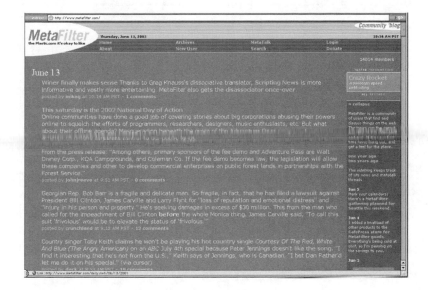

http://www.metafilter.com

MetaFilter is a fantastic group blog that anyone can contribute a link or a comment to. Although a typical blog is one person posting his or her thoughts on the unique things found on the web, MetaFilter breaks down the barriers between people to extend a blog beyond just one person and foster discussion among its members.

Matthew Haughey

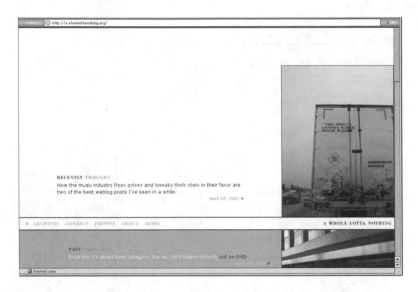

http://a.wholelottanothing.org/

Matthew is the creator of the group blog MetaFilter. This is his personal blog where he blogs about his life, his projects, and various goings-on in the web world.

Paul Bausch

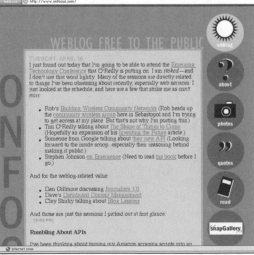

http://www.onfocus.com/

Paul is a web application developer and co-creator/developer of Blogger. He has a lot to say about blogs, and he's been working where databases meet the web for over six years. I like to check in on his blog from time to time because he takes and posts really great photographs.

The Popularity of Blogging

Blogging became a popular web publishing trend in 1999 and grew steadily into large numbers simply by word of mouth or, in this case, word of blog. From the beginning, blogs were on the breaking edge of news, but when news became a lifeline, blogs turned into so much more than simple web publishing.

Blogs in the Midst of Tragedy

On the day America was attacked by terrorists, most major news sites like CNN and the *New York Times* were overloaded and unreachable. Everyone had gone home to turn on the television or sign on to the web. With the big news sites all jammed up, people had to find an alternative. They found blogs. Bloggers were tracking developments as they occurred, and some were logging in with personal experiences from ground zero.

When the dust had settled and the media giants were back on track, more press about blogs started circulating. This was serious attention, and it launched a whole new wave of interest in blogs. The popularity of blogging continued to grow and hasn't stopped since.

Blogs Have Amazing Potential

The popularity of blogging is such that many projects have grown from the phenomenon. In fact, the gurus developing the applications that provide blogging services are usually very supportive of ideas and software that work together and enhance their offerings.

Many blog-related software projects will be covered in this book simply because they complement blogging so well—like user-commenting systems and content syndication. And some of the projects that have stemmed out of the blog phenomenon are just flat-out amazing work by some of the most talented visionaries working with the web today. Blogdex and Daypop, two blog search and statistics tracking sites, are harnessing the power of blogs and changing the way the web works (see Figure 1.5). Google, everybody's favorite search engine, loves blogs and is well aware of their true value to the web.

And people like Matthew Haughey, creator of the group blog MetaFilter, are working with blog-related technology to steer our baby web toward its true potential.

Figure 1.5

Daypop's Top 40 List of popular links in the blog world.

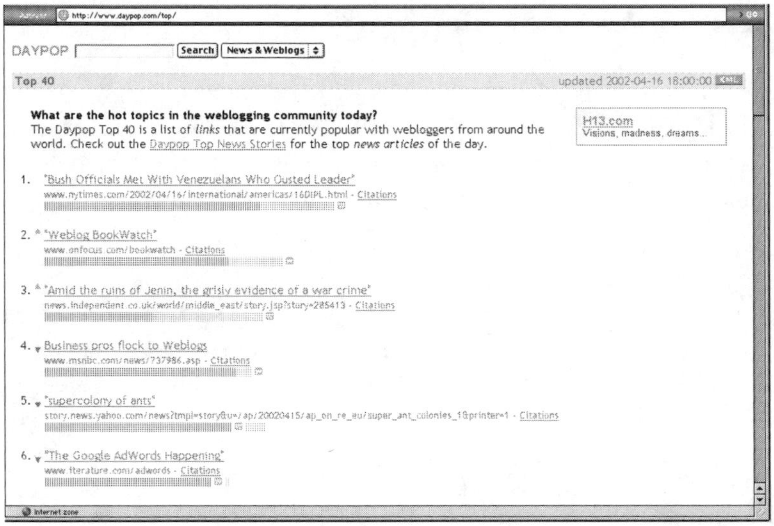

I think Wil Wheaton put it nicely when he gave me his personal assessment of the blog phenomenon, "It's another step in the evolution of communications, like the printing press or fortune cookies."

Chapter 2

Quick Start to Creating Your First Blog

This chapter assumes that you know nothing. Well, nothing about setting up a blog and its associated suite of web related paraphernalia, anyway. There are all kinds of add-ons and enhancements for blogs, but in this chapter, it's all about getting started. After you've tried blogging, you can decide what kinds of enhancements you'd like to make.

For consistency, and because I learned to blog with Blogger, this chapter focuses on getting started using Blogger and Blog*Spot. More blog providers are covered in Chapter 3, "Overview of the Major Blog Providers."

What You'll Need

For this chapter, you need access to the web. You can get access from anywhere: school, work, cybercafe, home, personal hybrid airship, whatever. It doesn't matter. A fast connection is nice but not necessary; a phone line connection with a modem will work fine. As far as software goes, Internet Explorer version 5.x (version 5 and beyond) for Mac or PC is highly recommended. If you have a favorite browser and you don't want to switch, give it a try, but IE 5.x is a better bet.

Getting Started

Many blog newbies are web publishing newbies as well. In other words, they can fill out forms and click buttons online, but the mysteries of actually building and uploading files to the web are beyond them. This is probably why Blog*Spot is such a popular destination for beginners. It's easy to set up and it's free.

Blogger is a leading blog provider that has been making publishing to the web in the form of a blog easy since 1999. Blog*Spot spun off a little later to accommodate the waves of people who wanted to get started without a learning curve. Blog*Spot is a fast and easy way to create a blog. It brings Blogger technology to people who don't already have hosting.

If you're new to blogging and web publishing in general, Blog*Spot is the place to start. So let's get started by creating a blog that doesn't cost you anything and doesn't require you to have web hosting.

Sign Up for an Account

First, you need to create a new user account at Blogger.com (see Figure 2.1). This is just like creating an account at any site. Simply fill out the forms and click Sign Up.

Figure 2.1

Join the Blogger revolution.

Type a name and password (twice) into a form, and you'll be taken to Blogger.com's home page.

> ### Can't Use That Username
>
> If the username you entered is taken, you'll have to pick another in the signup form along the right side of the Blogger.com home page.

Creating a New Blog

Now that you have a username and you're logged in, the next step is to create your blog. In the same area that you originally signed up, you see a Create a Blog link. The following steps take you through the necessary tasks for creating a blog:

1. The first step is to give your new baby blog a name, a description, and mark it as public or private (see Figure 2.2). You can change or edit these settings later. Don't take the "Private" thing too seriously; it only means that you'll be left out of Blogger's directory and recently created or updated lists, which means you shouldn't publish text you don't want anyone to read via Blogger.

Genius Tip

What Should I Put as a Description?
For your description, enter the topics you're most likely to write about on your blog. You can write a bit about yourself so that if people are browsing the directory, they'll get an idea of what they're going to find if they click your link.

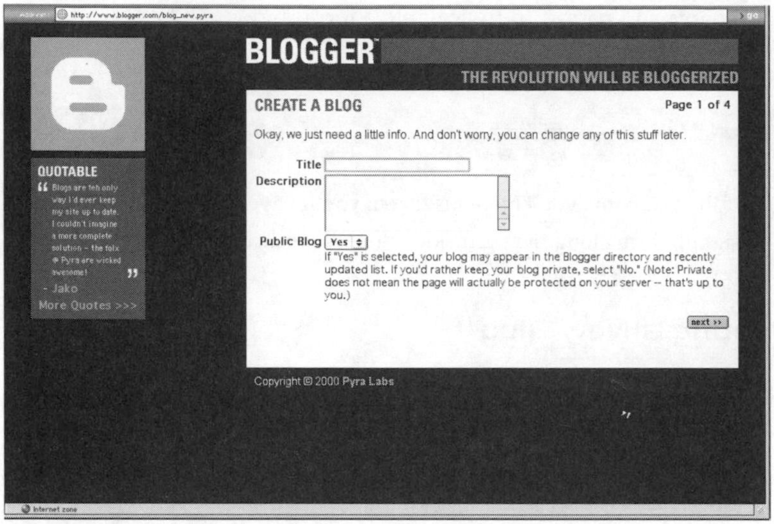

Figure 2.2

Enter your initial settings.

2. Choose to have your blog hosted at Blog*Spot (see Figure 2.3). Remember that Blog*Spot is only a free blog host; they do not offer email or file storage for anything but your blog, and they put banner ads at the top of your blog page. (Ads can be turned off for a small fee.)

Use Blog*Spot for Your Trial Run

Blog*Spot is a great way to try out Blogger and experiment with web building for free. If blogging gets you interested in publishing on the web and you decide that you want to build pages for essays, stories, poems, pictures, and the like, you can shop for a low-price hosting service that provides storage space for all these things, and you can still use Blogger to power your blog. (We'll get into that in a bit.)

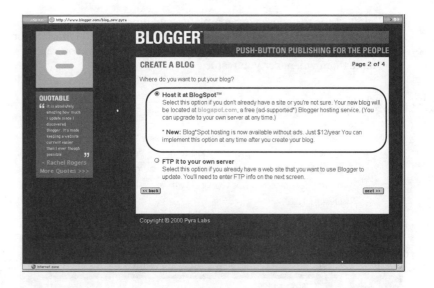

Figure 2.3

Choose BlogSpot.

3. Now, pick a name for your blog's address or URL (see Figure 2.4). It will be `http://yourname.blogspot.com` where yourname will be whatever you type in. As always, read and check the terms of service before you continue.

URL Naming Rules

No punctuation or special characters are allowed in your blog's name. You can change the name later in your settings, but your URL will not change.

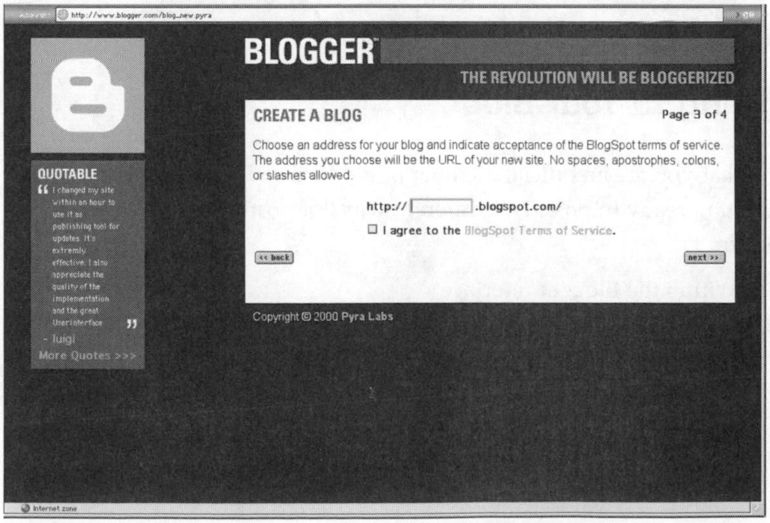

Figure 2.4

Enter the name for your URL.

4. Now it's time to choose your template (see Figure 2.5). The template is the design of your blog. Choose from many pre-designed templates or design your own. The great thing about templates is that you can change them whenever you want.

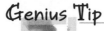

Genius Tip

Start with the Pre-Designed Template

It's best to choose a pre-designed template first to make sure everything is working right, and then swap in your own design later. You can find more information about working with templates in Chapter 5, "Blog Design 101."

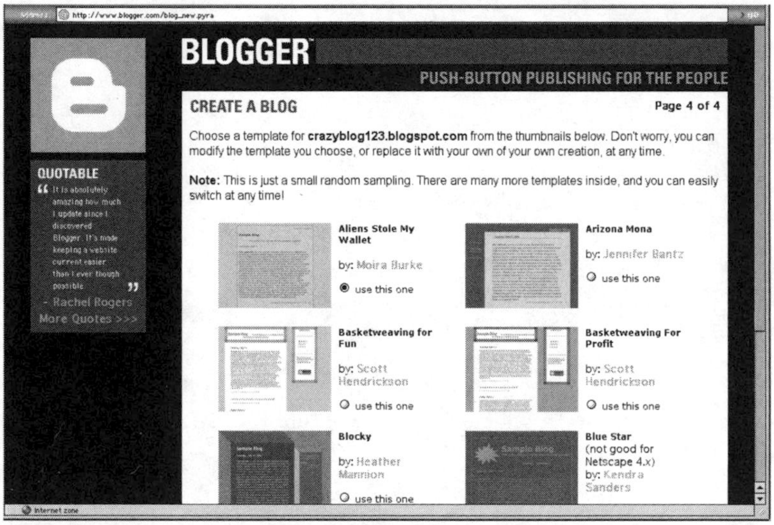

Figure 2.5

Choose your template.

![Screenshot of Blogger Create a Blog page showing template thumbnails]

Posting to Your Blog

Now that you are an official member of Blogger and your account is all set up, you're ready to post. Two different ways of posting are offered by Blogger:

- Within the Blogger interface
- Using the BlogThis! Bookmarklet

Posting from within the Blogger Interface

The easiest way for beginners to post is to use the Blogger interface. When you're signed in to Blogger, you see a list called Your Blogs on the right side of the page (see Figure 2.6). Click your blog's title (or pick one if you've got several), and you'll be "inside" Blogger. This is where you can post, publish, and access all your account settings.

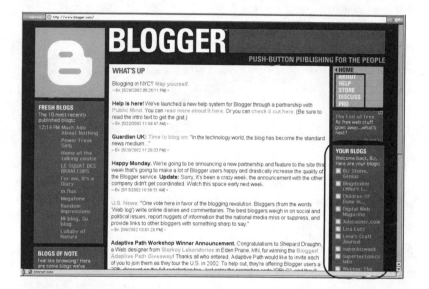

Figure 2.6

Click the titles to access your blogs.

Blogger Puts You There

You'll automatically land "inside" the interface after your initial signup.

Inside Blogger, the interface splits the screen. The top part is a form element you use to enter information, and the bottom part shows your posts (see Figure 2.7). Under each post in the bottom part is a little edit link. When you click edit, the post text is placed in the form above it so that you can work on it.

Figure 2.7

*Inside Blogger's edit-
ing interface.*

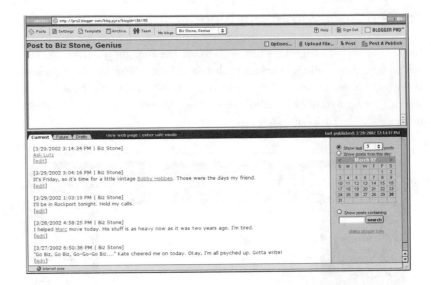

All you have to do is type inside that big empty box. When you're done typing, click the Post button in the upper-right part of the screen. Your text is
being posted to the bottom part, but it has not yet been "published," or sent
to your blog. This is a good time to check for errors and test your links. When
you have something posted but not yet published, an orange button will
appear on the right side of the middle black band that divides the page. After
you click Publish, Blogger sends the post to your blog. The Publish button
appears only when there is something different in your blog that hasn't been
sent to your site. Alternatively, you can click the Post & Publish button to perform both actions at once.

Once you've published, you are officially a blogger! Click the View web page
link, and you will be taken to your blog to see your post in all its published
glory.

Post versus Post & Publish

Clicking Post sends the page only to Blogger, and you'll have to go to
Blogger to publish it to your blog. Choose Post & Publish if you want the
page to show up immediately.

Using the BlogThis! Bookmarklet

The BlogThis! bookmarklet is a little JavaScript application you can put in your browser's toolbar so that you can post to your Blogger site from anywhere on the Net. To use BlogThis!, you'll first need to install it in your Favorites toolbar. BlogThis! is located in the Settings section within the Blogger interface. Simply drag it to your browser's toolbar, and it's ready to use.

Use BlogThis! whenever you discover a web page you'd like to link and comment about in your blog. When you click BlogThis!, a little pop-up appears, and it will already have a link to whatever page your are visiting. It's tricky like that. Just add your comments and click either Post, or Post and Publish. Again, Post only sends the post to Blogger; if you want it to show up right away, click Post & Publish.

Genius Tip

Highlighting Trick
If you highlight text on a page before you activate the bookmarklet, BlogThis! will include the link to the page plus whatever you have highlighted in the form of the pop-up.

Getting Started with FTP

If you already have a web site and you are interested in adding a blog to it, you need to tell Blogger that you want to FTP it to your own site. The process is the same as getting started with Blog*Spot—up until the part about hosting. At that point, you'll need to choose the option to FTP it to your own server.

If you were just testing out Blogger with Blog*Spot and you decide that you like it and would rather have the blog published to your existing or new hosting space, you can change a Blog*Spot-hosted blog to an FTP blog in the Settings tab in Blogger.

What's FTP?

File Transfer Protocol (FTP) is the protocol, or set of rules, which enables files to be transferred from one computer to another. When you use a web hosting company to host your blog, you'll have to set Blogger up to work with an FTP server.

FTP Settings

In Step 3 of the "Creating a New Blog" section, you get the opportunity to input your FTP information. You should be prepared to enter the following information:

- **Your Blog Filename**—This is the name of the file that will be generated by Blogger. This file is called blogger.html by default. To make your blog show up as your home page, you can name it index.html.

- **The Blog URL**—This is the new home of your blog, the web address you will give out to your friends. I prefer my blog to be my home page, so my blog URL looks like this:

  `http://www.bizstone.com/index.html`

- **The FTP Server**—An FTP server is the name of the FTP server where your site is hosted. Sometimes the name begins with the prefix ftp; in my case, it is the following:

  `ftp.bizstone.com`

- **Your Server Path**—This is the exact spot on the server in which you want your files to live. Leave this field blank if you want your blog to be your home page. Blogger will automatically place your file in the root directory of the account. If you'd like your blog in a more specific location on your site, be sure that the directory already exists. I created a blog for my friend Lisa, and this is the server path:

  `ftp.bizstone.com/lisa/`

- **Your FTP Username and Password**—For convenience, store your FTP username and password at Blogger. That way, you won't have to type them in every time you want to post.

Don't Know Your FTP Settings?

Contact the administrator of your web server if you are unsure of your FTP server name or path.

Genius Tip

Blog as Home Page

If you name your blog file index.html, it will show up as the page visitors see first when they type in `http://www.yoursite.com`. If index.html doesn't work, check your hosting company's conventions.

Inside Blogger—Navigating the Interface

Now that you're signed up and kicking the tires of your new blog, you'll soon
become familiar with the Blogger interface. It doesn't take long to get used to
clicking around inside Blogger just as you would click Back or Home on your
browser's toolbar. Remember that Blogger is software that runs in your web
browser, which means that its interface is the web page. The buttons along the
top of Blogger's interface (see Figure 2.8) are easy to spot and hard to forget.

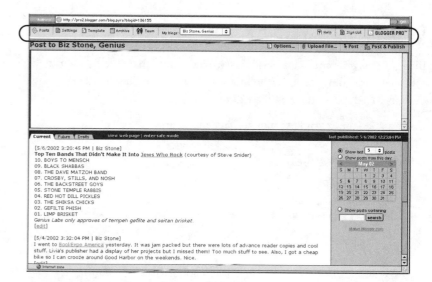

Figure 2.8

*Buttons of the Blogger
interface.*

Use Blogger's toolbar buttons to access the various parts of your account:

- **Posts**—This button takes you back to the default screen where you can
  write and edit your posts.

- **Settings**—Your settings include your Title, Description, and
  Public/Private Status. You can delete your blog from here, and this also
  is where you fill in all your FTP information.

- **Template**—The template area is where you can paste in your own
  design (as HTML) or select a new design. Blogger templates are like any
  kind of web page, but they have a special difference: blogger tags.
  Blogger tags enable communication between your blog's template and
  Blogger. For examples of Blogger tags in action, see the next section,
  "Blogger Tags." The Blogger template tags also are listed in Table 2.1.

- **Archives**—Archives are pages that contain past posts. They contain all
  of your posts, including those that may have scrolled off of your front
  page. Your archive index page contains links to all your archive pages.
  We'll discuss archives in Chapter 8, "Working with Blogger Archives."

- **Team**—The team page is where you can invite people to contribute to your blog or manage the people you've already invited. Adding team members to your blog is an easy way to create a group blog—many hands make light work!

- **Help**—Selecting Help brings you to Blogger's FAQ.

- **Sign Out**—Signing out is a good idea if you are on a shared machine. If you stay signed in, the next person who uses the machine can post to your blog.

Blogger Tags

Blogger tags are proprietary HTML style indicators that clue Blogger in to what you are going for. You don't need to know how they work right now; you just need to put them in the right place.

Listing 2.1 is an example of blogger tags in action.

Listing 2.1   Using Tags

```
<Blogger>
  <$BlogItemBody$><br>
  <small>posted by <$BlogItemAuthor$> on<$BlogItemDateTime$></small>
  <p>
</Blogger>
```

This tag would render your posts in the manner shown in Figure 2.9.

Figure 2.9

Blogger tags in a blog.

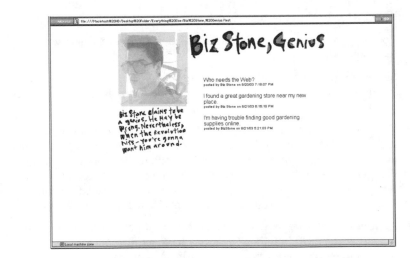

Table 2.1 lists the Blogger template tags.

Table 2.1   Blogger's Template Tags

Tag Name	Description
<$BlogItemBody$>	This is the text of an individual post.
<$BlogItemAuthor$>	The name of the author of a post is displayed wherever this tag is placed.
<$BlogItemAuthorNickname$>	Authors can have nicknames if they choose. This tag will render it.
<$BlogItemAuthorEmail$>	An author can have his or her email address automatically printed under a post.
<$BlogItemAuthorURL$>	The homepage URL of the author is great to display if there are multiple authors on one blog. Chapter 9, "Group Blogging," goes into further detail.
<$BlogItemDateTime$>	This is the date and/or time of a post. The display format is configurable in the Settings section.
<$BlogItemNumber$>	The unique ID number of the post comes in handy when you want to build permalinks (direct links to individual posts).
<$BlogItemURL$>	This displays the URL associated with the post if you have URL enabled.

Blogger How-Tos: Keys to a Successful Trial Run

Because this chapter is intended just to get you started with Blogger (that is, it is more of an introduction than a complete tutorial), I'm including a few key things in this section that might help you during your trial run.

How to Delete a Blogger Blog

Deleting a blog should not be taken lightly (unless you've only just created it and you want to start over fresh). Deleting a blog will delete all your posts and erase you from Blogger.com. If you host your own site and Blogger was FTPing the files to your server, your posts might still exist there. You will have to use an FTP client to erase those files from the web.

To delete a blog, follow these steps:

1. Click the Settings button in the toolbar.

2. Scroll to the bottom of the Settings page.

3. Click the button that says Delete this blog.

How to Change the Default Number of Posts on a Page

You can set the number of posts you'd like to appear on your blog or the number of days' worth of posts you'd like to see. To try this out, choose to have the last seven days' worth of posts displayed, or only the last 12 posts, regardless of how many days it has been. (The numbers are up to you, but if your choice results in a huge number of posts on the page, it might take a long time to load.)

To change the default number of posts on a page, follow these steps:

1. Click the Settings button in the toolbar.

2. Beneath the Formatting header, locate Show.

3. Enter the number of posts you want to display.

4. Select whether you want to display the Day's posts or the Latest posts.

5. Click Save changes.

How to Set an Author Nickname or Email Address

Having a nickname, email address, or URL is especially important when you have more than one member in your blog team. Without a name attached to the post, readers will not know who wrote it and the meaning may get lost. Also, many people who blog might want their email addresses displayed for feedback, or perhaps they'd like a link to their own blog if this blog were a group endeavor.

To change/add a Nickname, Email Address, or URL:

1. Click Teams in the top toolbar.

2. Click your name.

3. Click Edit my Profile in the upper-right corner.

4. Make changes and click Save profile.

How to Add a Subject or Headline to a Post

Chapter 4, "A Blogger's Guide to Simple HTML," goes into simple HTML in more detail, but here's a sneak peek. To create a subject or headline above your post, try using the headline tags provided in HTML. The code in Listing 2.2 shows what you would type.

Listing 2.2   Using Headline Tags

```
<h3>Headline of my post!</h3>
This is my post. I like to post posts.
```

Figure 2.10 shows Listing 2.2 in a blog.

Figure 2.10

Headline tag in a blog.

How to Add a Team Member

Team members and group blogging is a whole chapter later in this book (see Chapter 9, "Group Blogging"), but here's the quick way to invite another blogger to join your Blogger-powered blog:

1. Click the Team button in the toolbar.

2. Click Add Team Member.

3. Add the names and email addresses of people to whom you'd like to give permission.

4. They will receive emails notifying them of your blog.

5. After they accept the blog, they will have the ability to log on and publish.

Genius Tip

Store Your FTP Username and Password

It's best to store your FTP username and password in Blogger if you plan on inviting members. Otherwise, you'll have to give it out to each person you're inviting. Your FTP username and password can be stored in the Settings area. This is not necessary for Blog*Spot-hosted blogs.

How to Work in Safe Mode

Safe mode is there for you when you've forgotten to close a tag or if you've inadvertently entered some bad HTML. In these situations, your blog can get all screwed up, and sometimes the bad HTML can make it impossible to fix the problem. That's when safe mode comes in handy. Click the Enter safe mode link (to the right of the View web page link), and your posts will be displayed in HTML form so that you can find and fix whatever has gone wrong.

A simple example of bad code occurs when you forget to close a tag. So let's say you wanted to make a link in your post, and you didn't close the tag:

Please stop by and visit my `<a href="http://www.bizstone.com/">`Blog

There should be a `</a>` after the word `Blog` to close the tag. This would cause all the posts after this one to be linked in one giant never-ending link.

In regular mode, your computer can disable the Edit link under your post so that you are unable to fix it. But if you click into safe mode, your post will show up as HTML, and you will be able to repair the unclosed tag and carry on.

Now that you know a few ways to post and you've familiarized yourself with the Blogger interface, blogging is simply a matter of filling up that big empty form field!

Blogger is a great tool; I've been using it for years. You could use Blogger exclusively and never want for more. Several tools and software enhancements have been independently developed for use with Blogger, too; that's another reason why Blogger is a good choice. But if you're interested in finding out what other options await you, you're ready to check out Chapter 3, "Overview of the Major Blog Providers."

Chapter 3

Overview of the Major Blog Providers

Choices for blogging software on the web are already numerous—and they're growing. Within the blog community, you can even find individuals who have created their own blogging systems to suit their needs and often offer it to others for free. In this chapter, we'll look at the major blog providers and examine some of their key features. The definition of *major* here is simply providers that have been around a while and have a strong user base. The features of the software providers are often upgraded, enhanced, or changed— keep this in mind as you read this overview. More blog providers can be found in Appendix A, "Blog Web Links."

Blogger's Offerings

First there was Blogger, then came Blog*Spot, and finally Blogger Pro—a premium pay version of Blogger. Blogger is still free, and Blog*Spot is still providing a free spot for your Blogger-powered Blog. But Blogger Pro is a subscription-based service for users who are willing to pay for increased reliability, higher performance, new tools, and advanced features and flexibility.

Blogger

Blogger is the weblog provider that fueled the blogging revolution (see Figure 3.1).

Figure 3.1

Blogger is free. Go sign up!

Blogger still offers its original free software, which includes:

- **Instant Publishing**—Publish to the web without installing software. Simply enter information in a form and click Publish. It's like an instant message to the web.

- **Template Driven Design**—This gives you total control over the look of your blog. Design your own template and paste it in a form, or pick one of the many provided template designs. Great for integrating a blog into an existing site as a "What's New" page.

- **File Transfer Protocol**—The location of your blog is up to you. Blogger publishes your posts via FTP to your chosen location. The files are static HTML files that exist on your server.

- **Script Compatible**—If you're more sophisticated, your template can contain script, such as server-side `includes`, ASP, or Cold Fusion pages, and that script will still be processed after the Blogger content is inserted. The published Blogger file can even be an `include`.

The basic Blogger service is completely free. The only "payment" required is a link back to Blogger.com to help spread the word.

Blog*Spot

Blog*Spot enhances the Blogger offering and makes it easier for non-technical types to publish to the web. Basically, Blog*Spot is just a place to "park" your free blog, but it also has some unique features within that space:

- **Advertising**—You can advertise your own blog, product, service, or site to thousands of Blogger users and their readers on Blog*Spot for only 1/20th of a cent per impression ($0.50 CPM) and minimum of just $50 (100,000 impressions). It's as easy as deciding what you want your ad to be and filling out some forms.

- **Ad Free Blogs**—Because Blog*Spot is a free service, it hosts banner ads on the top of your blog. You can have these ads removed for $12 a year, which is cheaper than hosting (see Figure 3.2). Blog*Spot is a great place to blog if you're looking for something easy.

Figure 3.2

Get ad-free blog hosting for three pennies a day.

Blogger Pro

Blogger's premium offering takes Blogger to the next level (see Figure 3.3).

Blogger Pro has a more robust and still-developing feature set:

- **Spell Checking**—A well-spelled blog makes a good impression.

- **Title Fields**—An optional Title field is available in the posting form and in the template to save formatting time for people who like to give headlines to their posts.

- **Image Posting**—Upload and post photos (or any other type of file) from within the Blogger editing interface.

- **Post to the Future (or the Past)**—Adjust the time a post is published so that you can move items around on your blog—or even post to the future. Good for setting up an alibi!

- **Draft Posts**—Mark the post as a "draft." It won't be published until you to come back and finish it later.

- **BlogSend**—Increase reach, readership, and feedback by broadcasting your blog via email. Let readers subscribe to get your posts in their inboxes on a daily basis.

- **Post Templates**—If you routinely include similar text or HTML in your posts, create a Post Template and save tedious typing time.

- **Secure Logins**—For higher security, your password is encrypted via SSL whenever you sign into Blogger Pro.

- **Better Internationalization**—Ninety-two languages and locales are available for the date formatting, and a comprehensive list of time zones is available so that your time-date stamps will be geographically correct.

- **Better Archiving**—The overhauled archiving engine gives various date-formatting options, including the choice to archive daily or even to archive individual posts.

- **Post via Email**—Send an email to your blog, and it will show up as an entry on your site. Great for travelling—if you can email, you can blog!

- **RSS Generation**—Automatically generate RSS-formatted XML feeds of your blog. Huh? Basically, you syndicate your blog for inclusion in aggregation services, which translates into more traffic to your site.

- **Secure Publishing**—Publish via Secure Copy Protocol or HTTPS (SSL over HTTP) instead of FTP, to give you more security and allow you to post to servers where administrators don't allow FTP.

- **Moderation**—Blog team members can be limited to the ability to post "pending" items, which won't be published until they're approved by an administrator. This is good for zines powered by Blogger.

- **Priority Server Access**—Blogger Pro users have priority access to servers that carry a fraction of the total Blogger load, so they will be much less subject to performance and scaling issues.

- **Blog Search Access**—Blogger Pro users have access to the Blogger Search function unavailable to other users. This search is the only blog search on the web that indexes on the individual post level, and it is current up to the half hour, providing unique research opportunities.

- **Commercial Usage**—Original Blogger has always been free to personal publishers and corporate entities alike. But with the launch of Blogger

Pro, commercial users will be required to pay for the service to help support Blogger for everyone.

The planned price for Blogger Pro is $50/year per user. However, because they are still building out the functionality, the cost is $35 for a year for users who sign up early.

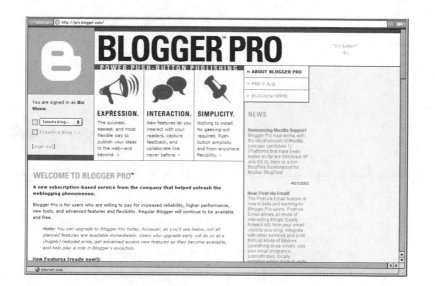

Figure 3.3

Blog like a pro.

Who Should Use Blogger?

Blogger is great whether you're new to blogging or you're a pro. I've been using Blogger for two years, and I like it. Blogger focuses on just the blog and, as you will see, isn't as concerned with site management as other blogging software providers are.

MovableType

MovableType is a sophisticated web-based personal publishing system designed to ease maintenance of regularly updated news or journal sites, like weblogs. It contains features common to many other such systems and includes a robust feature set. Notable for its amazingly clean and beautiful user environment (see Figure 3.4) and its highly configurable and expandable feature set, MovableType made quite a splash when it came onto the scene.

Figure 3.4

The MovableType interface is stellar user interface design.

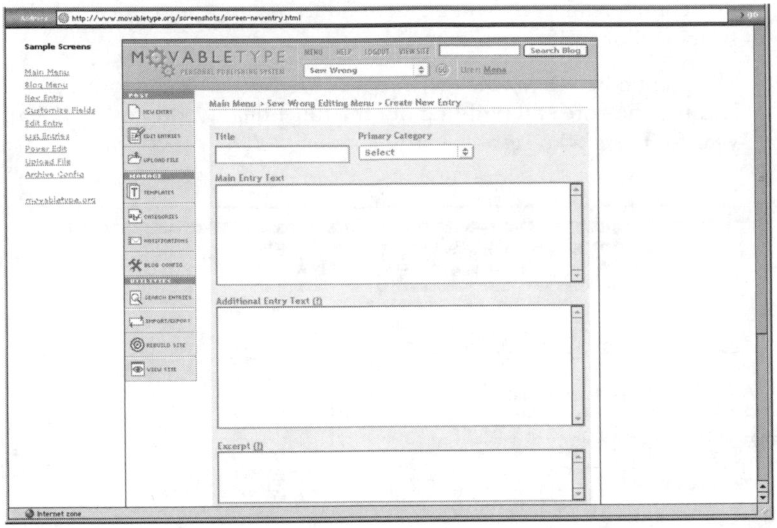

MovableType features include:

- **Data Import**—This feature allows you to import your entries and comments from other content management systems, such as Blogger and Greymatter, and then continue to manage those posts with MovableType.

- **Multiple Output Templates**—Enables one-click publishing to multiple destinations and formats from your site.

- **Multiple Author Support**—Register multiple authors and set their access levels using MovableType's role-based permissions system.

- **Entry Categorization**—Group your entries into categories for your own reference, for archiving purposes, and for display in your blog.

- **Search and Replace**—Save time by performing a global search-and-replace on all of your entries. Also use the search feature to look up a particular entry.

- **Multiple Archiving Options**—Create monthly, weekly, and daily archives of your content. Choose individual pages for each entry and archives by category. Archive file names and URLs are fully customizable.

- **Built-In Comment System**—Allow your visitors to post comments on your entries and engage in conversations. MovableType supports comments either inline in your blog or in popup windows. It also allows you to selectively exclude commenting on certain posts for those times when you don't want any "lip."

- **Email Notification System**—Maintain lists of users to whom notification messages will be sent when you post a new entry. Keep 'em in the loop!

- **Integrated Uploads**—Upload files and images, and seamlessly integrate them into new posts via MovableType's clean, easy interface.

- **Customizable Templating**—Combine MovableType's template tags with standard HTML (or whatever markup language you choose) to build and customize your site.

- **Flexible Dating**—MovableType allows you to override an entry's date stamp.

- **Delete Entries**—Clean out old or unwanted entries with MovableType's true entry deletion.

- **Draft/Publish**—Allow for content editorial and approval by setting entries to Draft. Then let an editor approve by marking Publish, at which point the entries will be published on your site.

- **Publicity and Notification**—When you have updated your blog, "pings" are sent out that place you on recently updated lists. More traffic!

- **Extensible Code**—If you have experience programming in Perl, you can write custom dynamic applications using the MovableType libraries.

MovableType Requirements

Because MovableType is more sophisticated than less feature-intensive blogger-ware, it has a few requirements beyond basic web access:

- An account on a web server that allows you to run custom CGI scripts.

- Perl, version 5.004_04 or greater.

- An FTP program to upload the necessary files to your web server.

- JavaScript and cookies enabled in your browser.

MovableType is donate-ware. They ask that you send payment via PayPal for the amount you feel the product is worth. In return, for every $20 donated, users receive a Recently Updated Key. This helps to promote your weblog each time you publish (see Figure 3.5). For donations of $45 or more, additional support is provided. For business sites, the cost is $150 for a commercial license. The terms of the current license apply to commercial usage in that you may not redistribute or charge for the software.

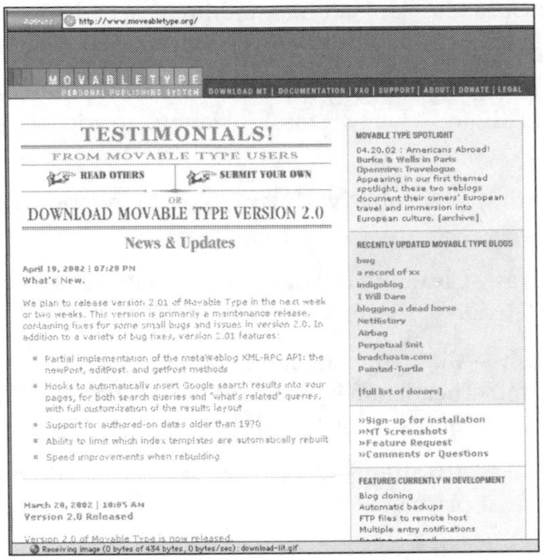

Figure 3.5

A donation to MovableType buys you a link in the Recently Updated section of the front page every time you post.

Diaryland

Diaryland is one of the original weblog providers and is simple to use. This group offers package blogging services in the form of an online diary aimed at a younger crowd (see Figure 3.6).

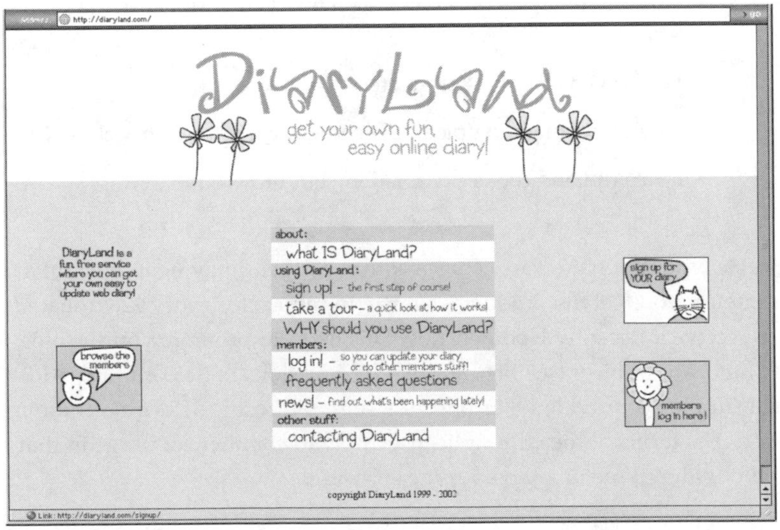

Figure 3.6

Diaryland has a fun and youthful façade.

With Diaryland, all you have to do is sign in, visit your "add an entry" page, type in whatever you want to say, and that's about it. If you're looking for an easy, free way to publish to the web, Diaryland offers you that. Diaryland features include:

- **Easy Web Address**—With a free Diaryland account, you get a simple `yourname.diaryland.com` web address for your diary.

- **Email**—Matching email address (`you@yourname.diaryland.com`).

- **No Ads**—No banner ads or pop-up ads.

- **Template-Driven Design**—Template-driven design control of your diary. Newbies can pick from existing templates; experts can go to town with their own designs.

- **Password Protection**—If you want to keep your diary private, you can password protect it so that only the people you give the password to can read it.

The signup procedure is quick and painless, and once you're signed up, you'll be able to start adding to your blog (diary) right away.

GrokSoup

GrokSoup offers blogging with a "news site" slant. It encourages users to create their own version of CNN, a blog, or an internal pressroom. Browser-based word processing style tools make it easy to add, delete, edit, and syndicate content with a complete feature set including:

- **Content Syndication**—Automatic XML-based syndication to broadcast your work.

- **Browser-based Content Editing**—Write and edit your work in a word processing style browser environment.

- **News Site Templates**—Preformatted designs to help with your blog design and layout.

- **Built-In Comments**—Users can discuss and comment on every article you write.

- **Calendar**—Easy calendar access to full story archives.

- **Bookmarking**—Comprehensive bookmark-management tools (see Figure 3.7).

- **Page Layout Control**—Full, HTML-level edit control over page layout.

- **Indexing**—Front-page profiles of top sites.

- **QuickSites**—An easy way to scan multiple news sites. Good when you've got writer's block.

- **Mailing Lists**—Another way to build a readership and community around your blog.

- **Display Formats**—Multiple display formats, including weblog, headline, and others.

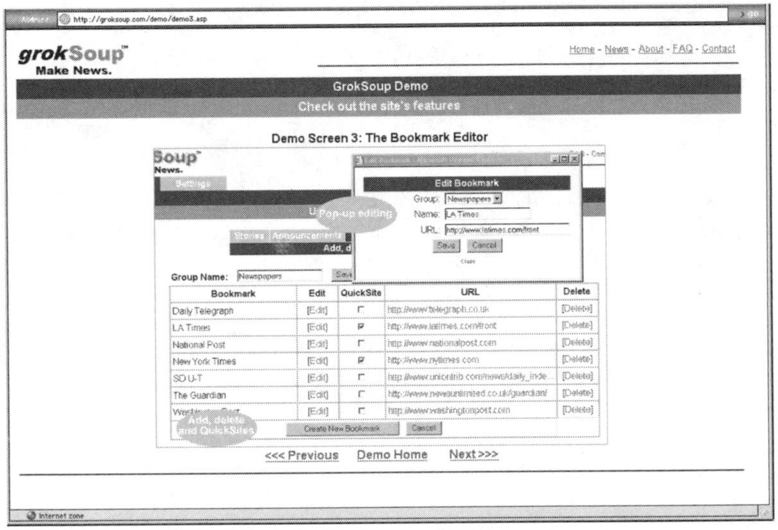

Figure 3.7

Bookmark management is bundled with GrokSoup's blogging features.

Userland Software

Userland is one of the heavy-duty players in the independent publishing and Internet development space. In fact, this group pioneered much of the technology that bloggers take advantage of today, and they're probably working on things right now that we haven't yet realized we can't live without.

UserLand's products make it easy to create, manage, and share content on the web and on Intranets, and they have contributed several important standards to the Internet developer community. UserLand's major weblog offering is Radio UserLand, a browser-based weblog tool that runs on a desktop (see Figure 3.8). With Radio, you can publish text, photos, and other documents, even if you think HTML might somehow stand for "How To Mow Lawns" and know nothing about web design. All you need to do is install the software, and you are developing content on the web in minutes.

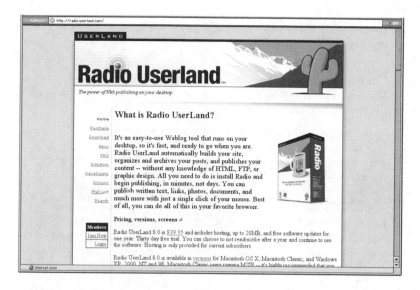

Figure 3.8

Radio doesn't actually come in a box.

Radio is helping blogs make an impact as knowledge management tools for schools and companies alike with intuitive software that enables students or employees to publish what they know on the web. Once on the web, that knowledge is accessible to others via search tools. Radio UserLand's blogging software offering is good stuff. Here's an overview:

- **Easy and Intuitive**—Use your browser to post items to your home page and write stories.

- **One-click Publishing**—Update your site through Radio's one-click publishing. Upstream files, documents, and pictures to your web site by dropping them in a folder. Let Radio do all the work.

- **News Provider**—Subscribe to hundreds of news sites and personal weblogs. Radio automatically gathers news from all of these sources and displays them on a convenient news page.

- **Automatic Syndication**—Radio automatically turns the content on your weblog into an XML feed that can be syndicated and subscribed to by other Radio users.

- **Your Own Web Address**—Every Radio user gets free hosting of their web site for one year with their purchase of Radio. No need to pay extra hosting fees.

- **Web Host Ready**—Radio sites can be sent to any ISP. All you need to do is enter your FTP account information.

- **Offline Friendly**—Edit your site while on the road or disconnected. Because Radio lives on your desktop or laptop, you can add to your site even when you're not connected. When you connect again, Radio makes all the updates for you.

- **Easy Navigation**—Radio enables readers to access back-issues of your weblog through a intuitive calendar on the homepage. Every day has its own URL.

- **Content Management**—Manage your templates, stories, and pictures. Macros and a complete scripting engine connect to Radio's powerful content management environment.

- **Quick Setup**—After downloading the software, you'll be editing your first site in the time it would take to get a cup of coffee. Or at most, the time it would take to get one of those good kosher dill pickles (light on the garlic) with a nice, clean crunch. I love those.

- **Design Control**—Change the look, fonts, colors, type, and more.

- **Friendly Community**—When you start your blog, you are joining a huge community of other webloggers. Radio includes information on your site's traffic, referrers to your site, and recently updated sites.

Radio UserLand costs $39.95 a year and includes up to 40MB hosting. (There is a 30-day free trial.) You can choose not to resubscribe after a year and continue to use the software, but hosting is provided only for subscribers. Radio UserLand 8.0 is available in versions for Macintosh OS X, Macintosh Classic, and Windows XP, 2000, NT, and 98.

Who Should Use Radio?

Radio UserLand makes it easy to post blog entries and gather news from around the web, and it's on par with Blogger, but it isn't free. Radio is a good tool for a blog that focuses on news and commentary.

Greymatter

Greymatter is a blogging application created by Noah Grey. Noah wanted more control than Blogger and other applications could provide, so he built his own and offered it to the world (see Figure 3.9).

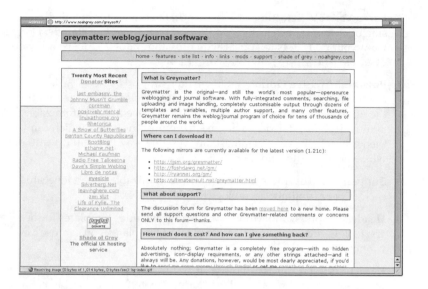

Figure 3.9

Greymatter is control-freak friendly.

Features include:

- **Server Control**—Greymatter runs completely on your own server at all times and is always under your full control; you're never dependent on the reliability (or privacy reassurances) of any outside source whatsoever.

- **Comment Posting**—Make your blog come alive by giving users the built-in capability to add comments directly to your entries (no PHP/SQL database required); every aspect of Greymatter's comments are completely customizable and controllable.

- **Built-In Search**—Allow visitors to search through your entries (with fully-customizable output). Also, perform internal searching from within Greymatter; authorized authors can search and replace text across all entries.

- **Built-In File Uploading and Easy Image Handling**—Upload files and images to your account from within Greymatter. Instantly create new entries with the files or images already linked to or displayed in your new entries. Make fully-customizable instant pop-up windows out of the images you upload.

- **Template-Based System**—Greymatter builds your blog with the templates you create and customize. Using template elements, Greymatter provides control over every aspect of the format and layout of your blog so that you can perform minute tweaks or sweeping overhauls.

- **Large Variable Selection**—More than 100 variables for detailed precision of elements such as the AM/PM on your time-date stamps. Do you want your AM/PMs to appear with or without dots? Upper- or lowercase? Not show up at all? That sort of thing.

- **Powerful Archive Options**—Greymatter supports a huge variety of options for dealing with archives, including archiving by the month or the week; using variables that allow you to place fully-customizable, automatically-updated lists of links to your entries (lists which can themselves be tailored in almost any possible way you could want) anywhere on your site; and more.

- **Support for Multiple Authors**—Fully customizable access levels for each of your (unlimited) co-bloggers.

- **Headers, Footers, and More**—Greymatter includes templates for headers, footers, sidebars, and 10 other custom templates you can use any way you want.

- **Karma Voting**—You can allow your visitors to rate your entries, if you want, with instant plus-or-minus "karma" votes. Also, you can control specifically which entries you want to allow karma voting or comment postings.

- **Censoring and IP Banning**—For family-oriented sites, Greymatter offers the ability to censor any words or phrases you want, as well as the ability to ban malicious visitors from voting or posting comments on your site.

- **Customizable Calendars**—Make monthly or weekly calendars linking to all your entries and customize them to your heart's content.

- **Full Editing Capabilities**—Instantly revise any entry—or visitors' comments—at any time.

- **Fully Configurable**—Dozens of configuration options allow you to instantly tweak how any aspect of your blog operates.

- **Connectibility**—If you like, you can connect a theoretically unlimited number of other files on your account to have Greymatter keep them updated with your blog information.

- **Polished Interface**—Greymatter features a clean, carefully organized interface designed both to be easy on the eyes and to provide the best working environment possible.

- **Built-In Diagnostics**—Greymatter offers a built-in Diagnostics & Repair function to ensure that your files are working and your paths are correct.

Greymatter is donation-based. Donations, although completely voluntary, are welcome and appreciated. You are not required to display an icon, banner ad, or any link on your site.

Requirements for Greymatter

Because Greymatter is more advanced than other blogging software, you'll need to have a few key ingredients:

- An FTP client such as CuteFTP (PC) or Fetch (MAC)

- A web account which offers full support for Perl 5 software

- A modest comfort level with HTML code (to customize the templates)

Who Should Use Greymatter?

Greymatter is for expert users. New bloggers will find Blogger more suitable to their needs; but for those who want maximum control or who just can't have enough tweaking and customization abilities at their disposal, Greymatter is the best choice.

Xanga

Xanga helps you build your blog and publish your thoughts instantly to the web. This product offers two versions of blogging software: a free version and a paid, Premium version. Xanga is great for beginners, experts, or bloggers with a yen for that warm fuzzy community feeling. These features are included in the free version of Xanga:

- **The xTools Browser Button**—Publish from anywhere, anytime, with a bookmarklet packed with most of the editing tools available when you are working at Xanga.com: hyperlinking, bold, italic, underline, HTML, and more.

- **Built-In Commenting**—Expect feedback with eProps and comments from visitors. eProps are Xanga's "currency of good will" used among members of the blogging community to give one another a kind of virtual pat on the back when they read a post they find interesting, entertaining, and so on.

- **Sites I Read Manager**—This feature provides control of Xanga blogs you enjoy most. You can even have them automatically emailed to you (see Figure 3.10).

- **Custom Design**—Xanga offers pre-designed templates, control over colors, fonts, links and the like, or complete template-level control with tags and variables. All comfort levels are represented.

- **Personal URL**—Xanga will host your blog for free at xanga.com/you, but they also have a unique feature that lets you buy a web address for $30 and have it mapped onto your blog. This means that your blog is hosted at Xanga, but the address is www.yourname.com. It's pretty tricky.

- **Blogrings**—Blogrings are unique to Xanga. They connect a circle of blogs with a common focus or theme. Themes can be a group of friends, a support group, a hobby, anything.

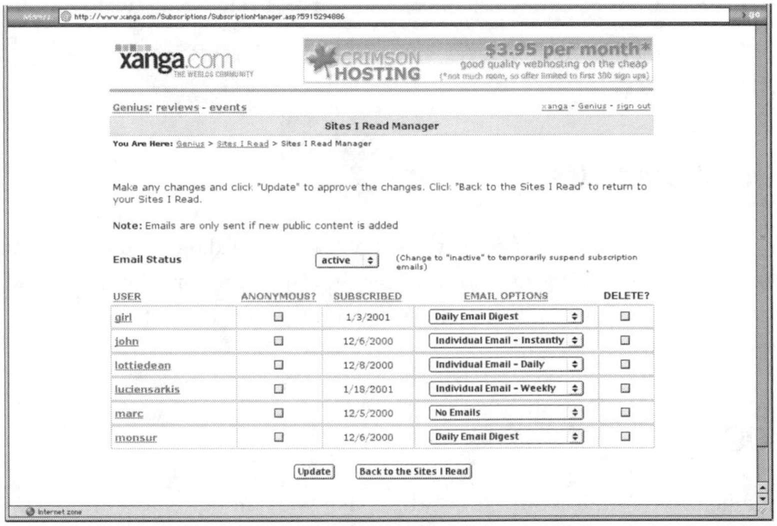

Figure 3.10

Manage the blogs you read.

Xanga Premium

Xanga's free blog feature set is robust, but if you'd like some enhancements and feel guilty about getting so much for free, you can upgrade to Premium and get the following features:

- **Better Browsing Tools**—Premium members can search the entire database of Xanga blogs for specific topics of interest or intrigue. They also can search the public entries on an individual member's site and all the public and private entries on their own site.

- **Better, Faster Editing Tools**—The Premium xTools editing interface works just like your favorite word processing program. Use point-and-click tools to change font style and sizes, add borders and fill colors, and easily insert symbols and smileys.

- **Image Hosting**—Upload images straight from hard drive to blog. Store hundreds of images.

- **Email Posting**—Posting to Xanga with Premium is as easy as sending an email to a unique address containing your Xanga ID. This means that you can post from the road or set up a very tech-unfriendly family member up with an email blog. This is also nice because you can use the word-processing capabilities of your email application to design individual posts.

- **Spell Checking**—Premium offers built-in spell checking to catch mistakes before you post.

- **Downloadable Weblog Archives**—Download a complete copy of your blog and store it on your own hard drive for safe-keeping.

- **Xanga Skins**—Xanga offers more control to designers who'd like to use all the features of Xanga but with their own unique design.

LiveJournal

LiveJournal.com is a behemoth of online journals. Created by Brad Fitzpatrick way back in 1998 as a database-driven method for updating his own blog, LiveJournal turned into a web-based application and soon grew into a huge undertaking.

Today, LiveJournal is a Webby Award-winning site, used by over 400,000 people worldwide. The site has become a member-funded open-source development project with numerous volunteers, developers, and a small paid staff. LiveJournal has expanded to allow easy creation of journals, weblogs, and interest-based online communities via the web, or by installing a small program on your Windows, Macintosh, UNIX, or BeOS computer. Some of LiveJournal's popular features include:

- **Built-In Commenting**—Optional built-in reader commenting on posts.

- **Communities**—Create your own online community or find users and communities by interest, location, etc. (see Figure 3.11).

- **Friends List**—A single page displays all the latest posts on every journal and weblog you find interesting.

- **Customization and Templates**—Change the colors or select from predefined system styles or choose from several highly customizable CSS-based templates.

- **Syndication**—Customizable RSS feeds as well as your own RSS feed.

- **To-Do List**—Helps you easily file projects and goals you want to accomplish.

- **Music Auto-Detection**—Music can be detected from Winamp, Sonique, Freeamp, Media Player, and the default Windows CD player and automatically posted to your blog. Great for a "now playing" module.

- **Works with Other Sites**—Embed your blog into another web page (or your existing home page) in a variety of ways.

Figure 3.11

LiveJournal is big on community.

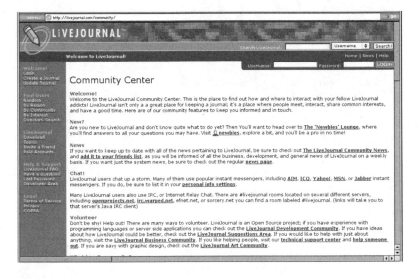

These features and more are part of LiveJournal's free accounts—although these days they are not giving them away as easily because of the high volume of users. To get a LiveJournal account, you'll need to be invited by an existing member or get a paid account. Paid accounts come with enhanced features like:

- **Email**—Mail to *your_username*@livejournal.com will be forwarded to your personal email address. Choose to display none, either, or both of your email addresses.

- **Personalized Domain Name**—Instead of the usual http://www.livejournal.com/users/*username*/, your blog will also be accessible by http://*username*.livejournal.com/ (shorter and more personal).

- **Fast Server Access**—Paid users automatically hit a group of really fast servers when they access any part of the site.

- **Advanced Customization**—In addition to just being able to pick the style of your journal and the colors, you'll also be able to create your own style using whatever HTML you like. This also lets you make new embedded styles that match your web site, never revealing that you're using LiveJournal.com as your journal mechanism.

- **Text Messaging**—If you have a pager or cell phone, you can get text messages (or numeric messages) right from LiveJournal. Set it to allow all users, registered users, or only your friends to page you. This is especially useful if you prefer to keep your cell phone private but want to be able to get messages on it.

- **Multiple User Pictures**—You're able to upload up to 10 pictures of yourself, and choose which one to use on each entry, in addition to your current mood/music, etc. For example, say you're feeling happy. In addition to the happy mood icon, you also can choose to use your "happy picture," which will then show up on everybody's journal that lists you as a friend for that one particular happy entry.

- **Surveys and Voting Polls**—A feature being worked on now will help users quickly and easily make voting polls and full surveys inside your journal entries, embedded right within your text.

- **Counters and Statistics**—Know when your visitors read your blog, how often, and what type of visitor they are—anonymous, another LiveJournal user, or one of your friends.

- **Customizable Comment Page**—This new feature will provide the ability to design the look and feel of your reader commenting area.

LiveJournal paid accounts cost $5 for 2 months, $15 for 6 months, and $25 for a year. So it works out to about two bucks a month if you pay for the year. Not bad if you're an avid journaler.

Free Upgrades

Blogging is a new phenomenon, and because these services are online-based software providers, they change often. This is a good thing because once you buy or subscribe the software, you keep getting the upgrades for free. You don't have to buy version 2.0, 3.0, 4.0, and up—just get in on the ground floor and let them handle the upgrades. Plus, the prices these blogging providers are asking for their paid versions are minimal compared to the cost of software you buy in a box. So get out there and try out some free blogging software. If you like it, buy a paid version—or don't, it's up to you!

Chapter 4

A Blogger's Guide to Simple HTML

Setting up a blog is simple. In a few minutes, you've got your very own digital printing press. Just type and click—*bam*, you're published! The more you blog, the more you'll want to blog. As you grow more prolific, you may want to take your posts a little further in terms of presentation. If you're new to web publishing, you might not know how to do some of the things everybody else already seems to know, like adding images to your posts or creating links.

Well, my friend, you have come to the right chapter. Use the HTML references here to blog with the best of them. From simple text formatting to displaying images within your posts, this guide covers the HTML that most new bloggers usually ask about. Although it's true that many blog publishing platforms offer What-You-See-Is-What-You-Get (WYSIWYG) text-editing interfaces that work just like an online version of Microsoft Word, it's still helpful to have a little bit of HTML knowledge. So here we go.

Some Basics

When the web was young, HTML was merely a way to format simple, get-the-job-done web pages. After people started designing with HTML, tweaking and bending it here and there to create interesting and functional layouts, HTML grew beyond its original scope. Using HTML within blog posts takes you back to some of that straightforward information formatting HTML was originally all about.

To use HTML in your blog posts, you need to know about tags. A *tag* tells the browser to do something, and sometimes, what's called an *attribute* goes inside the tag to tell the browser just how to do it. Most tags need to be placed around the text you'd like to format.

The tag for creating bold text is <b></b>. Here is an example of a tag in action using the bold tag:

```
<b>I want this text to appear bold</b>
```

The <b> opens the tag and the </b> closes it. It is very important that you remember to close a tag. If you don't close a <b> tag with </b>, for example, all the text on your blog that follows the opening <b> tag could end up being bold (or linked, or italicized—whatever tag you are attributing to the text). Not all tags need to be closed, but most of them do.

Making Links

When I set up a blog for my friend Lisa, she took to it quickly. She immediately started chronicling the secret behind-the-scenes action of a murder trial on which her friend was a juror. (I don't think she was supposed to be doing that. She can blog from jail, right?) Anyway, the first thing Lisa asked was, "How do I make links?" This is what I told her:

1. Put the cursor in front of the words you want to be linked.
2. Type the beginning <a> tag.
3. Add the HREF attribute.
4. Enter the exact URL of the link surrounded by quotation marks.
5. Place the cursor at the end of the text you want to link.
6. Type the closing </a> tag.

In Listing 4.1, the word *example* is linked to the website, imdb.com.

Listing 4.1   Link in Action

```
Lisa, here's an <a href="http://www.imdb.com">example</a> of a link
in action.
```

I told Lisa to use Listing 4.1 as a model for future links, and soon she was linking with wild abandon. Although Lisa is an accomplished screenwriter, she had never even thought about HTML when she started divulging courtroom secrets on her weblog. Many WYSIWYG blog interfaces make it easier to add links, but it is still good to know how to make it work for yourself.

Creating an Email Link

Lisa then decided to move away from courtroom drama and use her blog as an advice column. She wanted to know how to make a link that makes it easy for people to email questions to her. You, too, can make a link that, when clicked, launches your reader's email application and preloads your email address (or any address specified) into a new email message. Just follow the preceding steps for creating a link, but use a slight variation in Step 4: Instead of a URL inside the quotation marks, type **mailto:** plus the target email address (see Listing 4.2).

Listing 4.2   Email Link Example

```
<a href="mailto:biz@bizstone.com">Email me</a>!
```

Genius Tip

Sleazy Spam-Bots

If you don't want spam-bots (software that scans for email addresses to be used for junk email campaigns) stealing your address, but you do want feedback from your readers, don't use the `mailto` link. Instead, spell out your email address, like so:

```
Email me! My address is biz @ bizstone dot com.
```

Displaying Images in Your Posts

Finding just the right words to describe something succinctly is part of the joy of blogging, but sometimes you just need the power of a thousand words in one pixel-powered punch. One of the questions most frequently asked by new bloggers is, "How do I include an image in my post?" or something along those lines.

When you're blogging with images, you first have to realize that the image must already be uploaded to the web to be displayed in your blog post. Then, the site that's hosting the image needs to allow offsite linking of images. Many ISPs will give you web space with your Internet service. Check to see whether yours also allows offsite linking. If you'd rather not even think about FTP, you should choose a blog provider that helps you find and upload images from your hard drive.

Okay, so let's say the image is already on the web, and you just want to display it in your blog's post. Sheesh, that's why you're reading this in the first place. I'll cut to the chase. Here's how you include an image in your post:

1. Type the <IMG> tag.

2. After a space, type the src attribute.

3. Enter the exact location of the image inside quotation marks.

4. Close the tag.

Listing 4.3 shows what the HTML code would look like if you wanted to put a picture of me in your post.

Listing 4.3   Including an Image of Biz

```
<img src="http://www.bizstone.com/bizpic.gif">
```

Note that the img src tag is one of the tags that does not need to be closed. If you prefer to have the image aligned to the right, left, or center of your weblog post, you can do that using align=?, as you see in Listing 4.4.

Listing 4.4   Aligning the Image

```
<img src="http://www.bizstone.comx/bizpic.gif" align=right>
```

Hey, nobody said this was gonna be pretty (see Figure 4.1).

Figure 4.1

Align and resize images so that they enhance the post rather than dominate the screen.

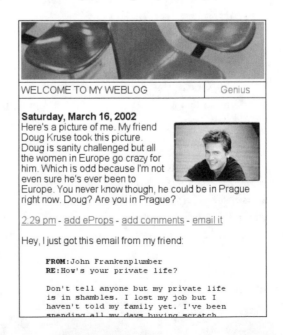

Setting the Image Width and Height

You can adjust the width and height of an image *visually* so it will fit nicely into your post by adding `height` and `width` attributes that are smaller than the original image dimensions (see Listing 4.5).

Listing 4.5   Adding Height and Width Attributes

```
<img src="http://www.bizstone.com/bizpic.gif" height=61 width=90
align=right>
```

Note that this does not change the file size or download time. Also, if you do not choose pixel sizes proportionate to the original image, you run the risk of distorting the graphic.

Genius Tip

Better Loading Pages
Including the exact pixel dimensions can be a good practice to get into because the browser will know how much space to give the picture even before it loads. This eliminates that awkward text re-flow that sometimes occurs when an image materializes.

Using an alt Tag on Images

Include an alt tag for people who have images disabled in their browser preferences. Type **alt="A picture of Biz,"** and your readers will at least have the benefit of descriptive text when the image doesn't appear.

Formatting Your Text

Blog posts tend to be short bursts of well-chosen copy, intended to deliver a thought, idea, or comment with a limited amount of text. Because of this, it often behooves us bloggers to make use of lists, indents, tables, strategically placed line breaks, and the like. Let's go over some of the ways we can whip our words into shape.

Section Headers

Headers are simple tags that help you attribute "importance" to your text. Traditionally, text that you want to give the most attention to would be level one header—the biggest header. The level six header is the smallest. I know, it seems backwards, but that's the way it works—think "priority." Headers are good if you want a simple way to title your individual posts.

There's not too much to applying a header tag. Just pick a size and go for it. Listing 4.6 shows what you'd type for the different sizes.

Listing 4.6   Section Header Examples

```
<h1>your text here</h1>
<h2>your text here</h2>
<h3>your text here</h3>
<h4>your text here</h4>
<h5>your text here</h5>
<h6>your text here</h6>
```

Figure 4.2 shows what a level one header looks like on a blog.

Figure 4.2

Use a level one header for a big, juicy title.

WELCOME TO MY WEBLOG   Genius

Saturday, March 16, 2002

My flight to the moon

Went to the moon today on a private experimental space shuttle. In fact, I'm still here because we ran out of gas. Help!

11:06 am - add eProps - add comments - email it

This is a level one header

Paragraph and Line Breaks

Some blog tools automatically convert your paragraph breaks, based on where you have pressed Enter or Return when typing data in the form. Knowing the HTML for separating your text is useful, just in case (see Listing 4.7).

Listing 4.7   Code for Creating Paragraphs

```
<p>Putting the paragraph tags around your text will guarantee that
it doesn't run together. This is some text that's got paragraph tags
at the beginning and the end. As a result, this text will appear in
miraculous paragraph form!</p>
<p>As a result, this paragraph is separated. I like paragraphs. I
remember in elementary school when we had assignments like, "Write a
paragraph on what you did this summer." The whole summer in one
paragraph! That's good stuff.</p>
```

If you only need a single line break instead the bigger double space associated with a new paragraph, you can use the <br> tag after the text where you want the break to occur (see Listing 4.8).

Listing 4.8   Code for Creating a Line Break

```
I <br> would <br> not <br> say <br> such <br> things <br> if <br>
were <br> you!
```

Figure 4.3 shows what the code in Listing 4.8 looks like in a blog.

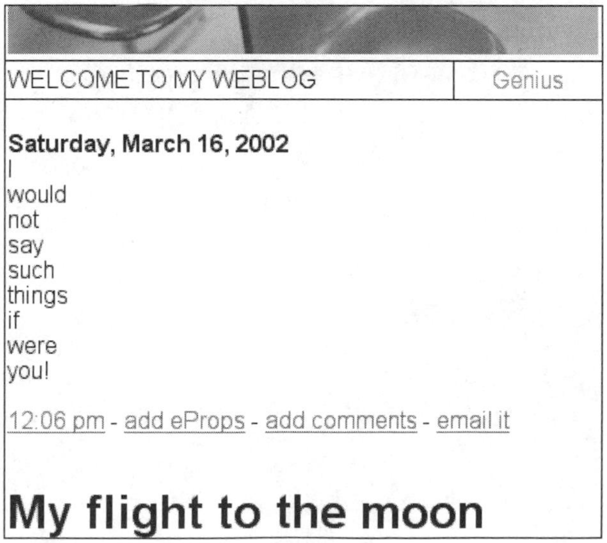

Figure 4.3

Use line breaks to boss your post around.

Creating Margins and Space

Good blog design tends to allow for plenty of white space right from the beginning—at the template stage. It is preferable to have plenty of margin space around your text because it keeps the eyes fresh and just looks better. But when you want even more emphasis, or you want to single something out within a post, blockquote works great. Blockquote together with the teletype tag works well when you want to display an email message, for example, and give it a different look from the rest of your blog's text.

To create this "emailed" look, follow these steps:

1. Put the cursor in front of the text you want to alter.

2. Type the opening <blockquote> tag.

3. Then, type the opening teletype tag, <tt>.

4. After the passage, close both tags with </tt></blockquote>.

Genius Tip

Staggering Tags

Remember that tags are "wrapped" around your text—they should never be staggered. For example, <b><i>your text here</b></i> is incorrect. The last tag opened should be the first tag closed, like this: <b><i>your text here</i><b>. You can think of your tags as layers of headphones on top of each other, if that helps at all.

Any text you type before or after the blockquote tags will appear with normal margins, and the text inside will be substantially more indented (see Figure 4.4).

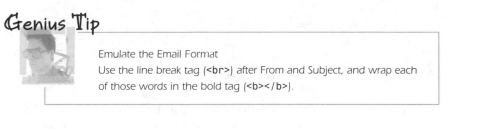

Figure 4.4

Always ask permission before you post a friend's email to your weblog.

WELCOME TO MY WEBLOG | Genius

Saturday, March 16, 2002
Hey, I just got this email from my friend:

```
FROM:John Frankenplumber
RE:How's your private life?

Don't tell anyone but my private life
is in shambles. I lost my job but I
haven't told my family yet. I've been
spending all my days buying scratch
tickets with my wife's credit card. I
know I can get the big score!

-Johnny F.
```

I love having a weblog that my friends and collegues read.
I'll put anything up here as long as it gets me more traffic.
I'm awesome!

12:35 pm - add eProps - add comments - email it

Genius Tip

Emulate the Email Format
Use the line break tag (**
**) after From and Subject, and wrap each
of those words in the bold tag (**<b></b>**).

Making Lists

There are two kinds of people in this world: good people and bad people.
Similarly, there are many kinds of lists on the web. We're going to talk only
about two of them: The Unordered List and the Ordered List. Both are good.

Making an Unordered (Bulleted) List

To make an unordered (or bulleted) list, follow these steps:

1. In your blog post, type the tag <UL>.

2. On the next line, type <LI> and enter a list item.

3. Repeat <LI>, followed by list items until you're done.

4. Don't forget to close each item with </LI>.

5. Close the list with </UL>.

So, the HTML that I'd enter into my blog entry area would look like Listing 4.9.

Listing 4.9   Unordered List HTML Code

```
Things I need to do (in no particular order):
<UL>

<LI>Sleep</LI>
<LI>Wake up</LI>
<LI>Get dressed</LI>
<LI>Eat</LI>
<LI>Go back to sleep</LI>
<LI>But before that, put on my pajamas</LI>
</UL>

Damn, I've got too much to do.
```

Making an Ordered (Numbered) List

The only difference between an ordered list and an unordered list in terms of HTML is the opening tags. The cool thing about the ordered list HTML is that you don't have to number the list. The browser will do it for you when it renders your HTML.

To make an ordered (or numbered) list, follow these steps:

1. In your blog post, type the tag <OL>.

2. On the next line type <LI>, and enter a list item.

3. Repeat <LI>, followed by list items until you're done.

4. Don't forget to close each item with </LI>.

5. Close the list with </OL>.

The HTML that I'd enter into my blog would look like Listing 4.10.

Listing 4.10   Ordered List HTML Code

```
Things I need to do (in this order):
<OL>

<LI>Sleep</LI>
<LI>Wake up</LI>
<LI>Get dressed</LI>
<LI>Eat</LI>
<LI>Put on my pajamas</LI>
<LI>Go back to sleep</LI>
</OL>

Damn, I've got too much to do.
```

Remember that if the blog application you are using doesn't automatically insert line breaks or paragraph breaks when you press Enter or Return, you will want to use the <br> or <p> tags where necessary.

Aligning Text

Your blog posts will be aligned according to your template design, but occasionally you'll want to center text within a post or otherwise align the text in a way that differs from your usual post format. To illustrate, let's say I want to center some text. Listing 4.11 shows what I'd type.

Listing 4.11   Centering Some Text

```
<center>
Home is where we grumble the most and are treated the best.
</center>
```

Creating Tables

Tables originally existed merely to "tabulate information." Then they were adopted by creative HTML authors who used the table tags to design layouts for entire web pages. Today, there are other choices for designing layouts, but tables still remain useful within individual blog posts for arranging information in tabular form.

Try to think of your tabular information with the table elements in mind. A table includes headings that explain what the columns and rows contain, rows for information, and cells for each item.

These are the table elements you need to know:

- `<table></table>`—These are the opening and closing tags for a table.

- `<tr></tr>`—Table row

- `<td></td>`—Table cell

- `<th></th>`—Table header

You also can adjust the look of your table a bit by using these tags (please note that in the following examples, I've used the # or % characters as place-holders for the numbers you will choose):

- `<table border=#>`—Sets the width of the border around table cells.

- `<table cellspacing=#>`—Sets the amount of space between table cells.

- `<table cellpadding=#>`—Sets the amount of space between a cell's border and its contents.

- `<table width=# or %>`—Sets the width of table, in pixels or as a percentage of document width.

- `<tr align=?>` or `<td align=?>`—Sets the alignment for cell(s) (left, center, or right).

- `<tr valign=?>` or `<td valign=?>`—Sets the vertical alignment for the cell. Use top, middle, or bottom in place of the question mark.

- `<td colspan=#>`—Sets the number of columns a cell should span.

- `<td rowspan=#>`—Sets the number of rows a cell should span.

- `<td nowrap>`—Prevents the lines within a cell from being broken to fit.

Listing 4.12 shows what the code for a very simple table with a rule would look like.

Listing 4.12   Simple Table with a Rule

```
<TABLE>
<table border=1>
<TR>
    <TH> Things I Love </TH>
    <TH> Things I Hate </TH>
```

```
    </TR>
    <TR>
        <TD> Coffee </TD>
        <TD> Smog </TD>
    </TR>
    <TR>
        <TD> Carrots </TD>
        <TD> Pain </TD>
    </TR>
    </TABLE>
```

Figure 4.5 shows Listing 4.12 in a blog.

Figure 4.5

A simple table.

Beware of Tables

Those new to HTML should be forewarned: Tables are very particular. You must make sure that every open tag is closed, or you could have major rendering problems—especially in Netscape. Don't be scared; just double-check your work.

Simple Text Decoration

Bloggers need to know how to use the simple text decoration tags covered in this section: bold, italic, underline, and strikethrough. These are probably the most common text decorations you will want to use when blogging.

I find strikethrough particularly useful when I blog something on Monday that turns out to be dead wrong on Wednesday. I could just go back and rephrase my post so that it looks like I knew what I was talking about at the time, but who would I be kidding? Nobody would buy that.

Bold Text

To create bold text, you just surround the words you'd like to appear bold with the <b></b> tags (see Listing 4.13).

Listing 4.13   Bold Text Example

```
I have a <b>bold</b> sense of self preservation.
```

Figure 4.6 shows Listing 4.13 in a blog.

Figure 4.6

Bold text in a blog.

WELCOME TO MY WEBLOG	Genius

Sunday, May 05, 2002

I have a **bold** sense of self preservation.

3:41 pm - add eProps - add comments - email it

Italic Text

Italic works the same way as bold; it's just a different tag, <i></i> (see Listing 4.14).

Listing 4.14   Italic Text Example

```
Just because I <i>said</i> you have a big butt doesn't mean I
<i>think</i> it's big.
```

Figure 4.7 shows Listing 4.14 in a blog.

WELCOME TO MY WEBLOG	Genius

Sunday, May 05, 2002

Just because I *said* you have a big butt doesn't mean I
think it's big.

3:43 pm - add eProps - add comments - email it

Figure 4.7

Italic text in a blog.

Teletype Text

Teletype text is good for when you want to re-create that typewritten feeling.
I like to use it to simulate an email message, a memo, or an old-fashioned
telegram. The tags for teletype are <tt></tt> (see Listing 4.15).

Listing 4.15   Teletype Text Example

```
<tt>Lost at blackjack. Please wire $10,000. Hope you're well.</tt>
```

Figure 4.8 shows Listing 4.15 in a blog.

Figure 4.8

Teletype text in a blog.

Strikethrough Text

Use strikethrough tags (<strike></strike>) to scratch items off a list or take back a statement (see Listing 4.16). Strikethrough is great because you can see the previous post, which helps add new meaning to the next statement.

Listing 4.16   Strikethrough Text Example

```
Go Yankees!
<strike>The Boston Red Sox are the best! They can't lose!</strike>
```

Figure 4.9 shows Listing 4.16 in a blog.

Figure 4.9

Strikethrough text in a blog.

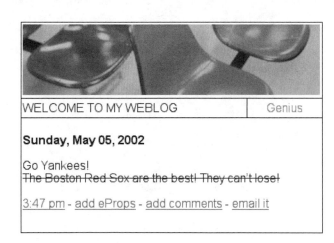

Underlined Text

Underlined text on the web tends to signify hyperlinked text, but not always. Underlining is as easy and straightforward as italic and bold (see Listing 4.17).

Listing 4.17   Underlined Text Example

```
I <u>strongly advise</u> against a definite course of action.
```

Figure 4.10 shows Listing 4.17 in a blog.

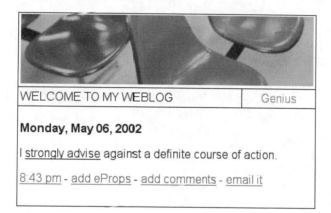

Figure 4.10

Underlined text in a blog.

Resizing Text

If you want to change the usual size of some text within an individual post, you can use the `<font size=?></font>` tags and replace the question mark with a number from 1 to 7, depending on which size you need (see Listing 4.18).

Listing 4.18   Resizing Text Example

```
That's when I shouted:<font size=5>STOP BITING ME!</font>
```

Figure 4.11 shows Listing 4.18 in a blog.

Figure 4.11

Resizing text in a blog.

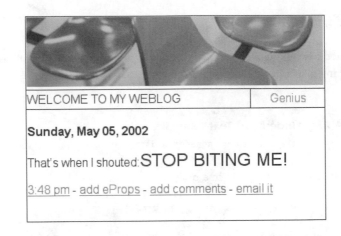

Colored Text

If you want to change the color of text within a post, you can use the `<font color=?></font>` tags and replace the question mark with a color name or hex value (see Listing 4.19). Also, see the "Specifying Colors" section in this chapter for a list of all of the colors you can choose.

Listing 4.19   Colored Text Example

```
Some prefer lighter hues, like <font color=silver>silver</font>.
```

Figure 4.12 shows Listing 4.19 in a blog.

Figure 4.12

Colored text in a blog.

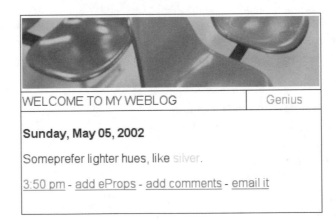

You also can combine both the color and size attributes to make an even bolder statement!

Horizontal Rules

Horizontal rules are one of the few graphic elements you can create with HTML. Use them to separate information within an individual post or just to jazz things up a bit. Additionally, there are a few different attributes you can use to change the way your rules look.

To create a rule, you type <hr> where you want it to go. The default horizontal rule is usually thin and has shading, but you can change the thickness (height), width, shading, and color of a rule. However, not all browsers will recognize every rule attribute.

These are all the rule tags you will need to know:

- <hr>—This is the tag you use to create the rule.

- <hr size="100pixels">—You can adjust the width of your rule as a fixed size in pixels, or

- <hr size="80%">—You can adjust the width of your rule using the more flexible percentage (of the browser window size) measurement.

- <hr height="4pixels>—You can change the height or thickness of your rule, too. The usual thickness of a rule is two pixels.

- <hr noshade>—Add noshade, and you'll just have a flat, graphic rule without the shadow.

- <HR color="blue">—This is how you add color to a rule.

Specifying Colors

Of the 216 "web safe" colors, there are 140 web colors that you can specify by name. After you have a few favorites, you will find that specifying colors by using their names is much easier. If a color name has more than one word, like "Dodger Blue," it's best to specify it as "dodgerblue" to make sure it renders correctly.

These are all the color names:

Aliceblue	Darkslategray	lightsalmon	Palevioletred
antiquewhite	Darkturquoise	lightseagreen	Papayawhip
Aqua	Darkviolet	lightskyblue	Peachpuff
Aquamarine	Deeppink	lightslategray	Peru
Azure	Deepskyblue	lightsteelblue	Pink
Beige	Dimgray	lightyellow	Plum
Bisque	Dodgerblue	lime	Powderblue
Black	Firebrick	limegreen	Purple
blanchedalmond	Floralwhite	linen	Red
Blue	Forestgreen	magenta	Rosybrown
Blueviolet	Fuchsia	maroon	Royalblue
Brown	Gainsboro	mediumaquamarine	Saddlebrown
Burlywood	Ghostwhite	mediumblue	Salmon
Cadetblue	Gold	mediumorchid	Sandybrown
chartreuse	Goldenrod	mediumpurple	Seagreen
Chocolate	Gray	mediumseagreen	Seashell
Coral	Green	mediumslateblue	Sienna
cornflowerblue	Greenyellow	mediumspringgreen	Silver
Cornsilk	Honeydew	mediumturquoise	Skyblue
Crimson	Hotpink	mediumvioletred	Slateblue
Cyan	Indianred	midnightblue	Slategray
Darkblue	Indigo	mintcream	Snow
Darkcyan	Ivory	mistyrose	Springgreen
darkgoldenrod	Khaki	moccasin	Steelblue
Darkgray	Lavender	navajowhite	Tan
Darkgreen	Lavenderblush	navy	Teal
Darkkhaki	Lawngreen	oldlace	Thistle
darkmagenta	Lemonchiffon	olive	Tomato

darkolivegreen	Lightblue	olivedrab	Turquoise
darkorange	Lightcoral	orange	Violet
darkorchid	Lightcyan	orangered	Wheat
Darkred	Lightgoldenrodyellow	orchid	White
darksalmon	Lightgreen	palegoldenrod	Whitesmoke
darkseagreen	Lightgrey	palegreen	Yellow
darkslateblue	Lightpink	paleturquoise	Yellowgreen

Web Link

These colors, along with their hexadecimal and RGB equivalents, can be found at

```
http://www.oreilly.com/catalog/wdnut/excerpt/color_names.html
```

One of the main advantages to blogging is that people who don't know HTML can get started in web publishing. Still, you will undoubtedly find yourself wanting to know the odd bit of HTML the next time you want to create a table or a numbered list of people you are planning on enlisting in your secret plot to take over the world. In that endeavor, I hope this chapter is your compatriot.

Chapter 5

Blog Design 101

When Steven Spielberg was shooting *Jaws*, he didn't have a dream budget. Ideally, Steven would have liked to film an incredibly lifelike mechanical great white shark attacking and consuming weak humans en masse. The problem was that an incredibly lifelike mechanical great white shark was incredibly expensive.

So he had to think of something else. Something creative. Something cheap. He decided to shoot the unsuspecting swimmers from the *shark's* point of view (with scary music), and it resulted in a classic memorable sequence.

While we're talking about Spielberg…remember the scene when Indy is approached by a sword wielding ne'er-do-well in the first *Indiana Jones* movie? The one where the bad guy flourishes his sword with practiced skill? The original screenplay called for a duel, but Ford had a bad case of diarrhea that day, and he could work only for a few minutes at a time before he had to run (pun intended). Ford consulted briefly with Spielberg, and when it was time to shoot the long, arduous swordfight, he brandished a pistol and shot his opponent. Another classic scene.

So what do all these Spielberg movies have to do with blog design? What's the connection? How do they relate? Alright already, stop with the questions.

The Biz Stone Theory of Limitations

When your back is to the wall, you get creative. It's as simple as that. Some of the most ingenious solutions have come into existence under circumstances with limited resources at hand. That's why those scenes in Spielberg's films are so good.

Create Your Own Limitations

If you're working for a client, you'll start out with limitations. They will most likely want you to use their logo and colors, match elements of an existing site, and impose other constraints. But if you're setting out to build a blog that's your own personal independent publishing endeavor, the canvas is totally blank.

This can be a problem. With no framework to work around, people can get lost trying to do everything and nothing at the same time. A blog heavy on graphics and tricked out with every possible web gadget or trying to dazzle with some kind of theme or concept just won't do.

In other words, if you find yourself thinking any of the following thoughts, you should slap yourself upside the head (in a friendly way):

- "My blog will look like a slightly open lunchbox, and the sandwich will be my entries!"

- "I love boats. My blog is a schooner, and you click the shark to go to my archive index page!"

- "Sherlock Holmes rocks. My blog is a big magnifying glass, and the words are huge!"

- "Everything on my blog will be backwards like Leonardo DaVinci's notebooks."

Actually that last one's kind of cool...as long as your readers have a mirror they can hold up next to their screen.

It's okay to riff off a concept, but the key is to give yourself a certain set of parameters and stick within them. For example, let's say that you have some Moorish tiles you pried off a wall at the Alhambra when you went to Spain (see Figure 5.1). Moorish tiles are beautiful, and you want your blog to be beautiful, too. Of course, because you are now cursed for life, this makes little difference. Nevertheless, we'll continue.

Figure 5.1

Do not pry Moorish tiles from the walls of historic sites.

First, create your limitations. Tell yourself that you are going to have a simple graphic header, default underlined links, black text in a column under your header, and that's it for now. Then, pick out colors from the tiles—let's say they have orange, green, and blue.

If you can scan in the tiles, that's great. You can use them as the graphic element in your header. Reverse your blog title out of a 600-pixel wide block or use a thin strip underneath the title. Make your title orange, your links blue, and your timestamps green. Put this all against a white background, and you'll have a clean, simple, museum-like blog with hints of Moorish colors and some tile work. Now you can blog your next trip to Spain in digital style. Of course, if your chosen blog topic is about flatscreen television technology, this design might be somewhat non sequitor. But hey, at least it's not a sandwich.

A clean, easy-to-read blog will prove more usable and, in the long run, will attract more regular readers than a bloated design. Plus, with a simple, streamlined approach, you have less chance of browser incompatibility and errors. When it's time to design your blog, think simple. You can always add on later.

Figure 5.2 is an example of a blog that makes dramatic use of emptiness. Lots of white space with Spartan gray text creates a page that at first glance doesn't look like it's really there. Readers are invited to lean closer and hear Jason Gurley whisper his unique, artful entries. When visiting the subtle `deeplyshallow.com`, you get the feeling that you are sneaking around in someone's mind. Those who stay long enough to investigate are in for a treat.

Figure 5.2

DeeplyShallow: Emptiness is sexy.

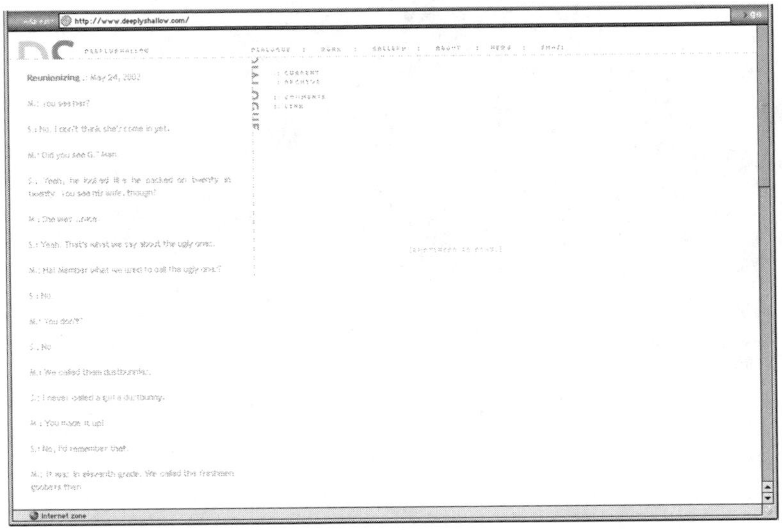

Elements of a Blog

Some elements are common to many blogs, so there is a kind of design precedent you can follow when you first start out. A classic blog design has a header, a simple date design, reader friendly body copy, easily discernable links, some modules in columns, and a footer. Each of these classic blog design elements is covered in more detail in the sections that follow. Sometimes it's great to have something to follow, just so that you can break the rules. Jason Kottke's blog, which is shown in Figure 5.3, has all the elements of a classic blog design.

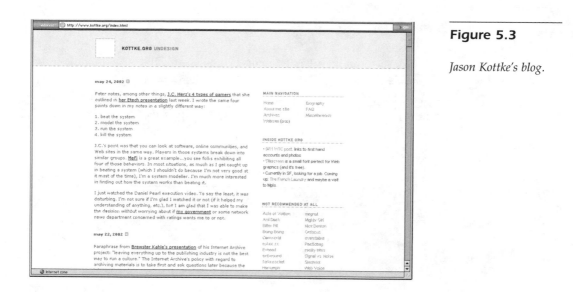

Figure 5.3

Jason Kottke's blog.

Page Header

The top part of your blog is usually the place where you introduce your "identity." It's generally the first to load, so it makes the first impression. For the best effect, have something simple yet memorable in this area, something that represents the "feel" of your blog. I've got a picture of me and a big, crazy, handwritten title that says *Biz Stone, Genius* (see Figure 5.4). To some people that probably means I'm some kind of big jerk. But people who know me or read my blog know that it's more funny than arrogant. I hope.

Figure 5.4

I claim to be a genius. Just go along with it.

Date Design

One of the most prevalent elements in a blog is the date. Although you can choose to display the date numerically or in a tiny point size after each post, many bloggers opt to present a date before each post (see Figure 5.5). Aside from breaking the information up nicely, it helps a reader see right away if there is a new post today. That being said, some bloggers deviate from the norm. Deviants are good.

Figure 5.5

Anil uses bold date headers. The little paragraph symbols are permalinks.

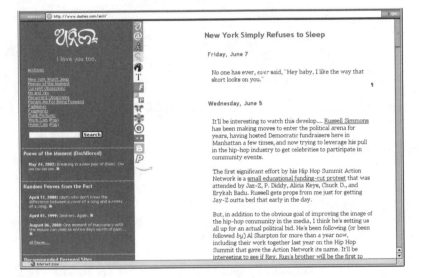

On his blog, "Nothing, and lots of it," Matthew Haughey doesn't put the date before the post. Instead, Matt has set up his blog so that the newest day is featured at the top of the page, and the days before it are placed in the lower "recently thought" section. You'll notice too that Matthew doesn't even have a header; he just starts right away with the post, and his navigational bar is used to separate new content from old content. Matt deviates from many of the blog layout conventions, but as you can see, it works (see Figure 5.6).

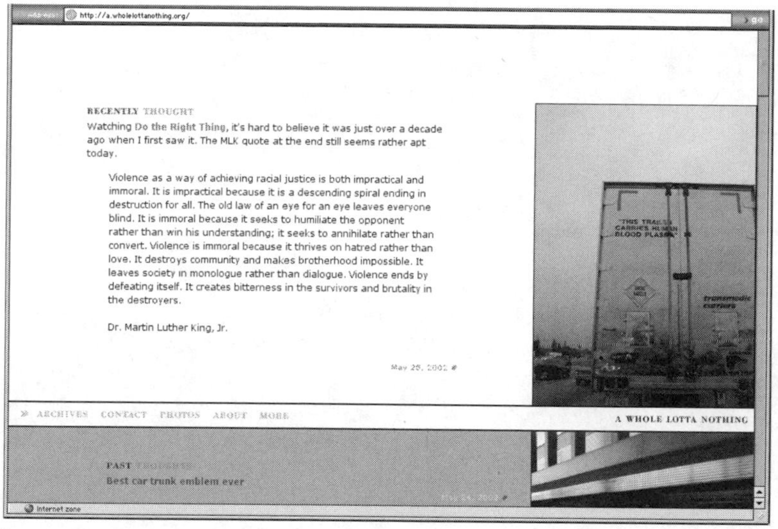

Figure 5.6

Matt Haughey is a deviant.

Body Copy

Your body copy is all the text on your blog; it's the main feature. We cover how to design your text for best results in some detail in Chapter 6, "Blogging with Style." Key things to remember are font size and ample space between lines. Don't make your text too small, and space your lines out a bit if you can. Don't be afraid of white space. Ample white space around and between the lines of your text helps make it more legible, and it also puts your words on display and makes them into a design feature. Type can be beautiful if it is thoughtfully arranged. Figure 5.7 shows the Fireland blog, which has small but soothing text.

Figure 5.7

Fireland is the Web home of Joshua Allen.

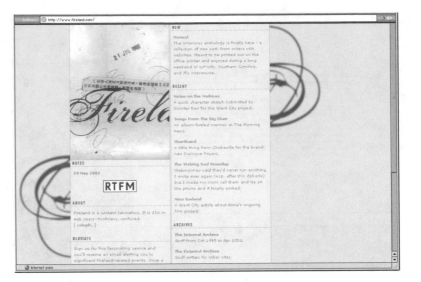

Links

Links are a huge part of blogging. A blog post is usually some form of commentary with a link to the subject being commented on. It's important that your links are easy to spot and that your readers recognize them as links.

In the early days of the web, a link was blue and underlined, and that was that. There was no question as to what was a link and what was text. Today, there are many choices. Your link color can be any color, it can be underlined or not underlined, have a rollover effect, and so on. Figure 5.8 shows Jim Romenesko's Obscure Store and Reading Room, which has a beautiful header, great body copy, and a different style of links in the boxes (also called *modules*) to the right.

Feel free to design your text and links as you see fit, but strive to present your links in a distinctive way that obviously separates them from the rest of your body copy. If your text is black and your links also are black but underlined, don't underline other words in your text that aren't links. It will confuse your readers, and they might think they have discovered a broken link.

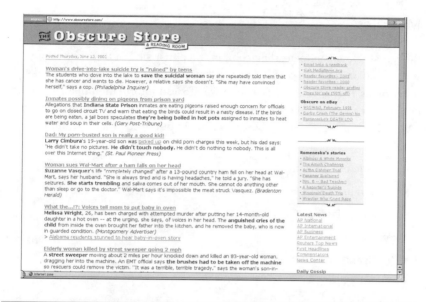

Figure 5.8

Jim Romenesko's Obscure Store and Reading Room.

Links with a Little Style

Get your toes wet with a bit of CSS. Add the code in Listing 5.1 to your blog template to turn off link underlines.

Listing 5.1   Turning Off Link Underlines

```
A:link {
  color: #0000FF;
  text-decoration: none;
  background: #FFFFFF;}
A:visited {
  color: #FF9999;
  text-decoration: none;
  background: #FFFFFF;}
A:hover {
  color: #999999;
  text-decoration: underline;
  background: #FFFFFF;}
A:active {
  color: #9999CC;
  text-decoration: underline;
  background: #FFFFFF;}
```

This gives you links that are blue without being underlined in the unvisited state. After they have been visited, the link color is salmon-pink (also without underlines), the hover state is medium-gray underlined, and the active state (the moment when the link is actually clicked) has a purple-lilac color and underlines. The hover state is not rendered in Netscape Navigator 4.xx, and active in NN4.xx is always red.

Modules

Bloggers have taken to creating columns on either side of their body copy with boxes or modules containing small amounts of information like links to other blogs. Using modules is a good way to add information that isn't quite enough for a whole new page without mucking up the clean, simple design of a blog. Here are some things bloggers usually put inside their columns or modules:

- Links to other blogs
- A short bio
- A "Now Playing" CD image
- Search box
- Navigation to other non-blog web pages
- Announcements
- Wish lists
- A "Now Reading" book image

There are even services for maintaining these lists. One such service is blogrolling.com. The web journaling service Upsaid.com also provides a feature called *Upsaid Columns* as part of their standard feature set:

> "The 'Upsaid Columns' are used to update your pages columns easily, without having to edit the html templates. We call 'columns' the list of links, information about you, etc., which web loggers usually display on their pages' sidebars."[1]

Figure 5.9 shows Upsaid.com's user interface for editing your blog columns. Fill in the fields and click Save to work on your column—there's no need to fiddle with your blog template.

---

1. *UpSaid Web Journaling Service. "Feature Description - Upsaid columns." May 2002. Available from the Internet:* www.upsaid.com/features.php?feature=col

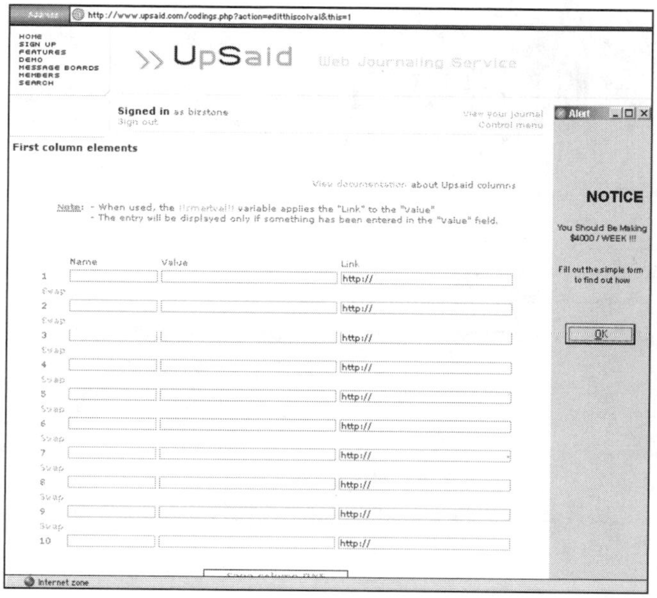

Figure 5.9

Edit your modules independently.

Footer

A blog's footer usually is just a few links at the bottom of the page. The links are often things like this:

- A copyright notice—for example, © Biz Stone, Genius 1999-2003 All Rights Reserved.

- An email link so that people can send you praise

- A link to the blogging provider (in lieu of payment)

- An optional "About This Blog" link

Some bloggers have adopted an old book-publishing standard and created a link to their colophon. Historically, a *colophon* is an inscription on the last page of a book with facts about the publication such as where the book was printed, who printed it, the typeface used, and things of that nature. Colophons are a nice way to enhance the perceived value of your blog. By dedicating a page for a written blurb about the software you use to publish your blog, who designed the blog, what typeface the copy is set in, and that sort of thing, your readers will get the idea that you have crafted something of value for them. Figure 5.10 shows a great example of a colophon.

Figure 5.10

Hack the Planet's colophon.

Bringing It Together

Designing a blog is a great way for anyone new to web design to get their feet wet, but for more experienced designers it's also a good exercise in working with constraints. The elements that make a good blog are the same elements that make a good, useable web page. If you do add more pages, or if you're working with archives enabled on your blog, you'll need to implement an easy-to-understand navigation system for your readers. A simple way to add navigation is to create a set of links inside a module. Put the module in a prominent location on every page—the blog, of course, but also the archive index page and any other pages you choose to build.

Keeping navigation links constant on every page is important; otherwise, users might become disoriented. However, it's best to unlink the name of the page the user is reading—this lets your readers know which page they are currently viewing.

When you break the blog into elements, like header, body copy, links, miscellaneous modules, and navigational elements, you are beginning to think like an information architect. Like many bloggers, you might eventually want to create more pages for essays or photos while you keep your blog as the home page of this new content-heavy web site. The streamlined, elemental thinking you've developed with your blog will translate well to future pages you might want to add. And if you decide to power your whole site with a blog-style content management system, you will already have the skills to make it so.

Part II

So, You Already Know How to Blog?

Chapter 6

Blogging with Style

Blogs are all about content, and this content is very often text. It's important for a blog to have a clean, readable type design yet still remain interesting and engaging. Back in the day when HTML was just a baby, your only font choice was whatever font the browser default displayed. Today's transitional HTML is a little more advanced with its font element and attributes, but for superior type control on the web, cascading style sheets (CSS) is the way to go.

Note that although style sheets provide a much wider number of design solutions, they also bring baggage to the situation—they aren't always supported by not-so-new browsers. Also, fonts specified in CSS must be native to the user's computer for them to appear.

A Brief Introduction to Typography

Before we get into the nuts and bolts of achieving beautiful type on your blog, let's take a quick spin through the world of typography as it applies to blogging.

Serif and Sans Serif

Type can be lumped broadly into two major categories—serif and sans serif. What is the difference? I'm glad you asked!

A serif typeface is one with "feet." Feet are the little extensions at the ends of the letter's strokes. A sans serif typeface does not have the feet. Sans means *without*. That's why people often say, "Biz Stone is an idiot savant *sans* the savant." It's a popular saying here on the East Coast.

Figure 6.1 shows an example of a serif font (Georgia), and under that is an example of a sans serif font (Helvetica).

Figure 6.1

Georgia has feet;
Helvetica does not.

The gods of typography generally agree that serif type is more readable than sans serif when you are dealing with copious amounts of text. Possible reasons for this could be that the feet of the serif face help guide the reader's eye along, the thick and thin variations in the strokes of the font make it more readable, or maybe it's just because we're all just used to it. There are no stone tablets that proclaim exactly why this is true, but open up a bunch of novels the next time you're in a bookstore and compare how many are set in serif as opposed to sans serif type.

These same gods have also been known to lean towards sans serif in cases where short bursts of type are required to provoke a instant recognition. Some uses of sans serif towards this end would be signage, headlines, or ad copy.

Fonts on the screen are different than printed fonts. A screen font is a mosaic of squares that tries its best to emulate the shapes in an alphabet. Screen type composition is not as exacting as print, and it can have various outcomes depending on the user's browser choice. I have found that, on the web, going against the gods works well for me. I often use Verdana, a sans serif typeface, for the body copy of web pages and blogs. Sans serif may work well on blogs because, by nature, a blog copy is usually formed in short lines and short paragraphs—not too dissimilar from advertising copy. And although I go against the gods, I haven't yet been struck by lightening. Once I did get a nice jolt from a coffeemaker, though.

Default Web Typeface
Times is the default typeface on the web. Designed in the 1930s for the Times newspaper in London, its design is based on the principles of typography, which have evolved since the Roman Empire (uppercase) and the 16th century (lowercase).

Measuring Type

When you are deciding how you want your blog type to look, it's helpful to have a general idea of how web font sizes and printed font sizes relate. In printed matter, size is straightforward, but on the web, there are various factors that influence the size of letters and words. These factors include monitor resolution (and how it's set up within an operating system), the web browser's default font size chosen by your reader, and finally, the actual size you specify for your typeface.

In the world of print, type is usually specified in points. Point size is the measurement between the bottom of the lowest descender to the top of the highest ascender, with a little bit added on. The most commonly used value for the typographic point is 1/72 of an inch. However, in print a 72-point letter is never exactly an inch high, because lines of type need to be set with additional space between them so that they don't touch.

When your word processing application asks the operating system for a particular letter at a particular point size, it is given a bitmap rendering of that letter. The size of the letter in pixels depends on the resolution of the output device. It is important to know that the type size, in pixels, for any specified point size is dependent on the resolution of the output device—this is as true for screen displays as it is for printers. Computer monitors typically range from 72 to 150 pixels per inch.

HTML Font Sizes and Point Size

The official HTML specifications leave it to the developers of browsers to decide the relationship between the <FONT SIZE=n> values and the actual type size in points. Microsoft Internet Explorer and most other browsers adopted the original Mosaic/Netscape default sizes. Table 6.1 shows the HTML font size and printed point size correlation.

Table 6.1   A Comparison of Web and Print Font Sizes

HTML Font Size	Point Size
0	6
1	8
2	10
3	12
4	14
5	18
6	24
7	36

One Space or Two?

In case you are wondering whether to use one space or two spaces after a period, use one space. Two spaces are a carryover from the age of the typewriter. On a typewriter, the letters are monospaced, which means that each character in the font takes up the same amount of space, including periods. This means that you needed two spaces in order to have a space show up at all.

The characters in most digital typefaces are proportional, which means that they each take up a proportional amount of space. For example, the letter *i* is about one-fifth the space of the letter *m*, so the single space after a period in a proportional font like Verdana is enough to separate it from the next sentence. There are a few fonts, such as Courier, that are monospaced to imitate the look of a typewriter—if you're using one of those fonts, you have my personal permission to use two spaces after the period.

Quote Me on That

Quoting is popular in blogs, and many people just hold down the Shift key and press " for quotation marks. This isn't really a quotation mark; it's an inch mark. And, ' is a foot mark. Here's an example of both in action:

> I am 5'11" tall, 6'1" if you count my hair when I wake up. That's when I look in the mirror and say, "My word, I look like Bird Man. Biiird Maaan!"

If you want to look like a type pro, use real quotation marks when you blog. On a Mac, the real punctuation for quotation marks can be secretly accessed on the keyboard like so:

- Opening double quote: " Option [

- Closing double quote: " Option Shift [

- Opening single quote: ' Option]

- Closing single quote: ' Option Shift]

Desktop publishing software sometimes AutoCorrects the quotes for you, but it's a good bet that your blog application won't. So, the next time you're quoting someone or something on your blog, remember your options.

Quotation Character Codes

If you want to really get into quoting, you can use the HTML character codes for quotations:

- &#147 —Opening double quote

- &#148 —Closing double quote

- &#145 —Opening single quote

- &#146 —Closing single quote

If you use the character codes, your quotes are sure to display correctly in all browsers.

Kerning for Fun and Profit

(Without the fun and profit.) Kerning is a design procedure employed to create visually consistent letterspacing. In many typefaces, each letter has a set amount of space on either side of it. Because of this, certain combinations of letters can appear to have more or less space between them, due to the angled or rounded shape of the letters and the impressions they create.

Ideally, every letter and every word would be adjusted for consistent visual spacing, but this is not going to happen in your blog. Although you cannot kern type by eye even with CSS, you can space out your letters to a comfortable degree. Why would you want to do this? Well, sometimes when you use italic, spacing gets a little tight between words. Also, skinny fonts such as Arial sometimes need a little breathing room.

Leading, AKA Line Height

Leading is a term from the olden days of printing. Up until the 1970s, printed type was set in hot metal. Every letter, (every letter!) of a book, newspaper, and so on, was cast onto a piece of lead backwards so that when it was inked and stamped onto the paper it would be facing in the right direction. The letters were grouped into words, and blank pieces of lead were placed between them for spaces. Later, words and whole lines were cast in lead, but the concept remained the same. Between the lines of type, more lead was placed to space the lines; thus the term, *leading*. In CSS, leading is referred to as *line height*, and although it doesn't involve metal, it's still hot. For a good example of leading in action, see Figure 6.2. Figure 6.3 shows a not-so-good example.

Figure 6.2

This blog has ample line height.

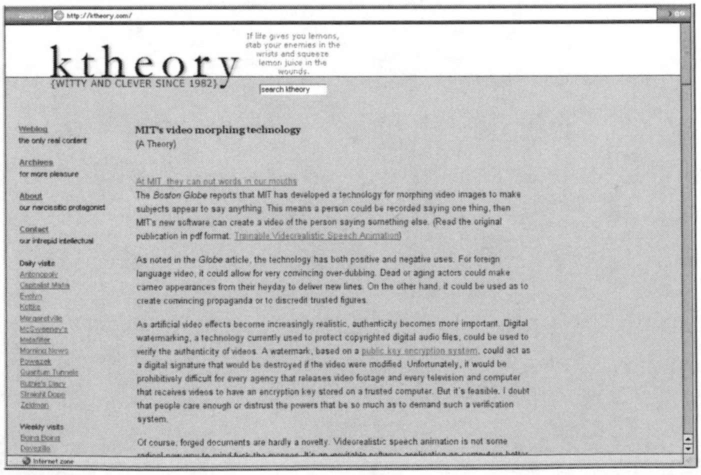

Figure 6.3

It's easy to lose your place when lines are tight.

Genius Tip

Setting Your Line Height

Ample line height improves readability. Set your line height at least 20% more than your type size. This means that if you choose 10 pixels for your blog body copy, use at least 12 pixels for your line height.

Working without Styles: Using the <font> Tag

Okay, we've covered type from a historical perspective and hinted at the potential of CSS. But, before we get into styles, let's cover the <font> tag because it's widely used and still very relevant to you as a blogger.

Specifying a Font

To specify a font with the <font> tag, you simply follow these steps:

1. Open the HTML of your blog template design.

2. Find the text (or proprietary tags that will call your entries).

3. Open the <font> tag.

4. Follow with an equal sign (=) and the attribute "face," which simply means the font you want to use. In this case, it's Verdana.

Like so (see Listing 6.1).

Listing 6.1   Specifying Your Font

```
<font face="verdana">
This will render my type in Verdana.
</font>
```

If you list multiple font names separated by commas, the user's browser will render the first font from the list that is native to their machine (see Listing 6.2). The idea behind choosing multiple fonts is to pick similar fonts so that if the people reading your blog don't have Verdana, they might have Geneva or Futura. This way, the general look of your blog will not be lost on them.

Listing 6.2   Listing Multiple Fonts

```
<font face="verdana, geneva, futura">
If you don't have Verdana, maybe you have Geneva or Futura.
</font>
```

Genius Tip

Another Option
Specify `"serif"` or `"sans-serif"` instead of font names for a broader way to ensure that users on different platforms can see your blog the way you want them to.

Specifying a Font Size

You have seven size choices with the <font> tag. These font sizes are not "absolute;" they're "relative." This doesn't mean you're obligated to visit them on holidays—it means that the size at which the font will actually appear depends on things such as screen resolution and computer platform.

The default font size is 3. This is the ballpark equivalent of 12-point type. You don't need to do anything to set the font at the default size, but if you want to change it, you need to add the size attribute (see Listing 6.3).

Listing 6.3   Adding the Size Attribute

```
<font face="verdana" size="2">
This font will be Set in Verdana and slightly smaller than the
➥default size.
</font>
```

It's easy to confuse header sizing and font sizing. In header sizing, 1 is the largest, and 6 is the smallest. In font sizing, 7 is the largest, and 1 is the smallest. Be warned.

Coloring the Font

When designing the text for your blog, you may want to set certain items, such as the date-time stamp, in a different color to help differentiate it from the text of the post. Adding color to a font, like specifying the size or font itself, requires the use of an attribute (see Listing 6.4). With color, you can use a (hexadecimal) number or the name of the color.

Listing 6.4   Using the Name of the Color As an Attribute

```
<font face="verdana" size="1" color="silver">
This font will be tiny and silver so as not to bother anyone.
</font>
```

When specifying color for your blog text, choose one that contrasts well with your background color. Light-colored fonts on a dark background or dark fonts on a light background will do the trick. Black type on a white background is old-school, but it works well in terms of contrast. Remember that you can use links to add a splash of color.

Working with CSS Style Sheets: Superior Type Control

What you can't do with type in HTML, you can do with CSS. In fact, type design is only the tip of the iceberg where CSS is concerned. It is very powerful. Before we get right into bossing our type around with style sheets, let's have a little look at how they work. You have three basic methods for creating styles. Don't worry about the CSS code; it's just there to serve as an example. I'll show you how easy it is to build a little style for your blog's type design in a just a bit. Here are the three methods:

- Linked style sheets
- Embedded style sheets
- Inline styles

These three methods are explained in the following sections.

Linked Style Sheets

The linked style sheets method allows you to keep your style sheet out of
your template. You build a separate document for the style, and then tell your
design to refer to the style sheet that is hiding in a folder somewhere out of
sight. Linked style sheets are great when you have many pages on your site in
addition to your blog (longer posts, essays, and so on.) because you can open
just the style document and change it, and then the changes are made
throughout your entire site. Here's how you'd create a style sheet for linking:

1. Create the style sheet. Here's an example of a simple style:

   ```
   H1 {color: #FF6600;}
   ```

   With this style, a level one heading will appear orange (#FF6600).

2. You should save a remote CSS file as something like "header1style.css"
   (not header1style.html), and save it in a folder called something like
   "styles."

3. To make the style work, you need to link it to your blog. To do that, you
   put the link syntax within the document head. Here's what the link
   should look like:

   ```
   <LINK rel=stylesheet href="styles/header1style.css" type="text/css"
   ```

Now, any level one headers you create when you blog will appear orange. I'm
not saying you should put orange headers in your blog; I'm just giving you
an easy example. With this method, you can develop a style for body text,
links, anything you want. The style will be more complex than this example,
but it will be just as easy to link to.

Sylloge uses a linked style sheet to achieve a strong type design with a serif
face and underlined links (see Figure 6.4).

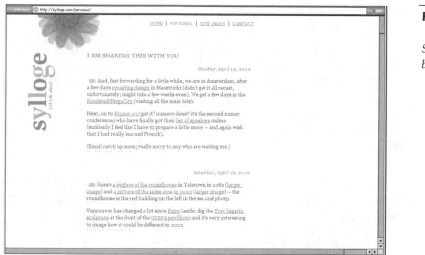

Figure 6.4

Stewart Butterfield's blog.

Embedded Style Sheets

Embedding the style sheets in your blog's template gives you page-by-page control of the styles. If you have only one page, you may want to go this route. All you do is create your style, and then make sure it's inside the document head. Listing 6.5 shows what a little embedded style sheet might look like.

Listing 6.5   Embedded Style Sheet Example

```
<style>
p {font-family: verdana; font-size=10pixels; line-height=12pixels;}
</style>
```

Keep in mind that an embedded style will override a linked style.

Inline Styles

Inline styles are ideal for perfectionists. They give you style control down to a single character by working directly within the HTML, using the style attribute. Listing 6.6 is what you'd be looking at if you wanted to go for the inline style.

Listing 6.6   Inline Style Example

```
<p>Inline styles are ideal for perfectionists. They give you style
control down to a single word or character by working directly with-
in the HTML using the style attribute.</p><p style="font-family:
chicago;" >So if you want to use a style to set a paragraph in
Chicago for your friends who use Macs, you can.</style>
```

Using CSS Style Sheets to Design Your Blog Typography

Using one of the three methods of creating a style and the background information on typography, you now can design the text of your blog for maximum readability and effect.

When you are designing your blog text, keep in mind that it is the main feature of your blog and that people (hopefully) will be reading it every day. You
want something interesting, but still easy on the eyes. Look at your type without reading it. Squint your eyes a little and think of it not as type, but as some
other element of design, like color. Does it look pretty? Is it clumped in deli-
cious, bite-sized paragraphs that are comfortably padded between the lines?
Are you getting hungry just looking at it? Maybe I should eat before I continue. Always remember that when you're designing for the web, different
browsers will display your work differently. Accept this fact, and you can be
happy.

Building Your Style

For this example, let's say you are using the embedded style method. This
means that you are going to design your main blog text using CSS, and then
you'll just paste it into the head of your blog template. The actual code for
your type design will be very simple, and when you're ready, you'll just paste
it into the document head.

So here's what you do:

1. Start by typing **<STYLE>**.

2. Type the open curly brace character (**{**).

3. Enter the various attributes you want to apply to your type. These
   should be separated by semicolons.

4. Don't forget to close the style tag with </STYLE>.

In this example, I'm using pixels (px) as my unit of measurement. Listing 6.7 shows how easy it is.

Listing 6.7   Using the Embedded Style Method

```
<STYLE>
{font: 12px verdana; line-height: 24px;}
➥a {text-decoration: none}
</STYLE>
```

In this example, I have created a style with the font Verdana set at 12 pixels, a line height (leading) of 24 pixels, and I used a {text-decoration: none} to turn off the underlining of my links. Some people believe removing the underline from links can cause confusion, but as long as the linked word or words stand out in some way—such as appearing in a different color—then you're fine.

More Information

Other attributes can be incorporated into your style simply by typing them inside the brackets with those you've already chosen. For more information on working with CSS you can visit http://www.w3.org/Style/CSS. If you'd like to be personally guided through the world of type online, visit Andy Crewdson's blog *Lines and Splines* at http://www.linesandsplines.com (see Figure 6.5).

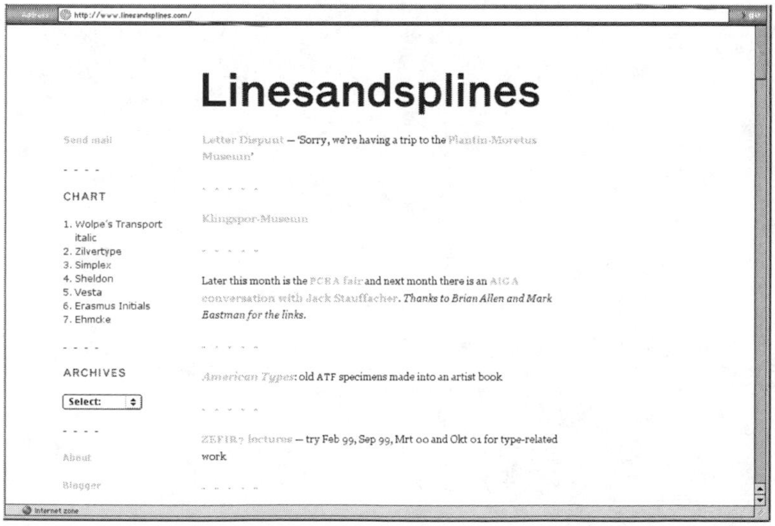

Figure 6.5

Lines and Splines is a blog dedicated to typography.

Since we've already cracked into type design, we might as well get into the design of your blog as a whole. To do that, we're going to need a whole new chapter.

Chapter 7

Blogging for Dollars

You've put in some time building your blog into something more than just a plain old web page. So much so that your significant other is starting to think that you're up to no good on the web. People are coming back regularly to read what you've posted, and maybe you've even registered for an ISSN, and your blog has become a *bona fide* periodical. (ISSNs are covered in Chapter 18, "Blog Goodies.") In other words, you're working on your blog, and you wouldn't mind getting paid for it.

Well, guess what? You can. I'm not saying you're gonna buy a new car with proceeds generated from your blog, but you stand to cover your hosting or "premium" fees and maybe even get a gift or two sent your way for a job well done.

For most bloggers, setting up their own payment processing system is virtually impossible, not to mention that it costs big bucks. But why do it yourself when someone else has already done it? There are lots of great ways to accept payments on the web.

Some methods for generating a cash flow with your blog are micropayment systems, affiliate programs, merchandising, ad hosting, and wishlists. Micropayments are direct fees for content, but the other methods bring a little more to the table in terms of offering something in return. Incorporate one or all of them, and you'll be actively engaged in blogging for dollars.

Micropayments

Micropayments are fees that range from a few dollars down to fractions of a cent. With a micropayment system in place, consumers are charged these fees for each instance of accessing a web site. In theory, if you can impose a small charge for some of the hits on your site, those pennies could eventually add up to dollars. This pay-per-view arrangement is an alternative to ad banners or subscriptions, and is thought by some to be the Holy Grail of making money on the web.

There has been much debate on the issue of micropayments on the web. Those who are pro-micropayment say, "Hey, we pay a few cents a minute when we're on the phone. Why not on the web?" On the other side, those opposed to micropayments simply state, "Users hate them. They will never work."

When you provide a useful service, however—whether it's software you've developed, helpful tutorials and essays, or a much-needed chuckle every morning—people are not completely averse to dropping you a little something every now and then.

Donations as a "thank you" may not work for big companies trying to generate a consistent and dependable revenue stream, but for us individual media baron wannabes, a few coins in the jar now and then can be a big help.

Take, for example, the unfortunate case of blogger LaVonne Ellis. LaVonne found herself sounding the micropayment alarm at the end of a lean month in 2002.

> 1/31/2002: "rent party"
>
> Back in the hippie days, there was a charming custom called the "rent party" borrowed from Harlem years earlier. If you couldn't pay your rent, you'd just invite everyone you knew [and a lot of people you didn't know] to a party at your place, and charge them a few bucks to enter.
>
> Of course, you'd offer a live band, free beer, and the chance to meet lots of attractively disheveled guys and/or long-haired hippie girls. And all the dancing, mingling, and groping a horny young person could hope for.

Oh, yes, and dope. Plenty of dope. Amazing how cheap marijuana was
in those days, not to mention acid and mescaline. But you wouldn't
have to pay for it; you could count on many of your guests to bring
their own and pass it around to the freeloaders. There were lots of freeloaders, but no one seemed to mind. It was a sweet, innocent time.

I only attended one of these parties, unfortunately. It was 1967 in the
local version of Haight-Ashbury, the Seven Corners district, a run-down
Minneapolis neighborhood of tenements and factories that is now quite
fashionable. There was nothing fashionable about the place then, and
that's what made it so exotic to me. After all, this was once the stomp-
ing ground of a young Bob Dylan.

The loft apartment was huge, dark, dingy, and crowded. The music, by
a trio of blues singers who were said to have influenced the Beatles, was
outstanding. It was a whole new world to me, still in my Marlo Thomas
flip hairdo and Jackie Kennedy chemise dress. I may have had a beer or
two, but I certainly wasn't taking drugs at that point.

I was never the same after that party. I learned that some people held
rent parties every month; it was their way of living without having to
get jobs. There was a whole community of college students from the
university across the river who regularly made the rounds of rent parties and bars on the West Bank, the larger neighborhood where Seven
Corners was located. Who knew how many people survived this way?
Of course, rent in those days and that neighborhood was obscenely
cheap, $50-80 per month. I thought rent parties made a lot of sense.

Within two years, I was living near Seven Corners, my hair now long
and straight, chemise discarded for tattered jeans, but by then rent parties were over. I never attended another, or had the courage to throw
one.

I wish I had the courage now. The rent is due, I've lost my only client
[I'm self-employed and not eligible for unemployment] and I'm $200
short. Times are different and so am I. In short, a rent party is not an
option.

So I'm freaking out here. It's the last day of the month. I know there are
a lot of unemployed bloggers out there and I hope they're okay, but I'm
not. I hope you will forgive this naked pitch for money and that you
will consider this little story entertaining enough to be worth $5 or $10.

I promise to pitch in when it's your turn.

Thanks for anything you can spare.

LaVonne Ellis is a freelance writer and avid blogger.
(http://surreally.com/bornfamous/)

Within minutes of publishing her tale of flip hairdos, drugs, and the blues, LaVonne had raised $100 from her blog readers—half of what she needed. She had to dig the other half up in the real world. Still, half is better than nothing, right?

LaVonne used the Amazon Honor System. It gives users access to Amazon.com's patented payment technology to collect online payments as small as $1.00. To date, they have nearly 30 million people signed up for the system.

How the Amazon Honor System Works

First, you'll need to sign up. Just go to Amazon.com and scroll all the way down to the bottom of the main page. Then, click the link that says Join Honor System (see Figure 7.1).

Figure 7.1

The Amazon Honor System home page. From here, you can manage your PayBoxes and PayPages.

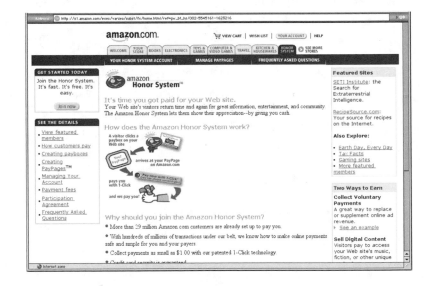

After you're all signed up, you'll get a code for a PayBox to put on your blog. A PayBox is a graphic image that links to the Amazon Honor System. People click the PayBox, and then arrive at your Honor System PayPage. You can customize your PayBox shape, size, and color, and select its message. Because they're served by Amazon.com, your PayBox will even greet Amazon customers by name.

The PayBox brings users to your PayPage—your personalized page at Amazon.com where people come to pay you. This page is like a product detail page at Amazon.com. "Customers" come to your PayPage, get the information they need to make a payment decision, and then click a button to send you money with a credit or debit card. You can put a title, image, and text description on your PayPage. You can also add a goal chart or a payment tracker.

Amazon transfers your Amazon Honor System earnings directly into your checking account. You can "initiate a disbursement" at any time, as long as your account balance is at least $1.00. In addition, they automatically pay you every 14 days. You can track your earnings and review your transactions online. Also, know that Honor System payments are voluntary—a payer may request a refund for any reason with no questions asked for up to 30 days after a payment is made. Doh!

The Amazon Honor System does not charge registration fees, setup fees, or fixed participation fees. They do, however, charge transaction fees based on the amount of money you receive. For each payment you receive, they charge $0.15 plus 15% of the total transaction amount. The person making a payment is not charged any fees other than the huge donation they are giving to you because you are such a fantastic person and talented blogger.

So how does the money get from someone's credit card into your bank account? Surely not by magic? No, by your checking account (which is like magic because everything in it always disappears). Amazon provides a secure page with fields for inputting your checking account number. After you do this, your earnings can be disbursed directly into your checking account.

Using PayPal

PayPal charges 2.2% plus $0.30 per transaction. Many small businesses use PayPal as their only payment process because it looks professional and is more customizable. It's just as easy to set up as an Honor System account (see Figure 7.2).

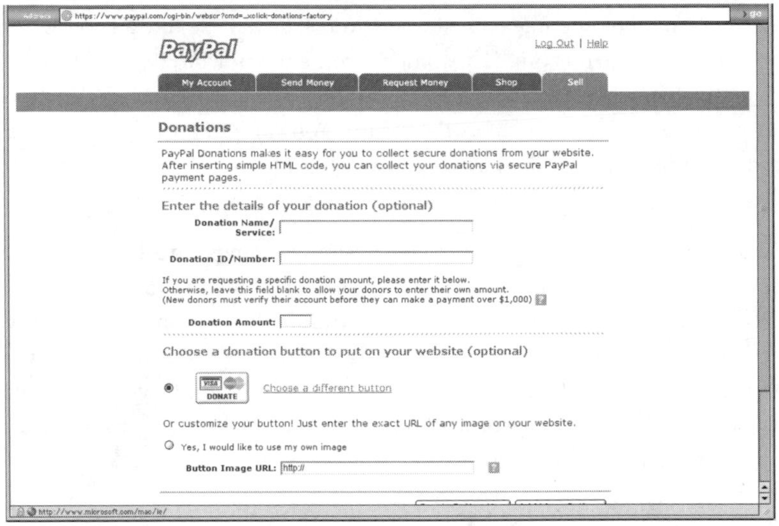

Figure 7.2

Setting up PayPal to accept donations is easy.

After you've signed up and filled out all the necessary information, PayPal generates the HTML code for your "payment button." You can select one of their buttons or use your own image to customize the look. Anyone who wants to send you a little cash just clicks to pay. They'll arrive at a secure payment page to enter their name, credit card, and billing information.

After someone pays you by credit card (or bank or checking account), the money will appear in your PayPal account right away. You can then withdraw the money by requesting a personal check from PayPal or by requesting an electronic funds transfer to your bank account. When finished, your generous benefactors will see a "Successful Transaction" page and can click to return to your blog. You'll both receive email receipts detailing the transaction.

Micropayments in the form of "thank you" tips are not out of the question. LaVonne waited until she was desperate and cried out for help, but it's not unreasonable to keep a PayBox or button somewhere on your blog at all times. Dedication to your blog and your loyal readers doesn't have to go unrewarded.

Affiliate Programs

If you have friends who read your blog, you've most likely got web-savvy friends who probably shop online. Something you should do the very day you launch your blog is sign up for an affiliate program like the Associates Program at Amazon.com.

Amazon Associates earn up to 15% of the sale price on individually linked books that you feature on your site and 5% on anything else that is purchased through your links, including CDs, videos, DVDs, toys, consumer electronics, and more. It's free to join, and there are no hidden quotas or performance tiers to reach before you start earning the highest level of referral fees.

Whenever you link to something available for purchase, make sure your affiliate code is in the link (right after the ASIN number). That way, anyone who clicks through to Amazon and eventually buys something will earn you a referral fee (see Figure 7.3). Do this every time you are blogging about a book, an album, software, or whatever, and you'll increase the likelihood of your readers buying something—especially if you've recommended it. If they are loyal readers, it stands to reason that they value your opinion.

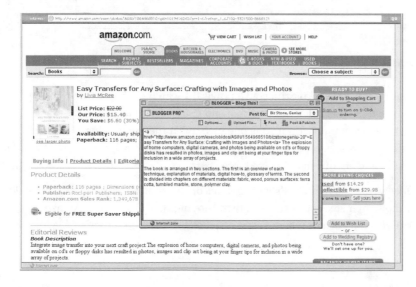

Figure 7.3

When you blog an item at Amazon, make sure your affiliate code follows the ASIN number in the link.

When you get into the habit of affiliating your links, you'll forget about it until the financial quarter comes around and you find that you've made enough to buy the new Harry Potter book, book 12, *Welcome Back Potter.*

Incorporating Affiliate "Modules"

When you're signed in to your Associates Program headquarters, you have many choices on how to display affiliated products on your blog. Banners, graphics, buttons, and boxes abound. Because of the vertical, often very "tall" aspect of blogs, modules or side boxes, together with the occasional posted link, work best (see Figure 7.4).

Figure 7.4

An affiliate module featuring The Lord of the Rings *blends well on the right side of megnut.com.*

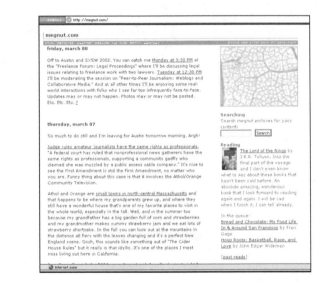

Search Box

Visitors can access Amazon.com's powerful search engine from your blog, a feature that adds tremendous value and convenience to your site—and 5% affiliate revenue for you if someone buys what they're looking for. Search boxes are great because you never know what your readers may want to look for outside of your usual posted fare.

Once you've signed in, it's just a matter of choosing the size, shape, and color of the search box you want, and then copying the HTML from Amazon so that you can paste it where you'd like it to be rendered on your blog.

Amazon Recommends™

Amazon Recommends™ links deliver new content and pricing to your blog on a timely basis, thus ensuring that your page stays fresh and up-to-date— just like your blog.

Once added to your template, this code communicates with an Amazon server each time a visitor arrives on that page. This displays specific content on your site based on the topics you select. The content and pricing within the links will change over time.

Building the box is as easy as creating any other affiliate module. Amazon builds the code for you, and you paste it where you want it displayed. You also can customize the colors of links and set them to open in a new window.

Build a Dynamic Affiliate Module

Bloggers are always coming up with unique ways of publishing their opinions, and many bloggers are handy with HTML and JavaScript. The following project is best undertaken if you have a basic knowledge of HTML and a familiarity with JavaScript. But even if you don't, it's worth tinkering with because you're bound to learn something or develop an interest in the effort!

The Recommends program at Amazon is great because it delivers fresh, dynamic content and saves you a lot of time. If your needs are more specific, however, you can use JavaScript to rotate affiliate-linked product images and text inside a custom-built module. In this way, you can dynamically present exactly the products you want to recommend to your visitors. Alternatively, you can make some of the products in your wishlist more visible by building them into this module.

This exercise shows you how to build a module that displays a different snippet of HTML each time a user views your page. In this case, the snippets are products at Amazon.com. The number of snippets you use is up to you.

Step 1: Create Your Content Array

Your content array is the HTML you want to rotate. The HTML contains descriptions and links to the products you are displaying. This array contains links to other books about blogging (books you don't need, of course, because you've got this one). Make sure that your links include the affiliate code necessary for generating your referral fee. In this example, I've used my affiliate code, `bizstonegeniu-20`. Save this file in Listing 7.1 as `booklist.js`.

Listing 7.1   Content Array (booklist.js)

```
var urls =
newArray("http:\/\/www.amazon.com\/exec\/obidos\/ASIN\/0738207411\
/bizstonegeniu-20",
"http:\/\/www.amazon.com\/exec\/obidos\/ASIN\/0596001002\
/bizstonegeniu-20",
"http:\/\/www.amazon.com\/exec\/obidos\/ASIN\/073820756X\
/bizstonegeniu-20");
var images = newArray("http:\/\/images.amazon.com\/images\/P\
➥/0738207411.01.MZZZZZZZ.jpg",
"http:\/\/images.amazon.com\/images\/P\/0596001002.01.MZZZZZZZ.jpg",
"http:\/\/images.amazon.com\/images\/P\/073820756X.01.MZZZZZZZ.jpg");
var titles = new Array("We\'ve Got Blog: How Weblogs are Changing
Our Culture", "Running Weblogs With Slash", "The Weblog Handbook:
Practical Advice on Creating and Maintaining Your Blog");
var authors = new Array("Editors of Perseus Publishing, Rebecca
Blood", "Chromatis and David Krieger", "Rebecca Blood");
var taglines = new Array("A collection of essays about weblogs,
edited and introduced by Rebecca Blood", "A technical how-to book
that teaches readers how to tap the power of the open-source
codebase that powers Slashdot", "The title says it all: this book is
an overview of the how to start a weblog, and how to take care of the
everyday details, like finding hosting and building traffic");
```

Step 2: Save the JavaScript File

Save the following code in Listing 7.2 in a file called `rotate.js`.

Listing 7.2   Rotating HTML Script (rotate.js)

```
/* Specifies the period of time between updates:
    month - once a month
    date - once per every day of the month (repeats the next month)
    weekday - once per every day of the week (repeats the next week)
    hour - once per hour (repeats the next day)
    request - once per browser request (default)
*/
var updatePeriods = new Array("month","date","weekday","hour",
"request")

// Invoked to display rotated HTML content in a Web page. The period
// argument should be an element of the updatePeriods array.
function displayRotatedContent(period) {
```

```
var updatePeriod = -1
for(var i=0;i<updatePeriods.length;i++) {
 if(period.toLowerCase() == updatePeriods[i].toLowerCase()) {
  updatePeriod = i
  break
 }
}
var s = selectHTML(updatePeriod)
document.write(s)
}

function selectHTML(updatePeriod) {
 var n = 0
 var max = urls.length
 var d = new Date()
 switch(updatePeriod) {
  case 0: // Month (0 - 11)
   n = d.getMonth()
   break
  case 1: // Date (1 - 31)
   // Scale to (0 - 30)
   n = d.getDate() - 1
   break
  case 2: // Weekday (0 - 6)
   n = d.getDay()
   break
  case 3: // Hour (0 - 23)
   n = d.getHours()
   break
  case 4: // Request (Default)
  default:
   n = selectRandom(max)
 }
 n %= max
 var output = "<A class=\"sidelink\" href=\"" + urls[n] + "\"><span
 class=\"booktitle\">" + titles[n] + "<\/span><\/A><BR><span
 class=\"greytext\">by " + authors[n] + "<\/span><BR><BR><A href=\""
 + urls[n] + "\"><IMG border=\"0\" src=\"" + images[n] +
 "\"><\/A><BR><BR><span class=\"greytext\">" + taglines[n] +
 "<\/span>"
 return output
}

// Select a random integer that is between 0 (inclusive) and max
   (exclusive)
function selectRandom(max) {
 var r = Math.random()
 r *= max
 r = parseInt(r)
 if(isNaN(r)) r = 0
 else r %= max
 return r
}
```

Step 3: Insert Two Lines of Code

Include the two lines in Listing 7.3 in the document head of your blog.

Listing 7.3   Code for Document's Head

```
<SCRIPT language="JavaScript" src="booklist.js"></SCRIPT>
<SCRIPT language="JavaScript" src="rotate.js"></SCRIPT>
```

Step 4: Place the Display Function

Place the script in Listing 7.4 at the point where you want the content to be displayed and rotated.

Listing 7.4   Call to Function

```
<SCRIPT language="JavaScript">
displayRotatedContent("request")
</SCRIPT>
```

If you are averse to typing in all this scripting, don't despair. Builder.com offers a handy little Cool Tool to facilitate the writing of this script (see Figure 7.5).

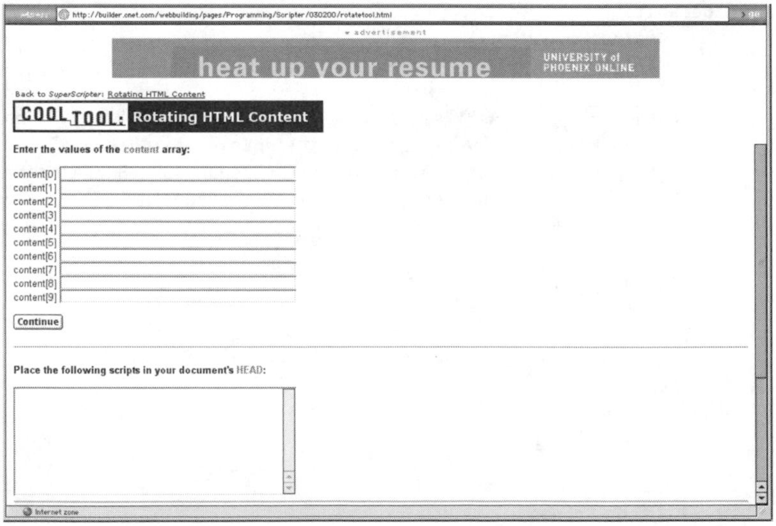

Figure 7.5

As an alternative to typing code, use the Rotating HTML Content Cool Tool at Builder.com to generate your scripts.

Visit Builder.com to see another way to do this project. All you have to do is provide your snippets of HTML, and the Cool Tool will to the rest. Here's the URL:

```
http://builder.cnet.com/webbuilding/pages/Programming/Scripter/030200/
```

Good luck!

Other Affiliate Programs

The blog community has a big appetite for media products like books, music, and movies. You might also have good luck if your blog is topical and you can find an affiliate program that matches up with your interests. Commission Junction is the place to go for this.

Commission Junction provides bloggers the opportunity to earn revenue from their audience on a pay-for-performance basis. You can partner with thousands of advertisers and access millions of ads from a single web-based interface. They track and report on every ad in the network, send you a monthly payment, and provide a suite of online tools to help optimize affiliate performance.

Payouts vary according to advertiser. One example is Overture. Formerly GoTo.com, Overture is a pay-for-performance search provider. One of the affiliate options they offer through Commission Junction is a search box. You copy the code and paste it into your blog template. Then, they pay you $.02 each search. If you have 50 searches performed each day, that's $30 a month—which should cover your hosting fees, at least. Not too shabby.

So, let's say you like to blog about traveling and you chronicle all your adventures. You could search for *travel* at Commission Junction and choose from participating affiliate programs (see Figure 7.6). Put one of them on your blog and you'll be offering your readers something they can use and making a little profit in the process.

Figure 7.6

There are 45 travel-related affiliate programs at cj.com.

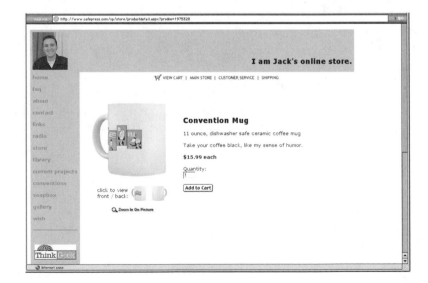

Merchandising!

When you have a blog that you've designed yourself and publish to on a daily basis, you've got a brand. An online store featuring merchandise celebrating your brand provides your audience a fun opportunity to say "thanks" as well as get something in return (see Figure 7.7).

Figure 7.7

"Take your coffee black, like my sense of humor." Wil Wheaton's store is fully co-branded to match his blog (and his sense of humor).

CafePress.com offers an outsourced solution that allows individuals, groups, and companies to sell a wide variety of merchandise without the typical hassles and overhead. Plus, they handle the product manufacturing, sourcing, fulfillment, and customer service. All you have to do is upload a .jpg, choose the products you want to sell, and customize your free hosted store to match your blog's design (see Figure 7.8).

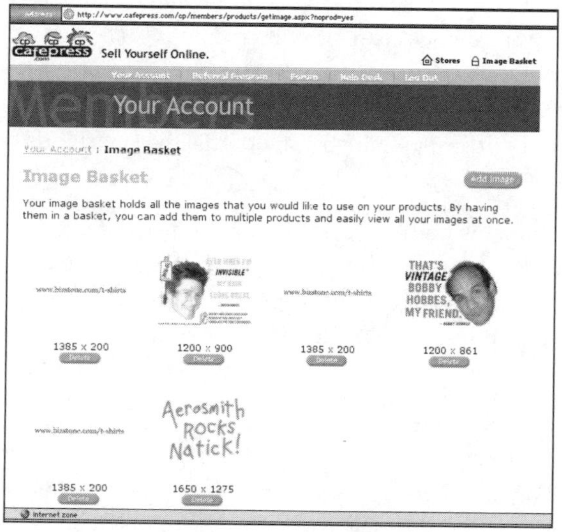

Figure 7.8

Managing your Cafepress artwork is easy. This is my "image basket." It Rocks Natick.

Using digital printing techniques, Cafepress puts your designs on t-shirts, sweatshirts, caps, mugs, mousepads, tote bags, and the occasional promotional item. I think they did a beer stein for Oktoberfest. *Mmm*, beer. Because Cafepress is free to use, you can go crazy and make shirts, caps, and mugs just for the heck of it. Here's an idea: Create a mug that says, "warning: this mug contains fatal poison" and then drink it in front of people to fake your own death. Fake death—that's where the real money's at.

Dream up a design and they'll print it, ship it, and handle the whole transaction online. They need to make a little money off the deal, but anything above that is profit for you. For example, say they need you to sell your mug for a minimum of $9. If you charge $15, then it's your six bucks. And the whole process costs you nothing.

Hosting Advertisements

The advent of text-based "microadvertising" has created a great (and cheap) new way to get the word out about your blog. We'll talk more about TextAds in Chapter 12, "Better Blogging." Right now, we're "blogging for dollars," so we want the money coming in, not going out.

Google pioneered the text-advertising field when they launched their adwords program. Anyone with a credit card and $20 could now buy key-word-targeted advertising on the results pages of the world's best search engine. Because ads on Google's image-free pages have yielded clickthrough rates five times higher than industry standards, the smart kids quickly cloned them.

When Philip Kaplan's traditional ad sales plummeted, he took a page from Google's book. By setting a small minimum purchase price on advertising and allowing people to launch campaigns using a credit card, Philip turned ads into "impulse buys." The result: his ad sales jumped back up again. Rather than rest on his laurels, Philip worked to make his ad program available for others to do the same. Thus, HTTP Ads were born.

HTTP Ads is a turnkey system for individuals to make money hosting advertising and taking ad orders on their own blog or web site. It's easy to set up and entirely web-based. As long as you can get online, you can approve new ad orders, view your stats, and manage your account.

Setting up HTTP Ads is as easy as 1, 2, 3.

To set up HTTP Ads at httpads.com:

1. Buy a zone (it's free). A zone is just ad space. Zones can be any size you want, and you can put them anywhere you want.

2. Set up a zone. This is where you set your advertising price. Again, this is your call. Set the price as high or as low as you want.

3. Put HTTP Ads on your site. To do this, all you need to do is paste some HTML into your blog.

HTTP Ads will take a percentage of your ad sales for providing this service, but it is substantially less than traditional online advertising fees.

After HTTP Ads, others followed. Adfarm.org, TextAds.biz, iDYA AdSystem, and then Bill Rini launched an open-source Text Ads program for anyone with Linux-based servers running PHP, Apache, and MySQL. URLs to these hosting services and more can be found in Appendix A, "Blog Web Links."

Wish Lists

Building a wish list online is like registering for a wedding. You preselect items that you would be happy to receive as gifts, and then make them available to your adoring public. Okay, so a wish list is not cash flow. However, if you were going to buy these things anyway, you're just skipping a step and saving a little time. And time is money, so there you go.

Wish lists make it easy for your blog readers to get you something they know you'll like during the holidays or for your birthday, or they can just be a way of paying you back for creating something they find valuable.

In the blog community, wish lists have taken on a life of their own. Bloggers have used Amazon.com's wish list feature to create elaborate Secret Santa events, matching people who have specified similar spending limits. Everyone who joins buys a gift and gets a gift—and everything is done online.

Creating an Amazon.com Wish List

Here is how you can create your own wish list on Amazon.com:

1. Shop around, and when you find a product you want, click the Add to my Wish List button under the Add to my Shopping Cart button on any product detail page.

2. Click the Create button and provide your name and shipping address for any gifts that are to be ordered for you. Your shipping address can be kept private.

3. Put a link somewhere on your blog so that your visitors can easily click to see your wish list.

Giving It Away

You've got a little revenue coming in, but you're not exactly puttin' on the ritz. At the same time, you don't want to just ignore the 10 or 15 dollars you've generated. Wish you could find something worthwhile to do with that revenue? Remember the affiliate code you place after the ASIN or ISBN number inside a link to a product page? Well, you can replace your code with one of GiveQuick's codes and team up with other bloggers donating their blog dollars to make a bigger difference.

GiveQuick.org has a directory of non-profits that participate in their program. The directory allows web site owners to funnel their commissions to the non-profit of their choice. This means that the non-profit's commissions will grow faster, using the fees generated by a growing number of bloggers like you. The combined affiliate revenue means much larger checks than they otherwise would have.

GiveQuick is different from online "malls" that aggregate referral fees and then redistribute the money among many non-profits. The money generated through their affiliate links moves directly from e-commerce retailers to non-profit organizations, so there is no overhead to be skimmed.

There are other ways bloggers can use affiliate programs to help raise funding for various causes. See Appendix A for a list of URLs to help you get started.

Whether you're keeping it, giving it away, or digging in and building a fancy JavaScript module, your goal should be to make it your own. Blog the items at Amazon that you have a perspective or opinion on. Incorporate books and music into your blog the same way you would talk about them with a friend over coffee, and they will move beyond just commercial links to products and take on your character. That's what blogging is all about.

Chapter 8

Working with Blogger Archives

Blogging every day means a lot of built-up content over time. You can't put all your posts on a single page; this would be too long. Instead, you need an easy way to manage your posts into archives. Blogging software automates the process of creating archives for your posts so that you and your readers will have access to them for years to come. This chapter takes a look at Blogger.com's archives and explores some of the different ways they can be configured.

What Are Blogger Archives?

Because you can't put all the posts you've ever written on one page, Blogger automatically saves them as permanent files, organized by week or month (your choice). If you choose to have your blog archived weekly, once a week Blogger automatically saves your files for you. If you choose to archive by month, the files are saved once a month.

Archives are a blessing and (sometimes) a curse. They are fantastic because they save all your work for posterity. But if you're a beginner trying to customize them, archives can be confusing. Getting "under the hood" is a great way to learn but if you'd rather just skip the tech stuff, automatic archiving and pre-designed templates are all you.

Essentially, when you create a Blogger account and choose to use archives, you will have three types of pages:

- **Your Blog**—You know what *that* is.

- **Your Archive Index Page**—That's a page similar to a table of contents for your archived files. You can link to it from your blog by including something like read my archives.

- **The Saved Files**—These files will look just like your blog, but they will contain only posts from the week or month specified—they're like a snapshot of your blog in time.

Don't Want an Archive?

You can choose to have "no archive," but I just can't bear the thought of all those entries slipping into the ether. Though I suppose it *is* kind of Zen-like.

When you have an archive, you'll notice as you happily blog away that posts from weeks or months ago are no longer on your blog. The posts are not deleted; they are saved as a set of permanent files so that they'll continue to exist even after your more recent work has replaced them in the limelight. Archives also come into play when building permalinks, which we'll discuss in Chapter 12, "Better Blogging."

By default, you set up a Blogger archive using the archive index page. Your archive index page points to all your saved files by way of hyperlinked dates. But as you'll see in this chapter, there are other ways to set up your archives in addition to the archive index page.

For Starters: How to Design Your Archive Index Page

Just like your blog, you can design your archive index page any way you like—you just need to add a tag that tells Blogger where to put the links to your saved files. Many people simply link to this index page from somewhere on their blog that says archive. From the resulting archive index page, readers can select a week or month they would like to see. Clicking a link to a week will bring up all the posts you created during that time.

You can customize the index page within Blogger by accessing a template area, similar to the way you can customize your blog template. To access your archive template area at Blogger.com, you must first be signed in. Then, you follow these steps:

1. Click the title of your blog from Blogger.com's front page on the right side.

2. Click the Archive button.

3. Click the Archive Template link.

Genius Tip

> **Save before Editing**
> It's always a good idea to highlight your template, copy it, and then save it as a text file on your desktop. That way, no matter what you end up doing, you always have the option of just pasting it back in, and you're back where you started.

In the template area, you can paste in your design. How should you design this page? You can design it any way you like, but here's a quick and easy suggestion: Use the same template as your blog, but replace the posting tags (the ones that look like this):

```
<Blogger>
  <$BlogItemBody$><br>
  <small>posted by <$BlogItemAuthor$> on <$BlogItemDateTime$></small>
  <p>
</Blogger>
```

With the archive tags that look like this:

```
<Blogger>
   <a href="<$BlogArchiveLink$>"><$BlogArchiveName$></a><br>
</Blogger>
```

Look for these tags and examples of how to set them up just beneath the form in which you paste the template. When you're done entering the template, click Save Changes. Remember that changing your template will never delete your posts.

Archive Settings

Archive settings is the area where you tell Blogger.com how often you would like your files saved. Your choices are these:

- No Archive
- Weekly
- Monthly

In the settings area, you also will need to tell Blogger where you want to save your files. Usually, people create a folder on their server called *archive*. Because Blogger generates a separate web page for each month or week of your archive, these files can multiply very quickly. Creating a separate directory keeps the archive files organized within your site. This server path must exist before you can tell Blogger where to find it. If you're taking care of your own hosting, you'll also need to indicate your FTP archive path. Most bloggers like to create a separate directory on their FTP site also called *archive*. Make sure this directory is created before you set up your blog archive settings. Blog*Spot users don't have to deal with the archive paths because Blogger takes care of that.

In the field that Blogger provides, enter a name for your archives like archive.html. Choose an archive index filename that is different from your blog filename. Also, note that Blogger uses the archive index filename to generate the name of each archive file, so if you enter **archive.html** in the area, your archives will be named like this: 2002_09_20_archive.html. Your archive index page will be located at archive/archive.html with dynamically generated links to all your individual archive pages.

So, to recap: Once you post and publish an entry using Blogger, you will have a main blog page, an archive index page (see Figure 8.1), and a bunch of archive files (see Figure 8.2). Whenever you post to your blog, the most recent archive page will be automatically updated, but if you decide to change your blog template or formatting, you'll need to republish all your archives.

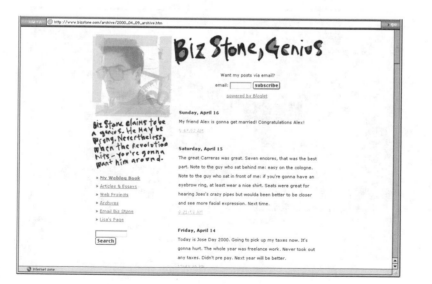

Figure 8.1

An archive index page with a template similar to the blog.

Figure 8.2

An archive file from the week of April 16, 2000. Darn, that reminds me—I still owe Alex a wedding present.

Republishing Your Archives

Archives are managed automatically by Blogger. If you edit an old post, its archive page will be published the next time you publish. However, if you make a change to your blog template, you should republish your archives to ensure that the change is made everywhere. To do this, you will need to click Republish All in the archive section of your Blogger account.

Presenting Your Archives

For beginners, the best and easiest route to take is that of the pre-designed blog template (see Figure 8.3). Pre-designed templates include the archive index page (see Figure 8.4) as well as the blog design, and they look great. Some template designs even implement a fancier type of archiving method—but we'll get to that in a bit.

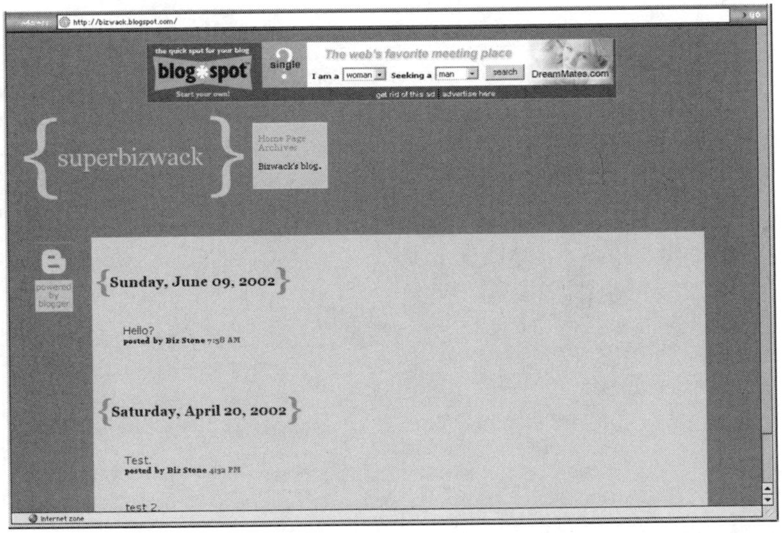

Figure 8.3

This template designed by Elaine Nelson is called Bracket Town.

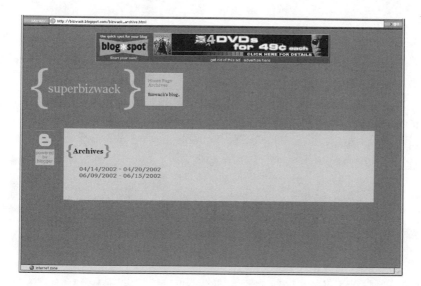

Figure 8.4

The Bracket Town template includes an archive index page.

If you're interested in creating your own blog design with matching archive index page, however, you're going to need to get into the template.

Standard Blogger Archive Index Page Template

Listing 8.1 is the standard archive index page template provided by Blogger.

Listing 8.1   Standard Blogger Template

```
<!DOCTYPE HTML PUBLIC "-//W3C//DTD HTML 4.0 Transitional//EN">

<html>
<head>
   <title>[Enter Your Blog Archive Title Here]</title>
</head>

<body>
<h1>My Weblog Archive</h1>


<Blogger>
     <a href="<$BlogArchiveLink$>"><$BlogArchiveName$></a><br>
</Blogger>

<!--
     if you like this service, please leave this button in -
     or link to us somewhere from your blog, thanks!
-->
```

```
<P><BR><BR><BR>
<a href="http://www.blogger.com"><img width=88 height=31
src="http://www.blogger.com/images/blogger_button.gif" border=0
alt="Powered by Blogger"></a>
</body>
</html>
```

If you paste the code from Listing 8.1 into your archive template area and save the changes, you will have a very simple looking archive index page that you can link to from your blog (see Figure 8.5).

Blogger Tags for Archives

Here are the tags that can be used in the archive index template:

- <$BlogArchiveLink$>—This is the filename of an archive page.

- <$BlogArchiveName$>—This is the name related to an archive page.

Note that case is important when using the tags. The tag <$BlogArchiveName$> will work, but the tag <$BLOGArchiveNAME$> will not.

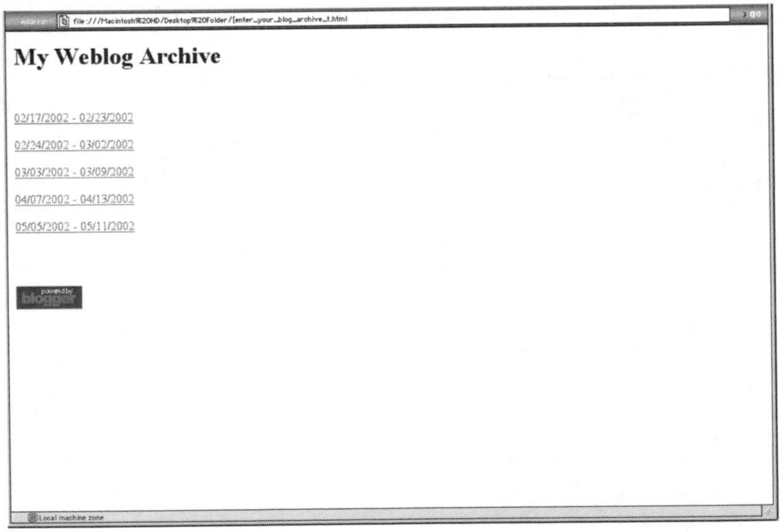

Figure 8.5

Blogger's standard archive index page is ultra-simple.

For example, the following Blogger tags:

```
<Blogger>
    <a href="<$BlogArchiveLink$>"><$BlogArchiveName$></a><br>
</Blogger>
```

Will produce the following output linked to the proper archive page:

```
8/22/99 - 8/28/99
9/19/99 - 9/25/99
9/26/99 - 10/2/99
```

Slightly Fancier (JavaScript) Archive Templates

Blogger's built-in archiving is great for no-frills, straight-up, get-the-job-done archiving, but the display is not as attractive as it could be. You can use a few JavaScript techniques to spiff up the default style of archive links. Let's take a look at some of them.

The following scripts can be used to alter the format of the dates on your archive index page. You also can use them to eliminate the need for the archive index page by placing the index somewhere on your main blog. We'll examine these scripts and walk through implementing them on your blog; but for an easy way to build custom archive templates with JavaScript, be sure to visit Phil Ringnalda's Blogger archive script generator at `http://www.philringnalda.com/scriptgen/` (see Figure 8.6).

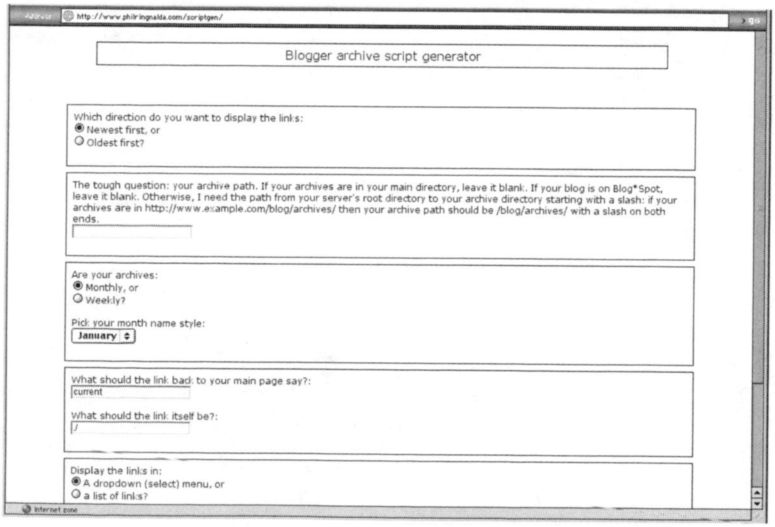

Figure 8.6

Phil Ringnalda's Blogger Archive Script Generator is good stuff.

Modifying the Date Format

You can use the following scripts to modify the format of the dates on your archive index page. Blogger provides only two choices for presenting the links on your archive index page, but these scripts allow you to present the links in few different ways. Please note that these scripts assume that you have named your archive directory **archives**.

The basic script, intended for monthly archives, writes links as May 2001. Listing 8.2 shows this basic script.

Listing 8.2   Basic Script: Month Names

```
<Blogger>
<!-- write the archive link-->
<a href="archives/<$BlogArchiveLink$>">
<script type="text/javascript">
// moname[0] = "January" ...
moname = new Array ("January", "February", "March", "April", "May",
"June", "July", "August", "September", "October", "November",
"December");
// tmp="05/01/2001 - 05/31/2001"
tmp="<$BlogArchiveName$>";
// get number for month
mo=tmp.substring(0,2);
// get number for year
yr=tmp.substring(6,10);
// change month number to name - remember January = 0
mo=moname[mo-1];
// set date to "May 2001"
newdate=mo+" "+yr;
// write it in the page
document.write(newdate);
</script>
<!-- if javascript is off, write the ugly date -->
<noscript>
<$BlogArchiveName$>
</noscript>
</a>
<br>
</Blogger>
```

Listing 8.3 writes a header of The week of... and then writes links as May 6, 2001.

Listing 8.3   Week of... Script

```
<!--Start with the text The week of... because otherwise it looks
like archives for just one day-->
The week of...

<Blogger>
<a href="archives/<$BlogArchiveLink$>">
<script type="text/javascript">
moname = new Array ("January", "February", "March", "April", "May",
"June", "July", "August", "September", "October", "November",
"December");
tmp="<$BlogArchiveName$>";
mo=tmp.substring(0,2);
day=tmp.substring(3,5);
yr=tmp.substring(6,10);
mo=moname[mo-1];
// if day is 01 to 09, take just the second character
if (day<10)
{
day=day.substring(1)
}
newdate=mo+" "+day+", "+yr;
document.write(newdate);
</script>
<noscript>
<$BlogArchiveName$>
</noscript>
</a>
<br>
</Blogger>
```

Listing 8.4 writes links as May 1-31, 2001, April 29-May 5, 2001, or December 31, 2000-January 6, 2001.

Listing 8.4   Written script

```
<Blogger>
<a href="archives/<$BlogArchiveLink$>">
<script type="text/javascript">
moname = new Array ("January", "February", "March", "April", "May",
"June", "July", "August", "September", "October", "November",
"December");
tmp="<$BlogArchiveName$>";
// assign first month
mostart=tmp.substring(0,2);
```

```
// assign last month
moend=tmp.substring(13,15);
// assign first day
daystart=tmp.substring(3,5);
// assign last day
dayend=tmp.substring(16,18);
// assign first year
yrstart=tmp.substring(6,10);
// assign last year
yrend=tmp.substring(19);
mostart=moname[mostart-1];
moend=moname[moend-1];
if (daystart<10)
{
daystart=daystart.substring(1)
}
if (dayend<10)
{
dayend=dayend.substring(1)
}
// format the new date
// did week cross new year
if (yrstart != yrend)
{
newdate=mostart+" "+daystart+", "+yrstart+"-"+moend+" "+dayend+",
➥"+yrend;
}
else
// did week cross new month
if (mostart != moend)
{
newdate=mostart+" "+daystart+"-"+moend+" "+dayend+", "+yrstart;
}
else
newdate=mostart+" "+daystart+"-"+dayend+", "+yrstart;
document.write(newdate);
</script>
<noscript>
<$BlogArchiveName$>
</noscript>
</a>
<br>
</Blogger>
```

The European style script for weekly or monthly archives writes the links as
6.5.2001 - 12.5.2001. Listing 8.5 shows the European-style script.

Listing 8.5   European-Style Script

```
<Blogger>
<a href="archives/<$BlogArchiveLink$>">
<script type="text/javascript">
tmp="<$BlogArchiveName$>";
// assign first month
mostart=tmp.substring(0,2);
// assign last month
moend=tmp.substring(13,15);
// assign first day
daystart=tmp.substring(3,5);
// assign last day
dayend=tmp.substring(16,18);
// assign first year
yrstart=tmp.substring(6,10);
// assign last year
yrend=tmp.substring(19);
if (daystart<10)
{
daystart=daystart.substring(1)
}
if (dayend<10)
{
dayend=dayend.substring(1)
}
if (mostart<10)
{
mostart=mostart.substring(1)
}
if (moend<10)
{
moend=moend.substring(1)
}
// format the new date as d.m.yyyy
newdate=daystart+"."+mostart+"."+yrstart+" -
➥"+dayend+"."+moend+"."+yrend;
document.write(newdate);
</script>
<noscript>
<$BlogArchiveName$>
</noscript>
</a>
<br>
</Blogger>
```

Archive Links in Main Page Scripts

The following Blogger archive scripts produce a JavaScript source file containing your archive index, which then can be included in your main blog instead of a separate archive index page with a <script src=...> tag. The script for the date display is pretty much the same. The difference here is that you also paste a bit of code into your main blog template so that the links to your archived files will show up alongside your current blog entries. Try incorporating the script into a module to the left or right of your blog text.

The basic script, intended for monthly archives, writes links as May 2001. Listing 8.6 is the archive template for this basic script.

Listing 8.6   Archive Template for Basic Script: Month Names

```
// moname[0] = "January" ...
var moname = new Array ("January", "February", "March", "April",
"May", "June", "July", "August", "September", "October", "November",
"December")
<Blogger>
// tmp="05/01/2001 - 05/31/2001"
tmp="<$BlogArchiveName$>";
// get number for month
mo=tmp.substring(13,15);
// get number for year
yr=tmp.substring(19);
// change month number to name - remember January = 0
mo=moname[mo - 1];
// set date to "May 2001"
newdate=mo+" "+yr;
// tell the script to write the archive link in the main page
document.write("<a href='archives/<$BlogArchiveLink$>'>");
// tell the script to write the date
document.write(newdate);
// close the link tag and go to a new line
document.write("</a><br>");
</Blogger>
```

Now you put this bit of code from Listing 8.7 into your main blog template wherever you want the links to your archives to show up.

Listing 8.7   Script Used to Include Your Archive Index on Your Main Blog: Month Names

```
<!-- Paste into your main template where you want the archive links -->
Archives:<br>
<script type="text/javascript"
src="archives/<$BlogArchiveFileName$>"></script>
<noscript>Javascript required</noscript>
<br>
```

The script in Listing 8.8 writes a header of Archives for the week of... and then writes links as May 6, 2001.

Listing 8.8   Archive Template for Week of... Script

```
var moname = new Array ("January", "February", "March", "April", "May",
"June", "July", "August", "September", "October", "November",
"December")
<Blogger>
tmp="<$BlogArchiveName$>";
// get the starting month number
mo=tmp.substring(0,2);
// get the starting day
day=tmp.substring(3,5);
// get the starting year
yr=tmp.substring(6,10);
mo=moname[mo - 1];
// if day is 01 to 09, take just the second character
if (day<10)
{
day=day.substring(1)
}
newdate=mo+" "+day+", "+yr;
document.write("<a href='archives/<$BlogArchiveLink$>'>");
document.write(newdate);
document.write("</a><br>");
</Blogger>
```

The bit of code in Listing 8.9 goes into your main blog template wherever you want the links to your archives to appear.

Listing 8.9   Script Used to Include Your Archive Index on Your Main Blog: The Week of...

```
Archives for<br>
the week of:<br>
<script type="text/javascript"
src="archives/<$BlogArchiveFileName$>"></script>
<noscript>Javascript required</noscript>
<br>
```

The monthly and weekly drop-down menus list archives from newest to oldest. Listing 8.10 shows this script.

Listing 8.10   Archive Template for Monthly Drop-Down Select Menu Script

```
var moname = new Array ("January", "February", "March", "April",
"May", "June", "July", "August", "September", "October", "November",
"December");
// we need the links and names in an array, so we can loop through
➥the options in the select menu
var archlinks = new Array;
var archnames = new Array;
var i = 0;
<Blogger>
tmp="<$BlogArchiveName$>";
mo=tmp.substring(13,15);
yr=tmp.substring(19);
mo=moname[mo - 1];
newdate=mo+" "+yr;
// put first link and name in archlinks[0] and archnames[0],
➥second in [1], ...
archlinks[i] = "archives/<$BlogArchiveLink$>";
archnames[i] = newdate;
i++;
</Blogger>
// change current location to archlink when selected from menu
function gothere(where)
{
location.href = where.options[where.selectedIndex].value
}
// tell the script to start a form - the \ before the " tells
➥javascript that you want to write a " rather
// than interpreting it as the end of the stuff you want to write
document.write("<form action=\"\">");
// tell the script to start a select menu that calls the gothere
➥function when it is changed
// change the class= to change the appearance of the menu, but leave
➥the \" before and after your class
document.write("<select name=\"archivemenu\"
```

```
➥onChange=\"gothere(this)\" class=\"links\">");
// this is the first, nonfunctioning option, that tells the viewer
➥what the menu does
document.write("<option value=\"\">Archives</option>");
// this is the option for your main, current page: if that isn't the
➥default page for the domain then you
// have to change \"/\" to your location - for
➥www.domain.com/me/blog/index.html use \"/me/blog/\"
document.write("<option value=\"/\">Current</option>");
// starting with the last link, and looping until we run out of
➥links
for (i=archlinks.length-1; i>=0; i--)
{
// write an option tag with the link and the name of the month and
➥year
document.write("<option
➥value=\""+archlinks[i]+"\">"+archnames[i]+"</option>")
}
// close the tags for the form
document.write("</select></form>");
```

Include the code in Listing 8.11 into your main blog template wherever you want the drop-down menu to appear.

Listing 8.11   Script Used to Include Your Archive Index on Your Main Blog: Monthly Drop-Down Menu

```
<!-- Because there is a "current" option for your main page, this
replaces both the archive link and the home link -->
<script type = "text/javascript" src =
➥"archives/<$BlogArchiveFileName$>"></script>
<noscript>Javascript required for archives</noscript>
```

For the weekly drop-down menu style archives, use the script in Listing 8.12.

Listing 8.12   Archive Template for Weekly Drop-Down Select Menu Script

```
// paste this into your archive template, and remember
// there should be absolutely nothing else in your archive template
// moname[0] = "January" ...
var moname = new Array ("Jan", "Feb", "Mar", "Apr", "May", "Jun",
"Jul", "Aug", "Sep", "Oct", "Nov", "Dec");
// we need the links and names in an array, so we can loop through
the options in the select menu
var archlinks = new Array;
var archnames = new Array;
var i = 0;
```

```
<Blogger>
// tmp="05/01/2001 - 05/31/2001"
tmp="<$BlogArchiveName$>";
// get the starting month number
mo=tmp.substring(0,2);
// get the starting day
day=tmp.substring(3,5);
// get the starting year
yr=tmp.substring(6,10);
mo=moname[mo - 1];
// if day is 01 to 09, take just the second character
if (day<10)
{
day=day.substring(1)
}
newdate=mo+" "+day+", "+yr;
// put first link and name in archlinks[0] and archnames[0],
➥second in [1], ...
archlinks[i] = "archives/<$BlogArchiveLink$>";
archnames[i] = newdate;
i++;
</Blogger>
// change current location to archlink when selected from menu
function gothere(where)
{
location.href = where.options[where.selectedIndex].value
}
// tell the script to start a form - the \ before the " tells
➥javascript that you want to write a " rather
// than interpreting it as the end of the stuff you want to write
document.write("<form action=\"\">");
// tell the script to start a select menu that calls the gothere
➥function when it is changed
// change the class= to change the appearance of the menu, but leave
➥the \" before and after your class
document.write("<select name=\"archivemenu\"
➥onChange=\"gothere(this)\" class=\"links\">");
// this is the first, nonfunctioning option, that tells the viewer
➥what the menu does
document.write("<option value=\"\">Archives</option>");
// this is the option for your main, current page: if that isn't the
➥default page for the domain then you
// have to change \"/\" to your location - for
➥www.domain.com/me/blog/index.html use \"/me/blog/\"
document.write("<option value=\"/\">Current</option>");
document.write("<option value=\"\">Week of:</option>");
// starting with the last link, and looping until we run out of
➥links
for (i=archlinks.length-1; i>=0; i--)
{
// write an option tag with the link and the name of the month and
➥year
```

```
document.write("<option
➥value=\""+archlinks[i]+"\">"+archnames[i]+"</option>")
}
// close the tags for the form
document.write("</select></form>");
```

Next put the code that calls the weekly drop-down menu version of your archives into your main blog template (see Listing 8.13).

Listing 8.13   Script Used to Include Your Archive Index on Your Main Blog: Weekly Drop-Down Menu

```
<!-- Because there is a "current" option for your main page, this
replaces both the archive link and the home link -->
<script type = "text/javascript" src =
➥"archives/<$BlogArchiveFileName$>"></script>
<noscript>Javascript required for archives</noscript>
```

Genius Tip

An Easier Way!

For an easy way to build custom archive templates with JavaScript, be sure to visit Phil Ringnalda's Blogger archive script generator at `http://www.philringnalda.com/scriptgen/` (see Figure 8.6). Thanks, Phil!

Trouble with Archives

If your archives are missing, broken, messed up, or just acting freaky, you can try two common cure-alls. They're not guaranteed to work, but they have been known to work on occasion. They're worth trying if you can pinpoint the problem. Here's what they are:

- **Republish Your Archives**—From the Blogger editor, enter your archive area and click the Republish All button. Cross your fingers and visit your archives when the FTP process has finished.

- **The On-Off Method**—In your archive settings area, change the archive frequency to No archive and click Enter. Then change the archive frequency back to what it was to begin with and click Enter again. Then republish your archives. (It's safe; this does not delete your archived posts.)

Archives are a great asset. They capture your content over time and make it available to you and your readers. Archives also can be a pain in the butt when you're first starting out. If you're worried about too much hassle, it's probably best to go with the basic default settings or use a pre-designed template.

Chapter 9

Group Blogging

One of the more interesting ways to "build out your blog" is to turn it into a group endeavor. A group blog can be as simple as adding one or two team members, or it can mean programming a serious online community. You can use a group blog to start a project with a friend, chronicle a developing subject with your peers, build an online community, or simply allow someone to post in your place while you take a break from your computer. Let's take a look at a few examples of group blogs. Remember that these are by no means the only ways to put the medium to use. In fact, bloggers are continually finding new and interesting ways to enhance the blogging experience.

> **Note**
>
> Not all blogging software providers have built-in tools for group blogging. Check with your provider to see whether this feature is available.

Create a Group Blog—I Did, Just for Fun

One day over coffee, my friend Jason and I agreed that it is fun to answer serious scientific questions with equally serious, thoughtful, yet entirely fake answers. Jason and I agree on many things of that nature. Together, we decided that the world was lacking a compendium of scientific misinformation, and the two-man blog, *Supertectonics*, was born (see Figure 9.1). All I had to do to get Jason on the "same page" with me was to invite him to join my blog.

Figure 9.1

Behind the scenes of
Supertectonics Labs.

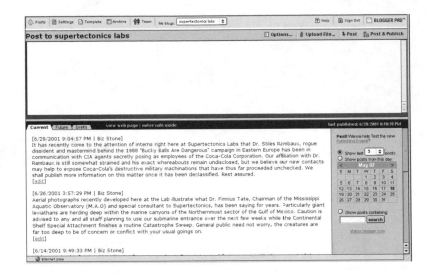

Adding Team Members to Blogger™

Blogger offers a team function that enables you to invite friends or colleagues to blog with you on one page. This is useful when building a fake science blog; it's also great for creating a mini-zine or for those times when you'd like to have someone guest-blog for you while you take a vacation from you computer.

To add members to your team, follow these steps:

1. Sign in to Blogger, and select the blog you'd like to populate with new bloggers.

2. Click the Team button at the top of the navigation bar, and choose Add Team Member(s) in the upper-right corner of your browser window.

3. On the resulting page, in the fields under the "New User" title, enter the name of the person you would like to add. Also, fill in the person's email address and an optional message.

4. Then, click Send invite(s), and the person will receive an email that explains what to do if he or she accepts your invitation.

Your team page then reappears showing the new user, listed with a pending status.

It's best to store your FTP username and password at Blogger so that you don't have to give them out to individual team members.

I created the now-infamous Supertectonics Labs at Blogger.com and invited Jason to be a team member (see Figure 9.2).

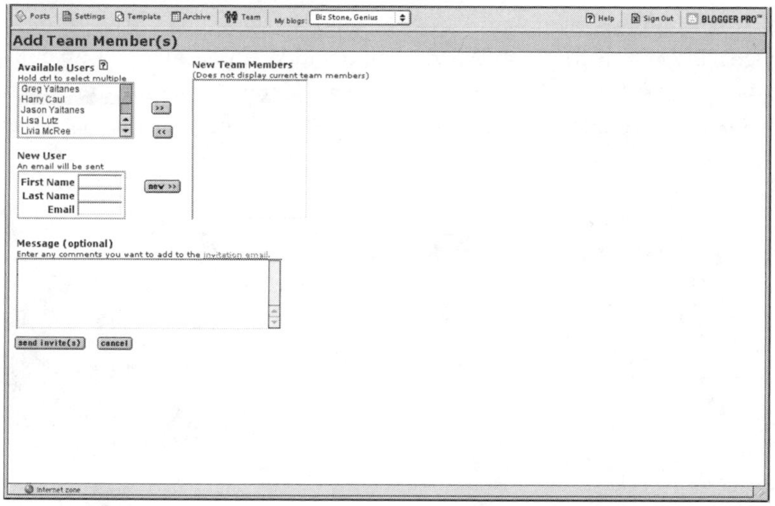

Figure 9.2

It's easy to add team members.

Before long, we were fielding questions daily and publishing general warnings such as, "Particularly giant leviathans are herding deep within the marine canyons of the northernmost sector of the Gulf of Mexico. Caution is advised to any and all Supertectonics staff planning to use our submarine entrance over the next few weeks while the Continental Shelf Special Attachment finishes a routine Catastrophe Sweep. General public need not worry, the creatures are far too deep to be of concern or conflict with your usual goings on."

Supertectonics is a good example of how easily a conversation over coffee can turn into a world-class scientific endeavor using simple blog-o-matic technology. But alas, it was more of an exercise in amusement than a serious micro-content management approach to aggregate useful knowledge and information.

Famous Group Blog Examples

A group blog is still a blog, but it is different. Because there is more than one author, it transcends the singular voice of one person. A group blog is a collaborative voice that brings a spectrum of opinions to its readership and covers more ground.

The End of Free

The End of Free is a classic example of a topic-based group blog that works well. Contributors Adnan Arif, Tara Calishain, Konstantinos Christidis, Jason Shellen, Olivier Travers, Evan Williams, and Todd Zimmerman dig up daily doses of pertinent information that chronicles the transformation of many free web offerings to paid versions. Figure 9.3 gives an example of this popular group blog.

Figure 9.3

The Internet is growing up, and it wants more allowance.

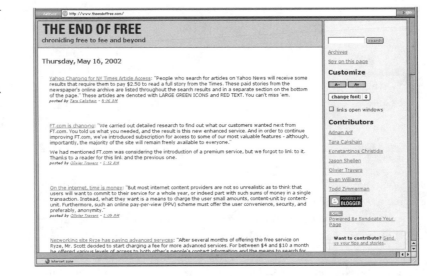

The End of Free group blog also is enhanced with a few neat tricks common in the blogosphere. They've built in an Atomz search engine (You can too! See Chapter 11, "Adding Dynamic Features.") so that readers can find what they're looking for. The End of Free also offers a customizable design, which is a nice touch that offers readers their choice of font and font size for preferred readability. The blog group also has included a "spy on it" feature, offered by spyonit.com, which is a service that automates the process of announcing new posts to anyone who signs up for it. The End of Free also is available as syndicated content via RSS (see Chapter 14, "Syndicating Your Blog").

Metafilter

Metafilter is the ultimate group blog. It's big, it's blue, and it always has something going on. MeFi, as it is affectionately called, is a blog that anyone can contribute a link or a comment to. Its creator, Matthew Haughey, writes that it "exists to break down the barriers between people, to extend a blog beyond just one person, and to foster discussion among its members."[1] Metafilter is more involved than your ordinary group blog in terms of programming, but it serves as an example to aspire to.

Metafilter newbies are encouraged to take a look around before participating. You can look at the archived posts to get a feel for the site before registering as a member. You have to register if you want to post comments or customize the look and behavior of the site.

Matthew Haughey has built Metafilter so that readers can post links to the main page only after posting a few comments and being a member for at least a week. Again, he's done this to allow new members to get used to the site. There are so many MeFi members that even if less than 1 percent of the members posted links every day, it would be overwhelming. Contributors are urged to take "extra special care when selecting a link for the front page."[2]

Posting on Metafilter

A good post at MetaFilter contains a link to something most people haven't seen before, something with interesting content that might spark discussion. Posts, also called *threads*, are the starting points for discussions at MetaFilter. These are ideally unique, interesting, and valuable links accompanied by commentary that generates comments from other members. Links and comments are the soul of MetaFilter. After a thread is started on the front page, any member can throw their two cents into the conversation by posting comments. The best comments often include new links that relate to the topic being discussed or personal experiences that might let other members see the topic in a new light. The biggest *faux pas* you can make at Metafilter is to post to the front page a link someone has already posted. Perform a search to make sure your link is original before you post.

---

1. http://www.metafilter.com/about.mefi
2. http://www.metafilter.com/about.mefi

Guest Blogging

If you know you're going to be away from a web connection for a week or so, or you are deliberately taking a break from technology (which isn't a bad idea every now and then), you might want to look into asking someone to guest blog in your absence.

Your readers read your blog every day, and they expect new content. If you know you've got some readers who would go into withdrawal if you didn't post for a week, and you've got a trusted friend or colleague who you think is up to the task, you're a prime candidate for inviting a guest blogger.

You can invite the person to blog, or you can simply share your password so that he or she can sign on as you. Only go this second route if you really trust your guest blogger. Also, your stand-in should make it clear to your readers that he or she is filling in for you. Otherwise, your guest blogger could go to jail for impersonation. Maybe.

Enabling Commenting on Your Blog

You can create your own little version of Metafilter by enabling commenting on each post of your blog. Some blogging providers offer commenting as a built-in feature, and all you have to do is choose whether you want comments turned on or off. Other blogging providers suggest that you go out and find an independent provider of commenting and add the feature to your blog yourself.

Adding commenting to your blog means that every time you publish a post, your readers can attach their response to the post (see Figure 9.4). This is an opportunity for interesting or entertaining dialog between you and your readers, which can grow from the original post and bring more content to your site. The worst-case scenario is a bunch of jerks heckling you on your blog. The chances of this happening are not so high if you know your audience and have a loyal following. Plus, you can always delete offending remarks—you're the boss!

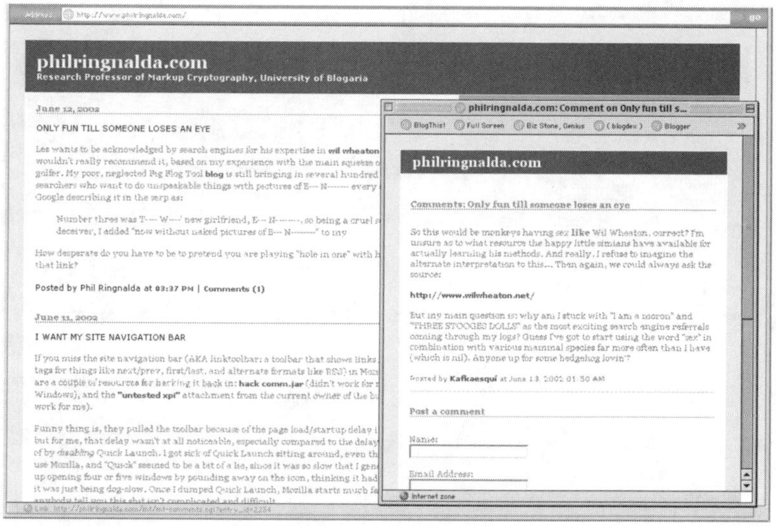

Figure 9.4

Phil Ringnalda's Comment pop-up.

Commenting System Example: YACCS

Many commenting systems for blogs exist, and more are being launched as blogs grow in popularity. Often, a commenting system will close membership when it reaches maximum capacity. Let's look at Yet Another Commenting System (YACCS) as an example of a commenting system (http://www.yaccs.org). As I am writing this, YACCS is still accepting new members, and they're over 16,000 users strong.

YACCS is great because you don't need a host that supports scripting, and you don't have to know anything about programming to use the service.

The system is easy to set up and use. In fact, it automatically installs itself if you use Blogger. Whether you're using Blogger or another blogging provider, you just sign up and decide what you want your Comments box to look like. Then, follow the instructions on which code to copy and where to paste it into your template.

If you use Blogger to power your blog, you can use the AutoInstaller. Figure 9.5 shows what the AutoInstaller page looks like.

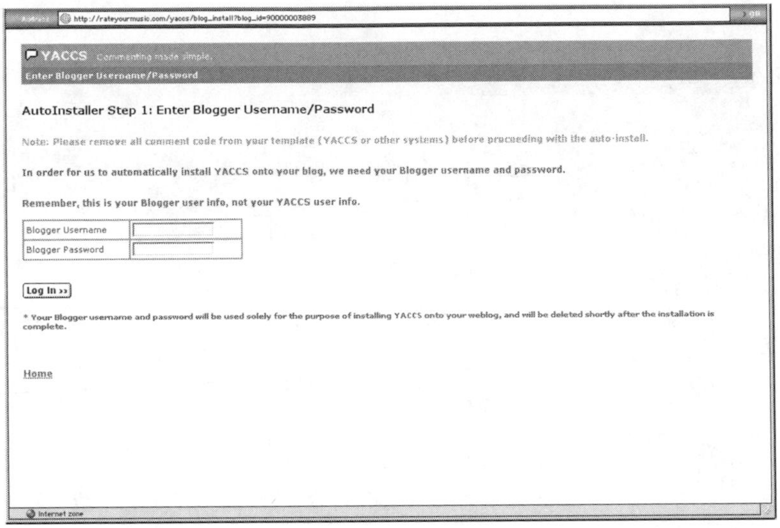

Figure 9.5

The AutoInstaller is a bonus for Blogger users.

For all other types of blogs, you are required only to paste a bit of code into your template.

YACCS works with blogs powered by Blogger, Radio UserLand, Big Blog Tool, or Scribble blogging software (see Figure 9.6). No matter which software you are using to power your blog, YACCS is easy to install. Just choose your provider, fill out a few text fields, and you're ready to copy the code for pasting into your blog's template.

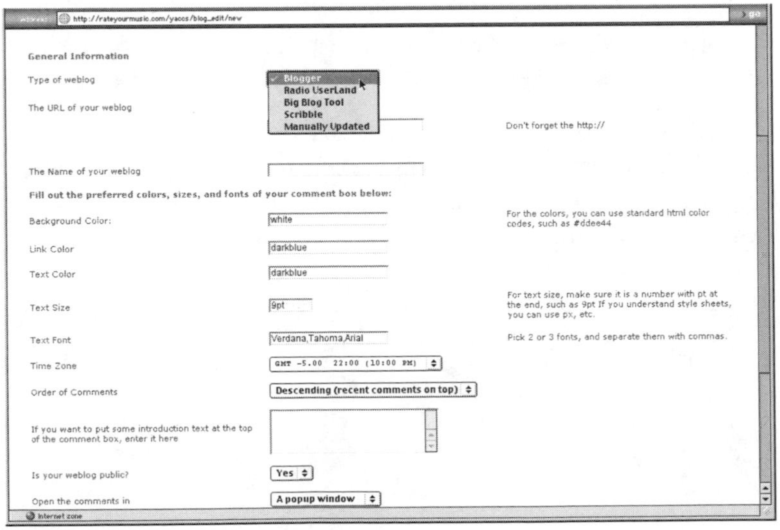

Figure 9.6

YACCS: Commenting made simple.

So, what else do you get? YACCS users get all of these benefits:

- It's available in 14 languages: English, Dutch, German, Spanish, Italian, French, Brazilian Portuguese, Tagalog, Esperanto, Korean, Persian, Hebrew, and traditional Chinese.

- Sports a comments counter on pages via JavaScript.

- Works with non-JavaScript browsers.

- Offers SPAM protection.

- Has fully customizable fonts, colors, and text sizes, and lets users customize the time zone, the order in which comments are displayed, and the introductory text message.

- Lets you make more advanced changes by customizing your Comments box to look *exactly* the way you want it to look. You can start from scratch or copy one of the 200+ templates that other YACCS users have created and customize it to your taste.

- Offers Permalinks, a feature that allows you to create individual comments with permanent links (marked by #) so that they can be referenced externally.

- Enables users to edit and delete posts, as well as ban users by IP address.

- Supports common HTML tags (bold, italic, strikethrough, etc).

- Remembers the name, email, and homepage used by your visitors so that they don't have to enter those items each time they visit.

- Gives you a fully customizable comments link.

- Gives you the option of opening comments in a popup window or in the same window.

- Includes a free counter.

- Provides a page where you can view and manage at once all comments for your blog.

- Allows you to search for your comments by name, email, homepage, IP address, or body.

- Includes an export feature so that you can move your comments off YACCS if you decide to host your own comments or move to a blog system with built-in commenting.

- Provides RSS-feed support.

System Requirements for Using YACCS

You can use the YACCS commenting system if you are using Blogger, Radio UserLand, Big Blog Tool, or Scribble as your blogging provider. To use this service, make sure that your browser is one of these:

- Internet Explorer 4.0, 5.0, 5.5, 6.0 (Win32) 5.0, 5.1 (Mac)
- Netscape 4.08, 4.7x (Win/Mac/Unix), 6.2 (Win32/Mac)
- Opera 6.0 (Win32), 5.0 (Mac)
- Lynx 2.8.2rel1 (Solaris, Linux)

YACCS Pricing

YACCS is free, but contributions through the Amazon Honor System or PayPal are welcomed (even if the amount is only a couple of dollars). Or, you can always mail an old-fashioned check to Hossein Sharifi, the mastermind behind YACCS.

You, the Center of the Universe

By inviting members or adding user comments to your blog, you are starting a little community with you and your blog as the cornerstone. Sometimes adding to your blog in this way can be a long, windy path to success—and sometimes it's an instant hit. You might also realize, after allowing others to be a part of your blog, that you don't like group blogging. It might not be right for you. If you have a popular site, it might take a lot of daily maintenance to weed out the undesirable elements and keep the crowd in check. Try group blogging if it sounds interesting, but if it isn't to your liking—hey, it was free.

Chapter 10

Corporate Blogging

The popularity of blogs as home pages, journals, digests, and other forms of personal publishing is obvious. But the emergence of corporate blogging—blogs maintained by companies in order to get the word out about products and services—is picking up steam as well.

Corporate Blogs at MSNBC.com

MSNBC.com is a major news portal featuring original journalism on the web. In June 2002, MSNBC.com launched a handful of blogs to help keep readers up-to-date with information that interests them from some of the site's top columnists:[1]

- In his *Altercation* weblog (www.altercation.msnbc.com), MSNBC.com political columnist and corporate blogger, Eric Alterman, reflects on media, politics, and culture. Eric Alterman recognizes that blogs are a chance to tap into a "collective intelligence" and that they provide an important "distribution network for news and information." Eric knows things.

- Chris Matthews' *Hardball* (www.chrismatthews.msnbc.com) is an insider's guide to how politics is played.

- Michael Moran's *World Agenda* (www.worldagenda.msnbc.com) focuses on international news and American foreign policy.

---

1. *Information in bulleted list found at: MSNBC.com, Peter Dorogoff. "MSNBC.com Launches Weblogs." (13 June 2002) Available from the Internet:* http://biz.yahoo.com/bw/020603/30447_1.html

- The *Cosmic Log* (www.cosmiclog.msnbc.com) is Alan Boyle's news forum for the latest advances in technology, science, space, and exploration.

- Jan Herman looks at news from the world of entertainment and the arts in *"The Juice"*(www.thejuice.msnbc.com). Figure 10.1 shows an example of this blog.

Figure 10.1

Jan Herman blogs the latest entertainment arts and news on MSNBC.com.

As noted in the MSNBC.com press release, "Users can offer feedback to the columnists by directly emailing comments from the weblog. Log onto the individual web sites for more information."

> ### An Executive Producer at MSNBC.com on Blogs
>
> Joan Connell, executive producer for Opinions and Communities on MSNBC.com said:
>
> "We see blogs as both a new literary genre and the next generation of online communities: A focused, information-rich environment in which a writer— famous, infamous or unknown—engages in the daily act of thinking aloud, in the ever-expanding universe of the Web....As our weblogs evolve, count on MSNBC.com to become a resource center and a platform from which bloggers can connect with one another and with the ideas that shape our world."[2]

Other Big Media Companies Who Blog

In addition to MSNBC.com, there are other "big media" companies you might recognize which also have added blogging to their offerings as well:

- Slate
- Salon
- FoxNews.com
- TechCentral Station
- Christian Science Monitor
- The Guardian UK
- MSNBC
- American Prospect
- Wall Street Journal
- National Review
- San Jose Mercury News
- L.A. Examiner

---

2. *MSNBC.com, Peter Dorogoff. "MSNBC.com Launches Weblogs." (13 June 2002)*
  Available from the Internet: `http://biz.yahoo.com/bw/020603/30447_1.html`

There is much debate—among bloggers, who like to debate—whether or not blogs are journalism. With actual well-known journalists like Andrew Sullivan (contributing writer for the *New York Times Magazine* and senior editor at the *New Republic*), the answer becomes clear: Some bloggers are journalists, and some aren't. A blog is whatever you make of it. It's not so much the content that makes a blog a blog—it's the structure. You've got to visit and read a blog before you decide what it is. That's the fun part!

Figure 10.2 shows Andrew Sullivan's blog.

Figure 10.2

Andrew Sullivan: pro journalist gone bloggin'.

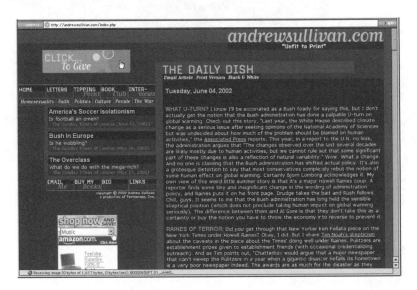

Blogs at Macromedia

One of the first major companies to go on record as officially using blogs as a corporate communications solution was Macromedia. When Macromedia, the company behind popular web authoring software Flash, Dreamweaver, and Shockwave, launched a few blogs as part of its strategy for introducing new services, it caused a ripple in the blogosphere.

Macromedia Community Manager, Matt Brown, on Blogging at Work

Here is what Matt Brown has to say about Macromedia using blogs:

"…The idea is that we can get information back to the community more rapidly than a lot of other channels. We do a lot of that anyway, but we do that mostly on a 1-1 basis or spread through a lot of other venues. This way we can bring in the important info to one place and get that out to people."[3]

Figure 10.3 shows Matt Brown's Dreamweaver Blog.

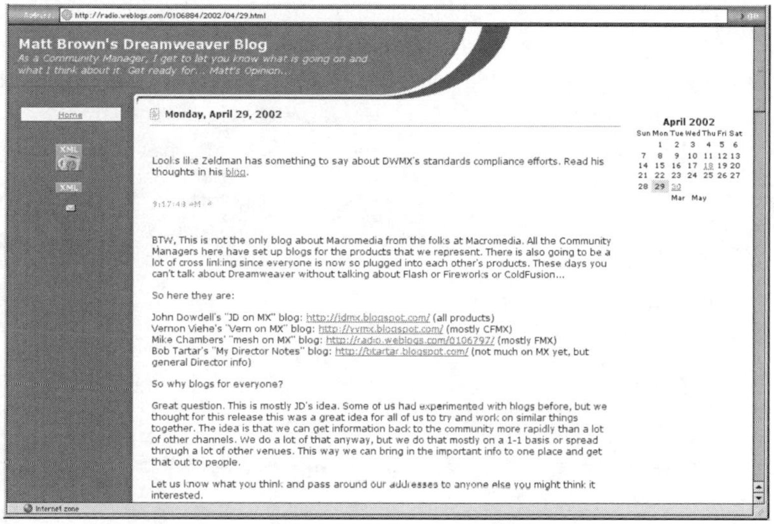

Figure 10.3

Matt Brown blogs for Macromedia.

The Reaction to Macromedia's Blogging Strategy

When *Wired News* reporter, Farhad Manjoo, published a story about Macromedia's decision to take blogging into the corporate environment, many bloggers had their first taste of corporate blogging.

3. Brown, Matt. *"Matt Brown's Dreamweaver Blog." (29 April 2002) Available from the Internet:* `http://radio.weblogs.com/0106884/2002/04/29.html`

Wired News Suggests More Companies Will Blog

Here is what Farhad Manjoo has to say about Macromedia using blogs:

"...These days, it's almost unfashionable for a self-respecting Webophile to not have his own blog; if Macromedia's effort is any indication, soon a tech company that doesn't embrace weblogs may seem equally dated."[4]

Most bloggers, myself included, were excited to see blogging being adopted by a mainstream company. Somehow it meant that all our blog evangelizing wasn't in vain. Although most bloggers thought the strategy was a good one, not all bloggers were as quick to warm up to the idea. Although she liked the general idea of it, long-time blogger Meg Hourian took issue with the fact that the blogs were hosted separately from Macromedia's corporate site. After a little initial skepticism, however, Macromedia's blogging strategy was a hit.

Macromedia's Blog Strategy Drew Some Initial Skeptics

"It seems like a mistake to separate the weblogs from the corporate site..."[5]—Meg Hourhian

"As important as the Macromedia blogs are, I still have to wonder about their veracity."[6]–Dave Rogers

"...they are biased and have a vested interest in product promotion."[7] –Al S.

4. Manjoo, Farhad. "Flash: Blogging Goes Corporate." *Wired News.* 09 May 2002. *Available from the Internet:* http://www.wired.com/news/culture/0,1284,52380,00.html

5. Hourihan, Meg. *"megnut.com: A Weblog by Meg Hourihan."* (09 May 2002) *Available from the Internet:*
http://megnut.com/archive.asp?which=2002_05_01_archive.inc

6. Rogers, Dave. *"Connect & Empower: Can Blogs Find a Place in Corpocracy?"* (17 June 2002) *Available from the Internet:*
http://dave_blog.blogspot.com/2002_06_01_dave_blog_archive.html

7. *"FCD/the weblog: Macromedia Blogs."* (03 May 2002) *Available from the Internet:*
http://fultonchaindesign.com/mt/archive/000125.html#000125

Blogger Anil Dash summed up the initial reaction well when he blogged his assessment of Macromedia's new blogging strategy:

> "The concern, of course, is that companies will astroturf the weblog world with hard-selling flacks whose links and posts would be the online equivalent of a cold-call at dinnertime. But it seems that the people in this first wave of corporate promotional weblogs understand that they have to be part of the community and fit within its mores in order to be successful."[8]

Overall, Macromedia's blog strategy is a success. The community leaders use the blog format to get information more rapidly to the people who need it and bring the important stuff to one place, or a few places anyway—their blogs. The cross-site discussions that blogs enable provide a great way for people to develop their ideas as they have them and share their experiences in a public forum that can be accessed by others.

The Company Blog

Small- to medium-sized companies will benefit from having a *company blog*— a blog operated by one person or a small team passionate about its work. The kind of blog I'm talking about is different than the organized "Community Leader" approach taken by Macromedia.

Here are some examples:

- Evhead (evhead.com) is the personal blog of Evan Williams, president and CEO of Pyra Labs, the company that makes Blogger™.

- Scripting News (scripting.com) is where Dave Winer, CEO of Userland (the company that makes the blogging software Radio™) puts his company's best foot forward.

- Joel On Software (joelonsoftware.com) is the blog of Joel Spolsky. Joel's company, Fog Creek, makes the blogging application CityDesk.

A company blog doesn't necessarily exist to answer questions or respond to bug alerts. A company blog may do some marketing or bragging, and it may post relevant updates, but it can also be humorous or even off-topic at times.

---

8. Dash, Anil. *"archive." (10 May 2002) Available from the Internet:*
   http://www.dashes.com/anil/index.php?blogarch/2002_05_01_archive.php
   #85077799

The idea is to get people coming back, to gain their trust and offer them something worth reading. At the same time, the company blog provides information about products or services. Once a following or readership has been established and people have built up trust, they feel they "know" the president of the company. And that's good PR without really trying to be. It's authentic.

Knowledge Management

The information dissemination that blogging offers and the subsequent retrieval of this information by people who need it, leads us to another blogging application: knowledge management. *Knowledge management* is the sharing and flow of information, usually within an organization or company. People are discovering that blogging makes knowledge management easy—especially when they think of blog posts as stories and stories as a fundamental method for understanding how things work.

The general idea behind knowledge management is to treat the cumulative knowledge of all past, present, and future employees of a company or organization as a valuable commodity. In this manner, the new guys don't have to keep discovering things that the previous staff already found out. Part of what makes this so tricky is that knowledge isn't always so cut and dried.

Genius Tip

Knowledge Management Group
To get more involved with blogging as knowledge management, check out the Yahoo! group dedicated to the discussion of Weblogs for Knowledge Management located at:
`http://groups.yahoo.com/group/klogs/`

Explicit versus Tacit Knowledge

Explicit knowledge is definable and easily documented, like the instructions that come with an IKEA do-it-yourself desk. *Tacit knowledge*, however, is the ethereal stuff in people's minds and practices—knowledge that hides itself in the subconscious yet is used every day. Tacit knowledge manifests itself only when it comes into use. You can bet your booty that an IKEA employee isn't going to include a page on "How To Un-Build That Which You Have Built Backwards and Also Nailed Together."

Managing tacit knowledge within an organization is nearly impossible because it's a bugger to get hold of something that even the people with the knowledge don't really know what they know. You know?

Blogs Impart Information over Time and Save Each Passing Day for the Future

The IKEA instruction sheet can only go so far. You're on your own if you go down the dark path of unrecommended fastening devices and superglue. However, if you had been reading a blog for the past year or so by a guy who loves building IKEA furniture on the weekends (a crazy person?), then you might have read about similar situations. In fact, you might even have avoided building an upside-down bench because you remembered a post by the strange IKEA blogger.

In this manner, a blog can serve as a kind of coach, imparting various experiences in the hope that it will be of use when you are faced with a similar challenge. Blogs work well as knowledge management systems because of their scalability, speed, archiving capabilities, and the fact that they provide context through links and other blogs.

Blogs are wellsprings of experience, personality, and tacit knowledge. We read the minds of bloggers through their blogs, and we get to know them. Through this exchange, we experience what they do, and the stories are passed down to us like ancient folk tales or cave paintings. Except without the ancient part. Or the caves. Or the paintings. But definitely—the folks and the tales.

The Future of Corporate Blogging

In larger companies and organizations, the various project teams—such as marketing, product development, research, or sales—will maintain their own blogs, similar to Macromedia's approach. In some companies, sensitive research and product development blogs will be confined to the Intranet, while others will be made available on the web in order to help publicize the company's expertise.

Chapter 11

Adding Dynamic Features

Blogs are friendly creatures. They like sharing the page with other interesting, useful features. Say you've been blogging away for a while and you've built up a readership; why stop there? Maybe you're looking to attract a higher number of repeat visitors—offer them more content and features. It's not hard to add some powerful, dynamic features to your blog.

Some of the more popular features to add to a blog are search, news headlines, and email subscriptions. Let's take a look at these features and find out how they can be integrated into your blog for maximum effect.

Adding a Search Feature to Your Blog

Is your blog searchable? Can a person who was telling a friend about something she read on your site return with the friend looking over her shoulder and bring up the comment? If you answered no to these questions, you should build a dynamic search feature into your site—but you shouldn't work too hard at it. Atomz search is a great way to plug search capabilities into your blog.

Atomz search is great, because it's free and it works. It's also easy. To build Atomz search into your site, just go to www.atomz.com, click Atomz Search, and then click "trial account." The trial account, Atomz Express Search, is all you'll need for your blog. The trial is surprisingly full featured:

- Limited to sites of 500 pages or less. (no problem)
- Can be used on any web site and is not time-limited by a trial period. (nice)

- Allows complete customization of look and feel to match your site's design. Only a small "Powered by Atomz" logo is shown above the search results. (fantastic)

- Includes site searching, search reporting, search result customization, on-demand site re-indexing, URL entry point and masking controls, and support for 15 languages. (and this is the *free* version)

With a free version like that, you don't need to shell out the dough to offer search capabilities to your users. Atomz Search works by "crawling" through your web site and following the hyperlinks from page to page. The resulting site index is stored within the Atomz network for easy retrieval and delivery to the web site's visitors. You have total control over how often this process is repeated, and you can either schedule the re-indexing of the web site or do it on demand.

Installing the Search Form HTML Code

To create the search form your readers will use to perform search queries, you'll need to add HTML code to your blog template. Atomz provides a standard search form and an advanced search form. I went with the standard form.

The Atomz web site will walk you through this, but basically all you have to do is select and copy the appropriate search form and paste it into the HTML of your blog template. Don't be afraid to modify the provided HTML to fit your design needs; I made the text input box a little shorter so that it would fit in my left column. Test it out after you change it to make sure you didn't break it. The good thing is you can always get the HTML again from Atomz if you need to.

Genius Tip

Copy/Paste Trick

You might hit a snag copying and pasting HTML code from the Atomz site into your HTML editor of choice. Sometimes, the code can mysteriously change in the process. If you run into this problem, try pasting it into Windows Notepad or SimpleText on the Mac; then copy it from there and paste it into your template.

The HTML for the standard search form is not complicated. Listing 11.1 shows what mine looked like when I pasted it into my blog template.

Listing 11.1   HTML for the Standard Search Form Example

```
<!-- Atomz Search HTML for Biz Stone, Genius -->
<form method="get" action="http://search.atomz.com/search/">
<input size=10 name="sp-q"><br>
<input type=submit value="Search">
<input type=hidden name="sp-a" value="sp1000f670">
<input type=hidden name="sp-f" value="iso-8859-1">
</form>
```

Designing Your Search Results Page

You can choose the ready-to-use templates (see Figure 11.1) for your search results page, change the basic look of the search results from the Atomz web site (see Figure 11.2), or design your own results display from scratch (see Figure 11.3). For the standard and basic modes, it's just a matter of filling out a few text boxes, and clicking a few check boxes. For the custom mode, you'll have to paste in your own template.

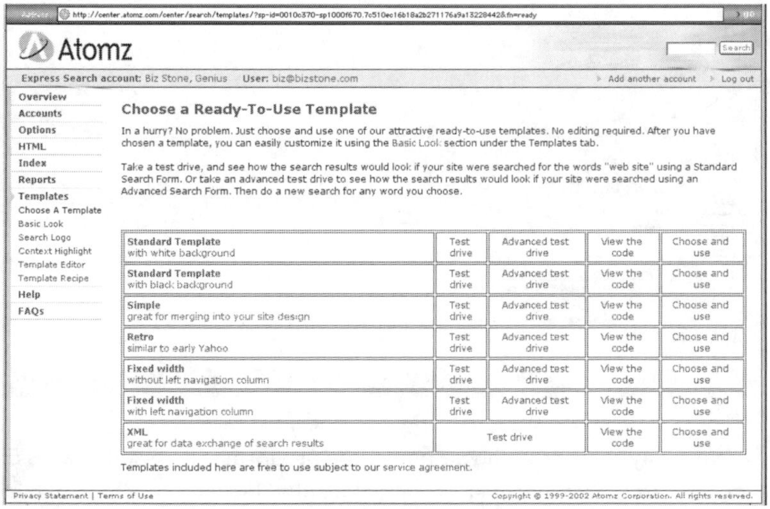

Figure 11.1

Choose from ready-to-use templates.

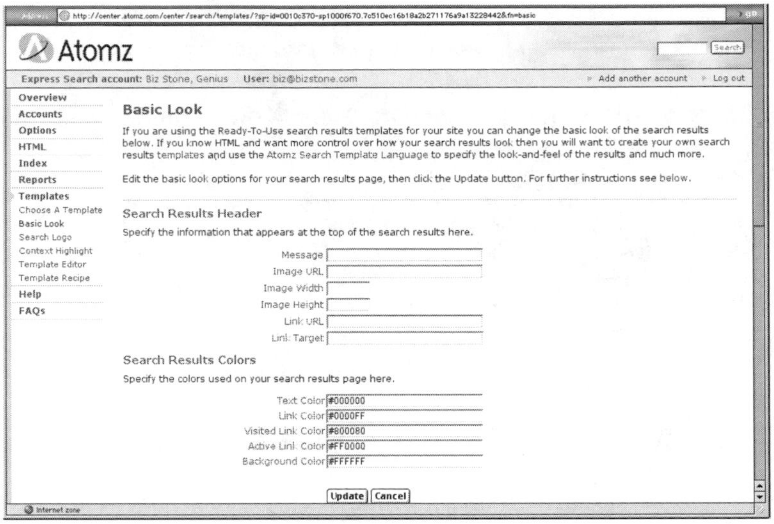

Figure 11.2

Edit your basic template.

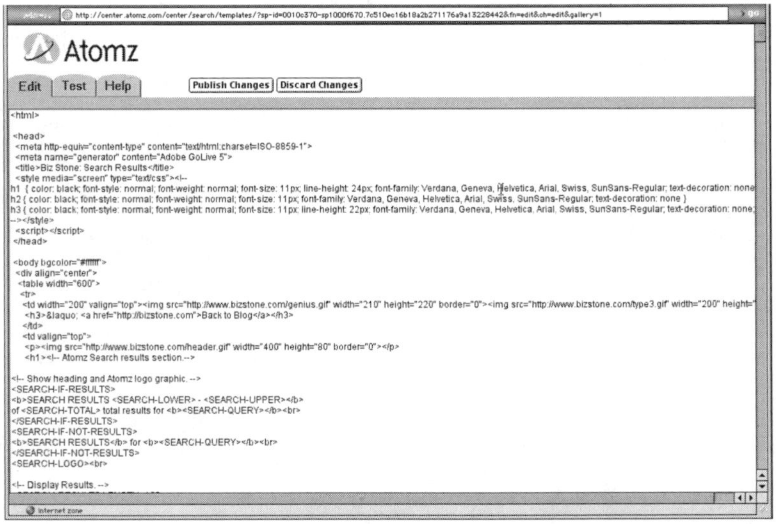

Figure 11.3

Create your own custom designed search results.

The easiest way to go is to choose one of the pre-formatted results pages like "Retro," which is a riff on an early Yahoo! results display, or "XML," which is good for data exchange of search results. You also can adjust pre-formatted pages in the Basic Look section. Editing your basic look is just a matter of choosing and submitting the following information:

- **The Message field**—This is the text message at the top of the search results. Typically, this will be your site name. If you are including an image URL, this message text serves as the alternate text for the image.

- **The Image URL field**—Enter a link here to the image you want displayed at the top of the search results (if you want one). Usually, this will be a URL that links back to an image on your own blog. Use this when you want to include a logo associated with your blog in the search results.

- **Image Width and Image Height**—These are fields in which you enter pixel numbers to indicate the size of the image used for the Image URL.

- **The Link URL**—This field specifies which URL should be linked from the image (or message) you have at the top of your results page.

- **The Link Target**—This is a field that specifies the target frame associated with the link you have at the top of the search results page. This should be changed only from the default value if you use frames on your blog. The default target is _self, which opens the link in the current frame/browser window. You also can specify target values reserved for browsers such as _top, _parent, _blank, or a custom frame name specific to your site. Don't worry about this if you aren't using frames.

- **Search Results Colors**—Choose colors for the text, links, and background. For best results, use color codes that match your blog design.

Using Your Own Template Design

If you know HTML and want more control over how your search results look, you will want to create your own search results templates. You can use the Atomz Search Template Language to specify the look-and-feel of the results. This method takes longer and is more involved than the other methods, but it provides superior design integration with your blog.

These are the main tabs that you need to know to navigate the Atomz Template Editor page:

- **Edit**—The Edit tab allows you to view and edit your template. While you are editing and testing, your visitors will continue to use your previously published template.

- **Test**—Use this tab to test the changes you have made. Enter any search term, click Search, and you will see exactly how your template will look and work with your site.

- **Publish Changes**—Use this button to publish your template, making it the template that visitors searching your site will use.

- **Discard Changes**—You guessed it; this button trashes any changes you've made.

For an example, refer back to Figure 11.3, which shows the Atomz Template Editor page.

Creating a template that matches your site isn't hard. In your web site editor of choice, you'll create an HTML page that looks exactly the way you want your search results to look. An easy solution for the layout of your search results is to use the template you use for your blog. Search results fill the page similarly to blog entries.

Genius Tip

Graphics and Your Search Results Page

If you use graphics on your search results page, use absolute URLs in `<img>`, `<a>`, and other tags that reference URLs to ensure that they render properly on the search results page. This is necessary because the page is being served by Atomz and not by you or your blog host. An example of an absolute URL is `<img src=" http://www.bizstone.com/misc/mylogo.gif">`.

Finishing the search template is now just a matter of copying and pasting. Paste your blog template into the space provided by Atomz, and then copy the search results HTML and paste it into your template where your blog entries would normally go. When you test it out, you should see a page that looks a lot like your blog. Instead of a blog, however, search results for the keyword you chose are displayed.

Once activated, your readers need only to enter a word or phrase in the search form. Atomz Search retrieves the list of relevant results from the previously created search index. The formatted search results then are displayed from the Atomz Search network. Because the search results page is customizable and matches the look and feel of your blog, the results are rendered in the same layout and design as your blog. Pretty sneaky, sis.

Adding Breaking News Headlines to Your Blog

Besides your thoughts and opinions lined up in a neat column of text and published daily to your adoring audience, there are additional, less obvious ways you can express yourself to your readers on your blog. A nice way to do this and add value at the same time is to build a customized news feed. The news headlines you choose to have piped into your blog are a reflection of your interests and/or an addition to your topic-based blog.

Several services provide free aggregated news headlines from hundreds of sources. They're dynamically displayed on your blog, and you need to spend only a few minutes to set it up. The news headlines from Moreover.com are a great way to go.

If you're interested in adding a news feed to your blog, visit Moreover.com and click the link in the footer that says Non-commercial Webmasters. From the resulting page, click Start Now to launch the Webfeed Wizard. In five minutes, you'll have a news feed all set up. For the techies out there, Moreover News Feeds also come in assorted formats, including JavaScript, Flash, XML, (RSS, CDF, WDDX, ColdFusion, and so on) WAP, TSV, and HTML.

Moreover allows you to choose from almost 1,000 predefined categories, or you can build a category from your keywords. There's no maintenance required because the news headlines update automatically—so there's no work for you to do after you have integrated the code.

Here's what you do:

1. Choose the kind of news you want on your site.
2. Design your "webfeed" layout.
3. Copy the HTML code.
4. Paste the HTML in your blog template.

Moreover.com provides an easy-to-use wizard for setting up your webfeed (see Figure 11.4).

In five steps, the Moreover Webfeed Wizard will construct a powerful module that brings breaking news headlines to your blog. You can choose any topic imaginable, and it all matches your design. If you don't feel like matching your design, you can choose from one of their pre-designed webfeed modules:

- retro
- red on black
- newsprint style
- alien side bar
- dark site
- white site

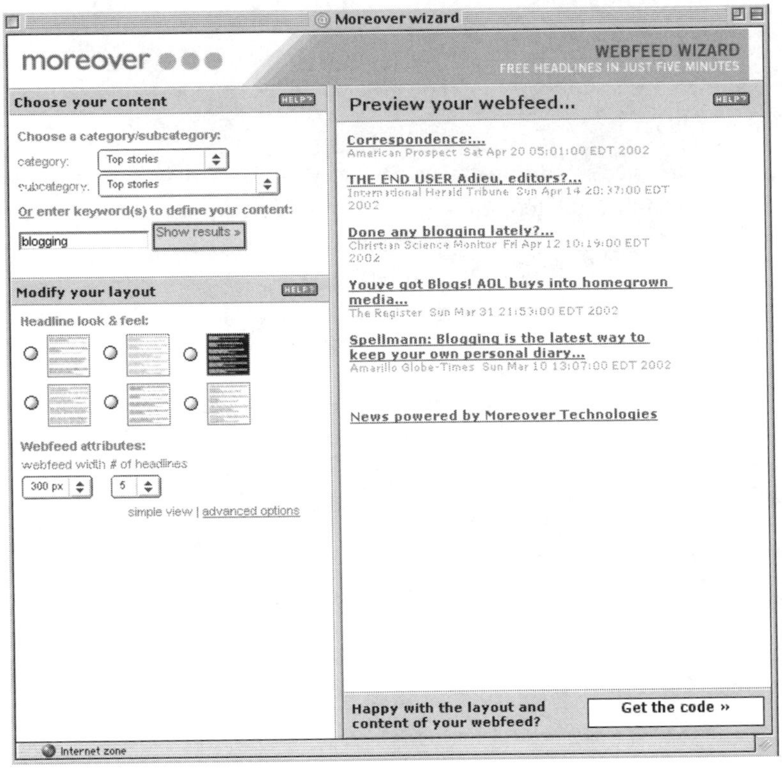

Figure 11.4

Moreover's Webfeed Wizard makes adding news headlines a snap.

You also can start with one of their designs, and then tweak it to suit your needs. Feel free to change the HTML around a bit to work with your blog, but make sure you don't break it! Go back and get new code if it's not working right after you've played around a bit with it. You'll find that a news feed is not only a valuable add-on for your readers, but it's also a great help when you're trying to think of something to blog about.

Placing Your Search Feature and News Feed

Are you trying to find the best spot on your blog to put your search feature and your news feed? Many bloggers find that a modular approach works best when adding elements like search and news to a blog. If the central text of your blog runs down the middle of your page, try putting the news feed in a column on the right, about 200 pixels wide. Figure 11.5 shows an example of a news feed column in a blog.

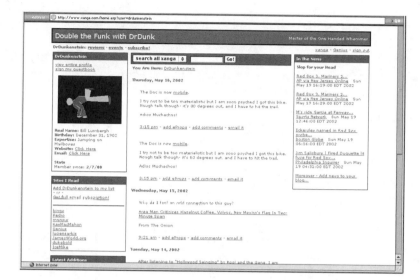

Figure 11.5

Dr. Dunkenstein features Red Sox news on his blog.

When choosing a spot for your search feature, think about where you would look if you came to a blog looking for something. You'll find that keeping the search "above the fold" (see Figure 11.6) so that users don't have to scroll down to find it makes it easier to spot right away.

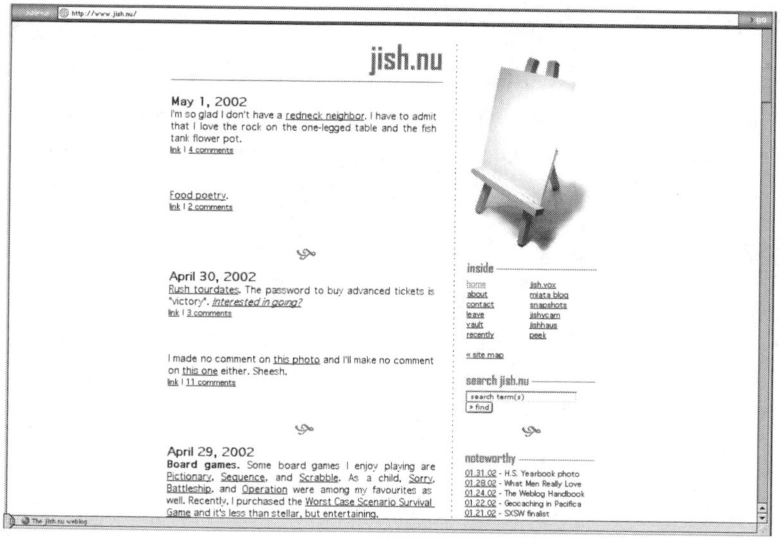

Figure 11.6

The jish.nu site places the search engine "above the fold."

Email Subscriptions

Another valuable feature available to bloggers is email subscriptions. Bloglet is a free service that you can use to make your blog entries available via email to anyone who signs up. Here's how it works:

1. Signup with Bloglet.

2. Put a subscription form on your blog.

3. Readers subscribe through the form.

4. Every day, readers receive a single email from Bloglet informing them of your site updates.

Although there is much more going on behind the scenes at Bloglet (more about that in Chapter 17, "Building a Blog-Related Application: Bloglet"), this is all you need to know. Like adding other dynamic features to your blog, Bloglet just involves signing up and pasting some code into your blog's template. Email updates are a great feature to add to your blog because daily emails remind your readers that your blog is still going strong and is worthy of a visit. Out of site, out of mind!

Manage Your Blog's Link Lists

Many bloggers keep a module somewhere on their site of other blogs they like to read. To edit or add a new blog to this list would require you to access your blog template, change it, and republish it. This isn't super-difficult, but it isn't too easy, either. That's where Blogrolling.com comes in handy (see Figure 11.7). Blogrolling.com provides an easy web interface for you to manage link lists on your blog. *Such* a good idea.

Just as the blogging community grows bigger and more diverse every day, so do the features available. Talented programmers are drawn to the blogosphere, and they often dash out valuable add-ons for bloggers just because they had an idea or felt like improving their portfolio (see Figure 11.8).

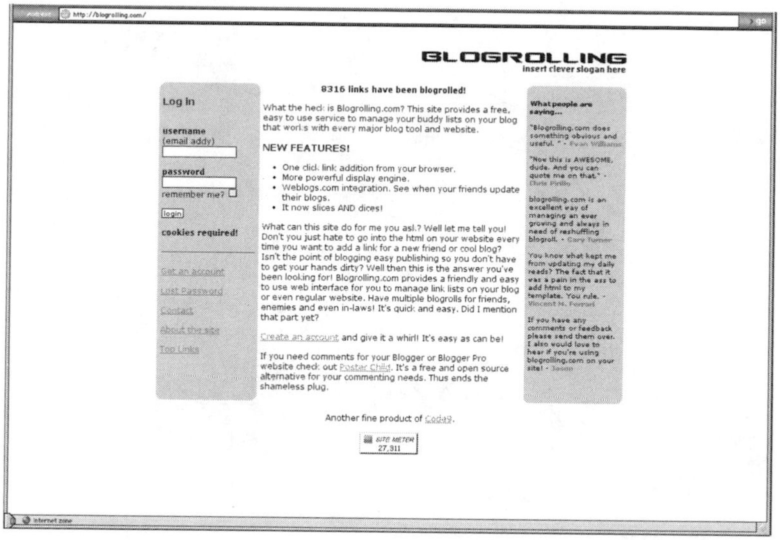

Figure 11.7

Manage your link lists with Blogrolling.com.

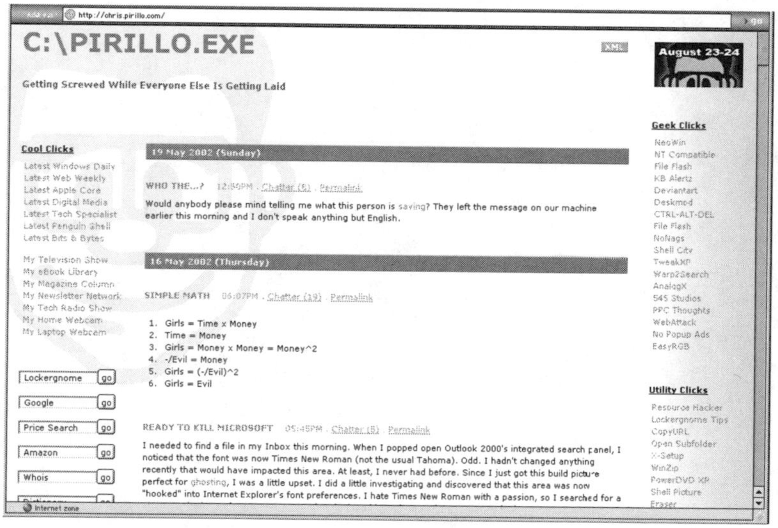

Figure 11.8

TV host Chris Pirillo uses Blogrolling.com to manage his blog's link lists.

As bloggers, we all win!

Chapter 12

Better Blogging

Blogging is an easy and fun way to publish to the Internet, and in many cases, blogging is an exercise for people who strive to write better articles, essays, or literature. In other words, it's a means to an end. The idea is so simple that there are many ways to approach blogging in terms of technique and execution. Let this chapter be an introduction to the idea of approaching blogging in a thoughtful, more precise way.

Finding Your Voice

For some people, writing is as natural as talking. For others, it takes a little getting used to. If you are new to blogging and you're not accustomed to writing for an audience, you might feel that your posts are awkward, clunky, and not really what you meant to say. This can result in a kind of writer's block where you repeatedly start and then delete sentences because they don't seem right.

Still other first time bloggers are afflicted with a kind of stage fright. Their thoughts, emotions, and opinions are going to be readily available to the entire world at the click of a button. And that can be intimidating. What if I come across as some kind of know-it-all? What if people don't "get" me and just think I'm a jerk? What if my sixth grade English teacher reads my blog and finds out that I'm still a bad speller? There are a million reasons not to venture forth in your new independent publishing career.

Relax. It's okay to make mistakes. It's okay if some people think you're a jerk, and it's fine if some people don't "get" you. There will be others who do. And you'll be happy once you get in and realize that the water's warm.

You just need to find your voice. Write to your blog as you would talk with a friend. This is a good way to ensure that your personality comes through in the prose. You can always go back over your work and clean it up a bit, but it's good to get it down initially in an off-the-cuff manner because that's when the good stuff comes out.

The more you blog, the more you will discover about yourself. You might be surprised to find that you are linking and commenting about a certain subject that you wouldn't ordinarily seek out. You might discover, like many people, that blogging is a path to new interests and a way to unlock thoughts otherwise lost in some corner of your brain. Blogging can take on a very intimate "journal" feel or a more "newsy" direction. Either way, the idea is that by putting your thoughts into words on a daily basis, you begin to see over time the kinds of things you gravitate toward. And those things often turn out to be different from what you expected them to be.

Finding your voice also makes for a good blog. Everyone is different, and blogs reflect their authors' personalities and opinions. That's why people read them, and that's why they can be so addictive. Sometimes you just have to tune in to a favorite blog to see what that person has said about the latest news story or to read his or her take on a movie you're thinking of seeing. Finding your voice is one of the perks of blogging that can really help you become a better writer. Don't think about it too much; just blog every day, and your voice will develop.

A Blogger's Style Guide

Blogging makes publishing so easy that anyone with a web connection and an opinion can be a published author. A disadvantage to this system, however, is that there is no one to check your work. Blogging has no editorial process. It's just your words straight to the web without the benefit of review for content or style.

A style guide can't get you your job back when you use your blog to allege that your boss is corrupt or save your relationship when you decide to blog about your various bedroom activities, but it can improve the quality of your blog. For example, some things you might want to keep in mind (but not always adhere to) while you blog are these:

- Get to the point early.
- Express one thought at a time.
- Go easy on the technical jargon.
- Resist excessive sarcasm.
- Back up your information.
- Link! That's what makes it the web.

Of course, having guidelines means you have rules to break! Blogger Matt Pfeffer has put together a helpful style guide starter that "seeks to serve as a resource for anyone writing or editing web copy, and to document some of the conventions that distinguish good writing, as published on the web, from writing published in other media."[1] Figure 12.1 shows part of the first page of Matt's style guide.

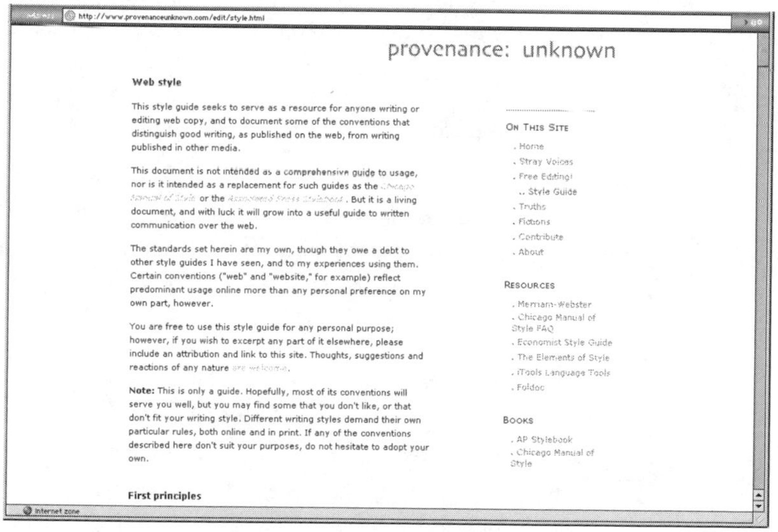

Figure 12.1

Matt is available for writing and editing services.

1. Pfeffer, Matt. "Web style." May, 2002. Available from the Internet:
   http://www.provenanceunknown.com/edit/style.html

Matt's document "is not intended as a comprehensive guide to usage, nor is it intended as a replacement for such guides as the *Chicago Manual of Style* or the *Associated Press Stylebook.*"[2] But because it's a "living document," Matt's work has the potential to adapt and grow into a comprehensive guide to written communication over the web.

Here are some examples and suggestions for better blog copy from Matt's site (`http://www.provenanceunknown.com/edit/style.html`):

bulleted lists

> Introduce a bulleted list with a colon. For example, *There are a number of things to keep in mind when writing a style guide:* … Capitalize the first letter of the first word of each bulleted item. Bulleted items must be parallel in construction. End bulleted sentences with periods (not semicolons or commas), and do not punctuate the end of fragments.

capitalization

> Avoid unnecessary capitalization. Only capitalize job titles if they precede the title holder's name. For example, *Chief Executive Officer Jack Welch.* Do not use all-caps for company names unless the name is an acronym. For example, *IBM, One Touch Systems Inc.* (not **ONE TOUCH Systems Inc.*).

company names

> Avoid unnecessary punctuation and symbols in company names. For example, *Yahoo, CNet, E-Trade Securities, Avanti.*
>
> Where a company name is spelled with an initial lowercase letter, do not capitalize the name at the beginning of a sentence. For example, *eBay.*

dashes

> Use em-dashes (either coded as a dash (—) or typed as two hyphens (- -)) to set off distinct thoughts within a sentence. In general, try to rephrase your thoughts to avoid this construction. Where used, treat an em-dash as a word, with a space on either side. For example, *No one disputes that Thom — who spells his name with an 'h' — is a totally rad dude.*

---

2. *Pfeffer, Matt. "Web style." May, 2002. Available from the Internet:*
   `http://www.provenanceunknown.com/edit/style.html`

dot-com

Minimize the usage of this term. Where possible, rephrase using *Internet* (adj.) or *Internet company* (n.).

email

Do not hyphenate. (Note: While there is little consensus on the spelling of *email*, it is not hyphenated on most major websites (such as Yahoo, for example). It is generally hyphenated in other media, however.)

emoticons

Keep to a minimum. Emoticons can be helpful in indicating sarcasm or good humor, but quickly become cloying and distracting.

hyphens

Use sparingly, and to avoid confusion. For example, *a high-net-worth investor; a highly intuitive solution; a more involved project.* Hyphenate complex phrases only to prevent ambiguity. For example, *some more-involved projects.*

irony

Always give your readers a hint (or some sort of confirmation) that a particular passage is ironic. Even the most obvious instances are often misunderstood.

jargon

Avoid technical terms if you can; most can be rephrased into meaningful English. If a term cannot be rephrased, it should be avoided, unless it is commonly used, accepted and understood.

measurements

Do not use " for inches or ' for feet: For example, *A 12-inch ruler; A 10-foot pole.*

Spell out the following:

inches	pages
feet	pounds
miles	yards

Use the following abbreviations (and don't spell out when preceded by a numeric value):

cm	(centimeter)
dpi	(dots per inch)
fps	(frames per second)
GB	(gigabyte)
GHz	(gigahertz)
Hz	(hertz)
Kb	(kilobit)
Kbps	(kilobits per second)
KB	(kilobyte)
KBps	(kilobytes per second)
KHz	(kilohertz)
Mb	(megabit)
Mbps	(megabits per second)
MB	(megabyte)
MBps	(megabytes per second)
MHz	(megahertz)
mm	(millimeter)
mph	(miles per hour)
ms	(millisecond)
ppm	(pages per minute)

Do not hyphenate adjectival phrases using measured quantities with abbreviated units of measure. For example, *He bought a 1200 dpi printer and a 10 GB hard drive.*

Do hyphenate such phrases when the units are not abbreviated. For example, *There was a 20-second delay before he dropped them both off the 200-foot cliff.*

numbered lists

Bullet points are preferred unless the exact order or the exact number of items is significant. Numbered lists follow the rules for bulleted lists outlined above.

offline

> Always one word, no hyphen, when used to mean "not connected to the Internet." In all other uses, spell as two words, hyphenated. For example, *The tracking system is still off-line*.

online

> Always one word, no hyphen, when used to mean "connected to the Internet."

publication names

> Italicize the names of newspapers and magazines in print. For example, italicize the name of the *Wall Street Journal*, but not WSJ.com.

punctuation

> Follow AP style, with the following exceptions:
>
> When a quote within a quote ends at the end of the full quote, separate the ending quotation marks with a single space. For example, *As Amy put it, "The guy was like, 'Do you want chips with that?' and I was like, 'Duh!' "*

quotations

> Edit quotations for grammar and house style. Exceptionally, a violation of good grammar and house style should be preserved if and only if it conveys the speaker's *deliberate* attempt to express a specific attitude, mood, or other contextual element.

sarcasm

> Writers are somehow tempted to employ sarcasm far more often when online than off. This is usually a mistake. Sarcasm should only be employed with reluctance, and should be identified as such, either with a parenthetical remark (saying, for instance, "(*Just kidding.*)") or a statement (or even an emoticon) indicating amusement.

web links

> Use hyperlinks selectively, and keep them short. When linking text, link from a noun or noun phrase if possible, but link to a verb phrase if necessary to avoid confusion.

website names

> In general, drop the www. For example, *MetaFilter.com*. Capitalize as the site treats its own name (avoiding excessive caps). For example, *CNet.com, craigslist.org*.

Permalinks

Permalinks are hyperlinks to your posts, and they're useful because they make your blog entries more link-friendly. If you build permalinks into your blog design, other bloggers will be able to link to a specific post, and the link will work even after the post has dropped off your front page.

Permanent links on a Blogger-powered blog work with archives, which means that you'll have to make sure you've got archiving turned on in your settings. For more information on archives, see Chapter 8, "Working with Blogger Archives."

How to Build Permalinks

To build permalinks, you'll need to add some tags to your Blogger template. The first tag is `<$BlogItemArchiveFileName$>`. When you publish your blog, this tag will be replaced with the name of the archive file where the linked post is permanently located. Used together with the `<$BlogItemNumber$>` tag, this is an effective way to link to individual posts.

Note that these tags must be located within the `<Blogger>` tags, but not within the `<BlogDateHeader>` tags or `<BlogDateFooter>` tags.

To build a permalink, follow these steps:

1. Sign in to Blogger.

2. Select the blog you'd like to work with, and click into your Settings area. (Make sure that you have archiving enabled and that you already have specified an archive name.)

3. Next, click into your Template area and find the section of your blog template where the `<$BlogItem$>` information is located.

4. Add the two tags, similar to the format in Listing 12.1.

Listing 12.1   Building a permalink

```
<$BlogScript$>
<Blogger>
<BlogDateHeader>
<h4><$BlogDateHeaderDate$></h4>
</BlogDateHeader>
<a name="<$BlogItemNumber$>"></a>
<$BlogItemBody$><br>
<small>posted by <$BlogItemAuthor$> on <$BlogItemDateTime$> |
<a href="<$BlogItemArchiveFileName$>#
<$BlogItemNumber$>">permanent link to this entry</a>
</small>
<p>
<BlogDateFooter>

</BlogDateFooter>
</Blogger>
```

Notice the addition of the <a name> tag at the top of each post. This allows you to point precisely to the post in the archive. Listing 12.1 would produce permalinks similar to those used on boingboing.net. See the example in Figure 12.2.

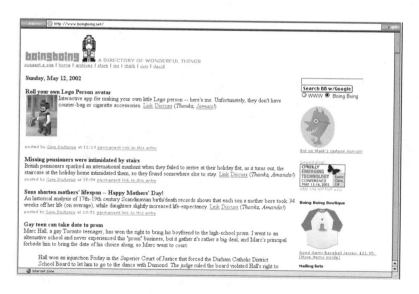

Figure 12.2

Boingboing.net's permalinks are written out.

Use the Whole URL

You might need to add additional path information to the link if you keep your archives in a different directory. Name your full URL to ensure that the path is valid no matter what directory the file is in. Here's an example:

```
<a href="http://www.bizstone.com/archive/"
<$BlogItemArchiveFileName$>#
<$BlogItemNumber$>">link</a>
```

Time Stamps as Permalinks

If you don't want to add any more information than necessary after each post, you can turn your time stamp into the permalink by placing `<$BlogItemDateTime$>` within the `<a name>` tag, as shown in Listing 12.2.

Listing 12.2   Turn your time stamp into a permalink

```
<blogger>

<blogdateheader><$BlogDateHeaderDate$></blogdateheader>
<a name="<$BlogItemNumber$>"></a><$BlogItemBody$>
<a href="http://www.bizstone.com/archive/<$BlogItemArchiveFileName$>#
<$BlogItemNumber$>"><$BlogItemDateTime$></a>

</blogger>
```

Figure 12.3 shows an example of this in action on the Biz Stone, Genius blog.

Figure 12.3

Go minimal: Time stamps as permalinks

Auto Text Bookmarklet

Bookmarklets are tiny JavaScript applications that pretend to be links. They run in your browser's URL field when you click them. Hundreds of bookmarklets are available at bookmarklets.com, and they are great (and free) little tools you can use to add functionality to your browser. There are bookmarklets for turning off banner ads, zooming in on images, changing background color, performing calculations, displaying the number of links on a page, and the list goes on. Bookmarklets are big in blogging. Blogger's BlogThis! bookmarklet generates a pop-up blogging form when clicked, as does Xanga's xTools bookmarklet. Most of the major weblog providers offer bookmarklet-enhanced blogging so that you can blog while you surf. Figure 12.4 shows Steve Kangas' bookmarklets.com site.

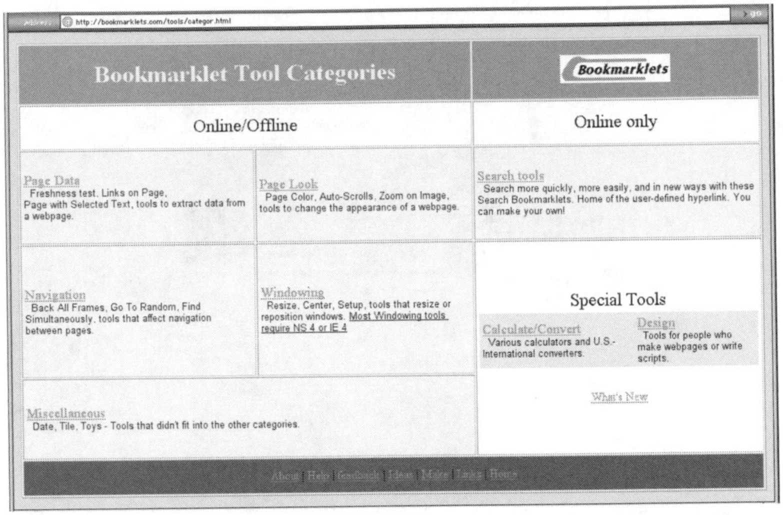

Figure 12.4

Visit bookmarklets.com *for all your bookmarklet needs.*

How to Build an Auto Text Bookmarklet

Blogger offers a handy bookmarklet builder that makes creating an auto text bookmarklet ultra easy (see Figure 12.5). Create and install a Blogger auto text bookmarklet to save yourself some typing while blogging. The auto text bookmarklet inserts text into the Blogger posting form so that you don't have to type the same thing in every time.

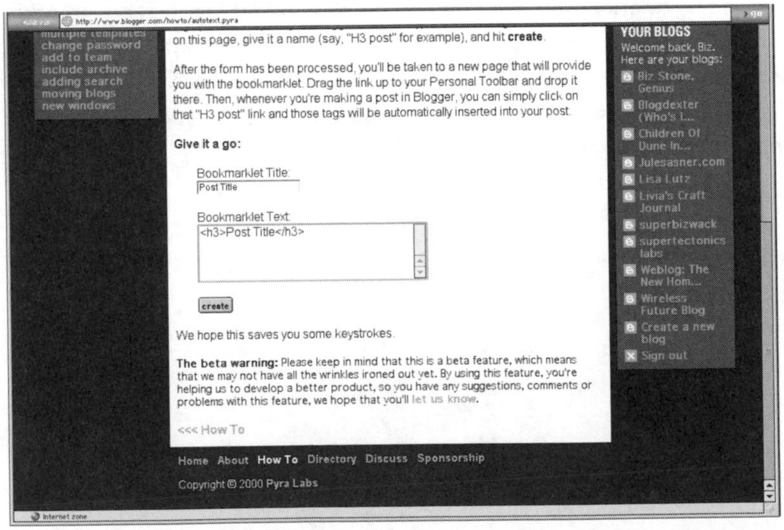

Figure 12.5

Blogger offers a helpful bookmarklet builder.

The auto text bookmarklet inserts text into the Blogger posting form when activated. The text is saved on your computer instead of the server, which means that it's ready when you need it. So let's say you want an auto text bookmarklet to help you create titles for your posts. Do this:

1. Name your bookmarklet Post Title.

2. Type the h3 tags into the bookmarklet builder form.

3. Click Create.

4. On the resulting page, drag your new bookmarklet to your browser's toolbar.

Now, whenever you're writing a post in Blogger, you can click that Post Title link, and those tags will be automatically inserted into the text field. Create as many bookmarklets as you like. Good stuff.

Chapter 13

Increasing Traffic on Your Blog

Monitoring your blog's visits and referrals can become a little addictive. When you log in to check your stats, you can see where visitors to your blog are coming from, how many visits you get each day, and even how long visitors tend to stay. Often, you can click on a link in your referral log and be transported instantly to another blog, where you can read what someone has written about you or a post you published. In a way, it's like being able to hear what people say about you when you leave the room. How often have you wished you could do that?

Measuring Your Blog's Traffic with Site Meter

One of the first things you should add to your blog is Site Meter. Site Meter is a free statistics tool you can paste into your blog template to get real-time reports on the visitor activity of your web site. Site Meter displays the number of visitors to your blog, as well as the referrals (links to web pages that have linked to your blog). It also keeps statistics on the number of visits each hour and every day and provides detailed information about these visitors (see Figure 13.1).

Figure 13.1

Sitemeter.com helps you keep up-to-date on your blog's stats.

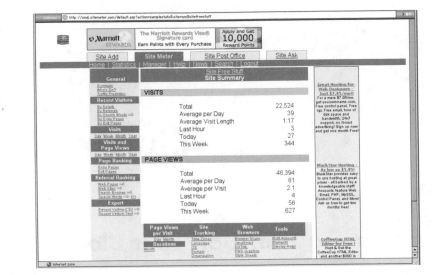

By now, you should know the drill. Find something you want to add to your blog, sign up, copy the code, and paste it into your blog's template.

Adding Site Meter is no different. Just sign up for an account, get the code, and paste away. The service is free, but you will have to put up with pasting a little linked graphic somewhere on your blog (see Figure 13.2).

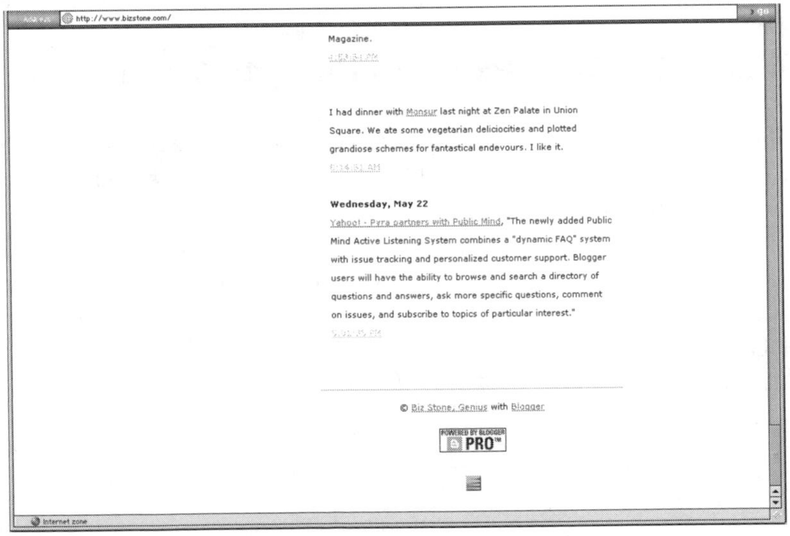

Figure 13.2

I use the free version of Site Meter for my personal blog.

If you'd rather not display the graphic, you can upgrade to one of the paid versions and choose an invisible site meter. Upgraded users can have statistics tracking without displaying a counter or the Site Meter logo on their blog. The utility costs $6.95 a month for up to 25,000 page views. Your credit card will be charged once a month, based on the traffic level of your site.

Site Meter is blog-friendly. If you have a Blogger or Blog*Spot-powered blog, Site Meter will add the HTML to the web page template in your Blogger account. All you have to do is sign in, click the Manager tab, click first HTML Code, and then Adding *Site Meter* to a Blogger or Blogspot site, and add the necessary information (your blogger ID, username, and password). After this, it's just a matter of clicking a button, and your Site Meter code is added to your blog. Nice.

Google: A Great Way to Get Traffic to Your Blog

Once you've added Site Meter, you'll have a good idea of your traffic numbers. You'll also be able to see where the traffic is coming from in your referral logs, which is even more fun!

After you've spent some time blogging, you'll start to notice that a lot of people are coming to your blog because they searched for keywords at Google. Why are there so many Google referrals? It turns out that Google favors blogs, in terms of delivering up links when people search the web. There are three reasons for this:

- **Blogs contain links**—Although it isn't mandatory to include links in your blog, the classic blog format is very simple: links with attached commentary. The original bloggers were like self-appointed editors of the web. They sought out interesting or obscure sites and pages on the web, linked to them, and added their thoughts. That's how blogs began, and that's the format that hundreds of thousands of blogs employ today.

- **Google treats links as "votes"**—Let's allow Google to explain how Google works: "In essence, Google interprets a link from page A to page B as a vote, by page A, for page B. But, Google looks at more than the sheer volume of votes, or links a page receives; it also analyzes the page that casts the vote. Votes cast by pages that are themselves important weigh more heavily and help to make other pages important."[1] Basically this says that if page A links to page B, then page B increases in popularity and climbs the ranks among Google's search results pages.

- **Google looks for fresh content**—Google wants users to have access to the most current information on the web, so they refresh millions of pages every day to ensure that search results include frequently updated pages, such as news portals and (you guessed it!) blogs.

---

1. `http://www.google.com/technology/`

Figure 13.3 shows an example of how blogs show up first in a search.

Figure 13.3

The number one result for "evan" on Google is a link to Evan Williams' blog.

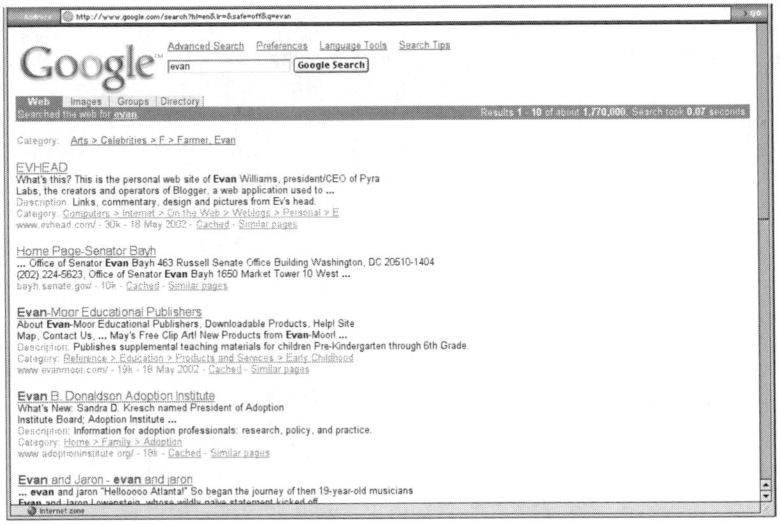

The end result is that Google acts like a funnel for visitors to your blog. This is great, because it's free and it introduces your blog to people who ordinarily might not have looked for it.

Micro-Advertising—Using Google's AdWords Advertising Program

Another way to increase traffic to your blog is to go the old-fashioned route and pay for visitors. Don't worry; it's cheap! Google started it with their successful AdWords program, which uses small, yet eye-catching modules with a few succinct lines of copy and a link. Anyone with a credit card and something to promote can create, preview, and then buy a small, inexpensive ad to appear along with the results of a keyword search. I'll let Google explain it exactly:

> "Google AdWords Program is a simple and quick way to purchase highly targeted advertising, regardless of your budget. AdWords are shown on the right side of the results page to Google's millions of users and are based on the keywords and phrases you select, which are relevant to the products or services you're advertising. Your keywords are matched against the search terms that Google users enter for a search. When a Google user enters the keywords or phrases that you've selected for your campaign, your ads are displayed.

Unlike other web sites that offer advertising targeted by general content or user demographics, Google AdWords Program lets you reach only those people who have expressed an active desire for information related to your products or services. Furthermore, with the AdWords program, you will be reaching Google users, who have some of the most sophisticated demographic profiles on the web.

Our experience with advertisers to date is that highly targeted keyword advertising produces, on average, four times the industry standard click-through rate. Many advertisers have even experienced returns significantly higher than that rate. While we cannot guarantee that your ads will perform at this high level, we can assure that you will be able to quickly discover the keyword search combinations most effective in driving traffic to your site."[2]

Instead of just buying space on a site, you are buying space on a page that people see only when they search for the keywords you have purchased. This highly targeted advertising, at such as reasonable rate, is one of the reasons why Google is going to be around for a long time. Figure 13.4 shows the Google page that will get you started.

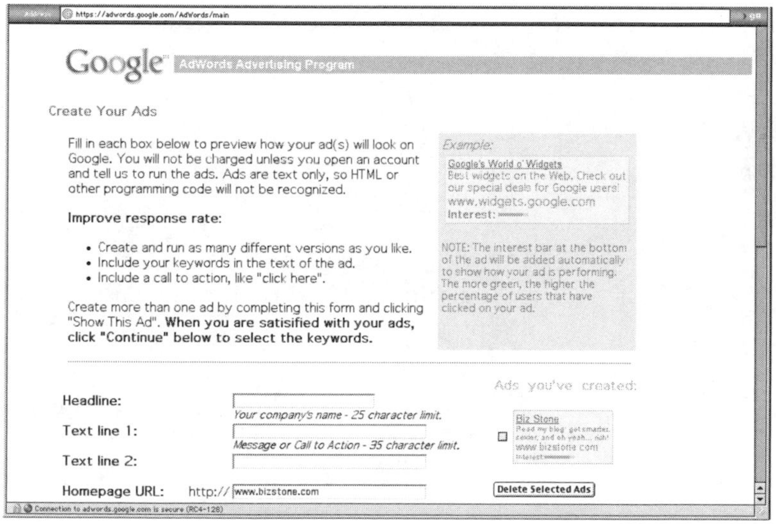

Figure 13.4

The Google Create Your Ads page.

2. http://www.google.com/ads/index.html

Google Ads are all based on keywords. You purchase keywords, and your ad is displayed whenever someone searches for those words (or word). So, to reach collectors of deadly, man-eating robots, you might buy the keywords *man-eating* or *deadly robots*. The more popular the keyword search, the quicker your impressions will sell out. Google even includes a status bar at the bottom of your ad, which gauges user-interest in your ad.

Pricing for AdWords is based on the position in which your ads are shown. Google positions your ad based on how many users click it over time. Current rates are between $8 and $15 per thousand ads shown, depending on positioning. There's no minimum deposit required, and accounts are opened with a credit card.

Google boasts unnaturally high click-through rates, so you're pretty much guaranteed a super-targeted audience. Hey, if a user searches for *inflatable alligators*, and you sell inflatable alligators, how can you not go for this?

Micro-Advertising and the Blogging Community

Once Google proved that this method of advertising worked, all the smart kids started building their own versions. The following sections give you some specific examples.

Genius Tip

Include **META** Tags in Your Blog

Not all search engines are as sophisticated as Google. You can give those engines a little help indexing your blog by using **META** tags. You can include keywords that relate to the things you'll be blogging about and a general description of your site. Here is how **META** tags are formatted:

```
<META name="keywords" Content="[place relevant keywords
here (separated by commas)]">
<META name="description" Content="[place description
here]">
```

Place these tags in your template between the <head> and </head> tags.

TextAds

The first person to jump in and set up a home-brewed version of the AdWord program was Matthew Haughey, designer and developer of the group blog, Metafilter. You can see an example of micro advertising in action in Figure 13.5.

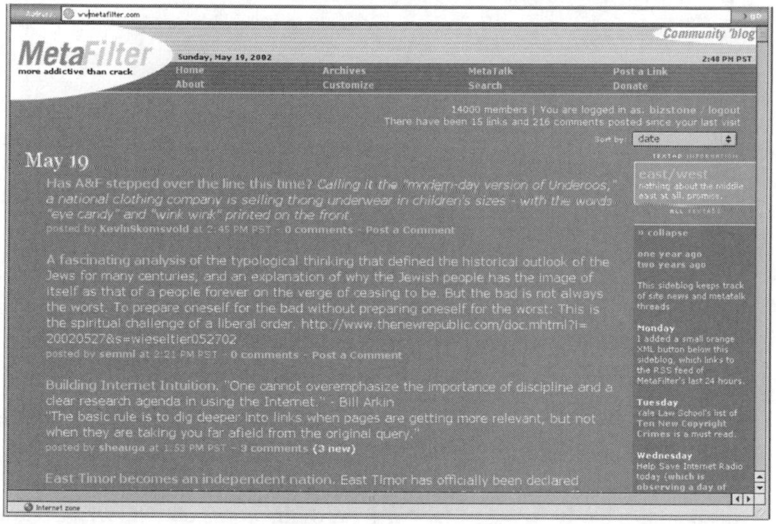

Figure 13.5

Owners of the Blog east coast/west coast bought an ad on Metafilter's front page.

Haughey called his self-serve advertising *TextAds* and billed them as, "A non-invasive, non-annoying, low-cost way to get your site in front of thousands of people."[3] I bought one immediately, and new visitors began dropping by my personal blog unannounced. It was great. TextAds are priced at $2 per 1,000 impressions, and you get your very own stats page, which displays click-through rates and other pertinent info. Metafilter contributors are notoriously hard to impress, but they welcomed TextAds. They saw TextAds as a way to give back to the community, while driving traffic to their own projects. Matt did a great job.

pyRads

The success of TextAds prompted Evan Williams and Jason Shellen to launch pyRads. They called their text-based ad offering "Web Advertising That Doesn't Suck." The first Pyra-product since Blogger, pyRads is an innovative way for the hundreds of thousands of bloggers to thank one of the last great free products on the web—and draw a crowd doing so. Figure 13.6 shows the pyRads main page.

---

3. http://www.metafilter.com/textads.mefi

Figure 13.6

pyRads: Web advertising that doesn't suck.

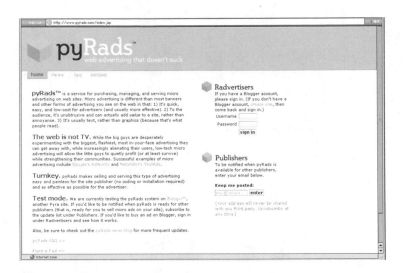

Like Google's AdWords, you can purchase pyRads with a credit card. They are priced affordably at $10 per 8,000 impressions—a great deal, considering that pitching to Blogger users is more like grass roots PR than straight advertising. "The unique thing about Blogger users is that they are all publishers themselves. Thus, if you show them something new and/or noteworthy, many of them are likely to pass the word via their blogs, the collective readership of which is potentially millions."[4] (Figure 13.7 shows an example of this.) And yes, I bought one of these, too. (I was doing research!) Anyway, pyRads brought a bunch of new visitors to my site.

Figure 13.7

Blogger is advertising its own advertising feature on the right side of their front page.

4. http://www.blogger.com/spons/micro_ads.pyra

Daypop

If you want to pitch your blog to a news-junkie-type crowd, you should advertise on Daypop. Daypop is a search engine that keeps track of both "living" sites like blogs and news articles. Advertising on Daypop is inexpensive, and the site is very popular with people looking for breaking news. Figure 13.8 shows the Daypop Ad Center page.

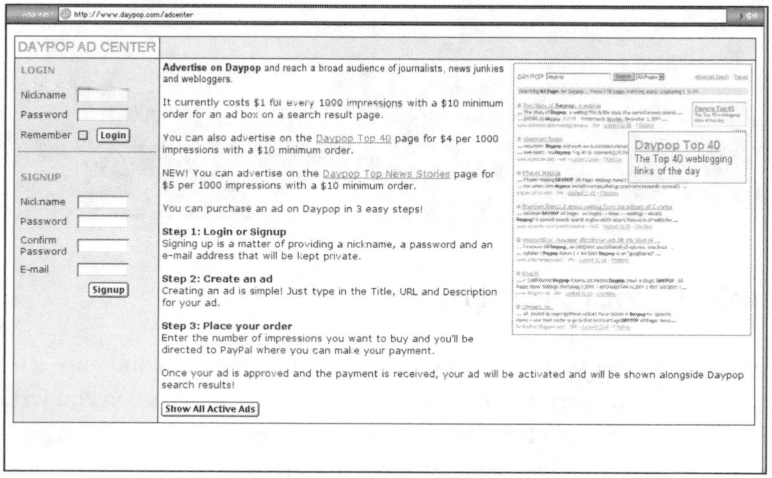

Figure 13.8

Advertising on Daypop is cool. Everybody should try it once.

BlogSnob—Free Micro-Advertising

Arnab Nandi, a 19-year-old college sophomore in Delhi, India, saw all this cool micro-advertising whoo-ha going on and decided to make it available to everyone for free. Figure 13.9 shows the BlogSnob home page.

As it says in the first paragraph of Arnab's site, "BlogSnob[tm] is an experimental service for members of the blogging community. It enables you to tell everyone Out There about your blog thru simple, text-based ads. It's free, it's fast, and it's downright simple. Besides, it's a great way to get to know about new blogs!"[5]

5. Nandi, Arnab. "BlogSnob HostingMatters." Available from the Internet: http://blogsnob.idya.net/

Figure 13.9

That Arnab Nandi is always thinking.

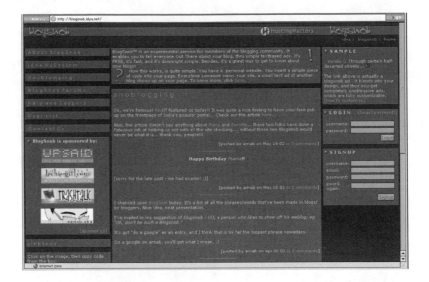

Think of Your Audience

As a general rule of thumb, it's always good to think of your audience when you blog. Blogs are very audience-specific. That means that when you write your blog, whether it's a topic blog or an open diary to the world, it has a unique voice—yours—which appeals to a certain audience. The worst thing you can do with your blog is try to please the masses and disobey your instincts. That will get you nowhere. Be yourself, and you're more likely to build a relationship with your readers. The same holds true when it comes time to compose your text ad; try to keep your key audience in mind.

Developing a distinctive voice with your blog is not a way to get an immediate boost in numbers; it's a more gradual approach. If you develop a few regular readers, there's a good chance they will spread the word about your blog through word of mouth, email, or perhaps a little publicity, if they are bloggers too. In any case, it doesn't hurt to give yourself a bit of a boost in readership with a text ad. Your readers will be glad to have discovered you!

Part III

Power Blogging

Chapter 14

Syndicating Your Blog

Bloggers are always looking for new ways to bring in more traffic. Knowing that people are reading your work is encouraging and prompts you to continue blogging. If you're looking for an even wider audience for your blog, you should consider syndicating your blog.

Syndication means that your posts have a second life after being published on your blog. When you syndicate, your blog posts become available to people via news aggregators (software that periodically reads a set of sources and displays the new content on a single page), email, or even other peoples' blogs, depending on how you choose to do it.

You can syndicate your blog a couple of different ways. One method employs some lightweight XML. Another method involves using JavaScript's `document.write` method and offering up a snippet of code to your fellow bloggers.

Either way, the idea behind syndicating your blog posts is to spread the word about your blog. You'll get your posts or the titles of your posts showing up all over the web. In essence, you're creating many doors to your blog—and many doors means higher traffic.

Syndicating Your Blog with RSS

RSS, also known as *Real Simple Syndication*, *Rich Site Summary*, or *RDF Site Syntax* is a lightweight XML format designed specifically for syndicating web content. Building your own RSS files requires some fairly heavy experience, but thankfully this process also can be automated by some blog providers.

Originally developed by Netscape, RSS has become a popular way to share content between web sites as well as blogs. RSS is a great syndication tool because not only can the big destination sites like BBC, CNET, CNN, Disney, Forbes, Motley Fool, Wired, Red Herring, Salon, Slashdot, and ZDNet use it for their content distribution services, but the blogging community also can make use of it to promote their work.

With RSS, your posts can be pulled from your blog and displayed on other web sites and information aggregation tools. After you've created an RSS file and posted it, you then can give the URL to sites and aggregation services as well as link to it from your blog.

How RSS Works

RSS defines a set of tags for sharing content. An individual RSS text file contains both static information about your blog and dynamic information about your latest posts—all surrounded by start and end tags. Each post is defined by an <item> tag, which has a headline title, URL, and description.

Evan Williams syndicates his personal blog automatically with Blogger Pro's syndication feature (see Figure 14.1).

Figure 14.1

Evhead.com's RSS is generated using a Blogger Pro feature.

Automatically Generate an RSS File for Your Blog

If you are using a major blog provider such as Radio or Blogger Pro, you don't need to worry about building your own RSS file because the RSS generation is done automatically. If you are using Blogger Pro, for example, all you need to do is set RSS up in the Settings section of your account. Check with your blogging provider to see whether the company offers automatic RSS generation. Figure 14.2 shows you how easy this can be.

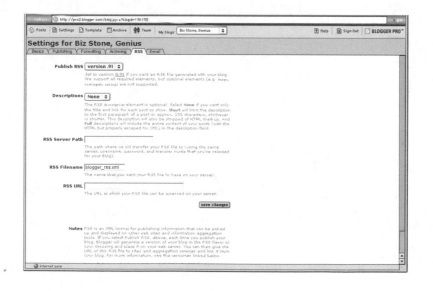

Figure 14.2

Generate an RSS file in a few clicks with Blogger Pro.

Blogger Pro and RSS

If you select Publish RSS in your settings, each time you publish your blog, Blogger Pro will generate another file on your Web server that is a version of your blog in RSS format. You then can give the URL of this file to sites and aggregation services and promote it on your blog. Many bloggers use an orange XML or blue RSS button to indicate the presence of an RSS feed (see Figures 14.3 and 14.4).

Figure 14.3

Standard RSS button.

Joel Spolsky
John Robb
Jon Udell
Pierre Kerchner
SATN.org (Frankston/Reed/ Bricklin)
TheFeature.com (Mobile)
WebWord.com (Usability)

archives

12/01/2001 - 12/31/2001
01/01/2002 - 01/31/2002
02/01/2002 - 02/28/2002
03/01/2002 - 03/31/2002
04/01/2002 - 04/30/2002
05/01/2002 - 05/31/2002
06/01/2002 - 06/30/2002
current

RSS

Figure 14.4

Standard XML button.

You can determine what shows up in the optional description element of the RSS file. On the RSS settings page of your Blogger account, select None for descriptions if you want to show only the title and link for each post. Short descriptions will limit the description to the first paragraph of a post or approximately 255 characters, whichever is shorter. This description also will be stripped of HTML markup. Full descriptions include the entire content of your posts (with HTML, but properly escaped for XML) in the description field.

> ### Titles Are Required for Blogger Pro RSS
>
> Titles are required in RSS, which means that only posts that have titles will be included in your Blogger Pro RSS feed. You need to use the title field feature when blogging to publish RSS with Blogger.

Use an RSS Editor When Automation Is Not Available

If you are using a blog provider that doesn't automate the process of generating an RSS file, you can use the RSS Channel Editor provided by WebReference.com to do the job (see Figure 14.5).

Figure 14.5

WebReference.com provides an RSS editor.

To create a customized RSS file, fill in as many blanks on the RSS Creator form as you can. You must fill in the Channel Title and Channel Link and at least one Item Title and Item Link.

If you want to edit an existing RSS file, you can type its URL into the RSS URL field and click the Fetch button. This will bring up the form with the values from your RSS file. You can then work on the file from the form.

When you're finished with the form, click any of the Build RSS buttons. Then save the file to your computer so that you can upload it to your site. After you have an RSS file, you can submit it to information aggregators so that it will be available to the general web populace.

> **Don't Use HTML Tags**
>
> Avoid using HTML tags in any of the fields; otherwise, the RSS file will be invalid. HTML tags and RSS files don't mix well.

Building a RSS File from Scratch

If you're a little more technically inclined and you'd rather do things the old-fashioned way, you can build your RSS file from scratch. If you've got a text editor—or even better, an XML editor—and some free time, you can use the information in this section to do just that.

Overview of an RSS document

A basic RSS document has a simple structure:

- **XML Declaration**—You aren't required to start XML documents with an XML declaration, but it's not a bad idea to do it anyway. The declaration does just that: it declares that the document is XML and also specifies the version.

- **The Container**—The container is the "root element," containing all other elements in the document.

- **The Channel**—The channel element is the place to describe the RSS channel; in this case, your blog. This is where you put your blog title, link, and description.

- **The Items**—This is the whole point of the RSS channel—the blog posts you want syndicated. The items are made up of only a title and link.

The Declaration

To start out with your declaration, here's what you do:

1. Tell the programs reading the file what it is:

   ```
   <?xml version="1.0"?>
   <rss version="0.91">
   ```

2. Then you begin to build your channel. The `channel` tag starts a new channel. The `title` tag names the channel, the `link` tag brings new readers to your blog, and the `language` tag in this case indicates US English.

```
<channel>

<title>Biz Stone, Genius</title>
     <link>http://www.bizstone.com/</link>
     <description>Biz Stone claims to be a genius. He may be
wrong</description>
     <language>en-us</language>
```

Adding Entries for Items

Normally, you need to add an entry for each page you want listed in your channel. With your blog, each item is a post. So to get this to work, you need to make a change to your Blogger template. At the beginning of every blog entry, you'll need the code `<span class="RSS:item">`. Then, at the end of each entry, close the span with `</span>`. This means that if you are using Blogger, your template will include this line:

```
<span class="rss:item"><$BlogItemBody$></span>
```

Genius Tip

Use the HTML-Encoded Versions
If you are linking to a URL that uses an ampersand, use the HTML-encoded version (&) instead of the character &. The same goes for quotation marks, which need to be marked up as ".

Finishing Up

Here are the last steps that you need to take in building a RSS file:

1. Close the channel and the RSS file:

```
</channel>

</rss>
```

2. Save your file with an .rss extension. Then upload it to a web server.

Promoting Your RSS File

To promote your feed, link to it from your blog. You can create a standard text link or post an eye-catching graphical link that announces your RSS feed. Actually, you might not even need to promote your RSS feed if the current trend toward auto-discovery continues to grow. *Auto discovery* is a new development in the blogosphere that allows RSS aggregators to automatically "see" your RSS file. You can find more information about auto discovery at `http://diveintomark.org/`.

RSS Aggregators

News aggregators are web applications that save you time online. Aggregators venture out onto the web and find you news stories or new blog posts and bring the headlines together on one page. Then you can simply bookmark that page and visit it when you want to get the lowdown.

If you are using Radio as your blog provider, you can enjoy the built-in aggregator that comes with the service. Beyond Radio, there are a number of aggregators out there that automatically pull RSS files from content providers and present the news in a variety of ways. Aggregators make it easy to drop an RSS feed into your site. Here are a few popular RSS aggregators:

- **AmphetaDesk** (`http://www.disobey.com/amphetadesk/`)—Written in Perl so that it works for both Windows and Mac users, AmphetaDesk sits on your desktop, downloads the latest news that interests you, and displays it in a customizable web page. There are thousands of channels to choose from.

- **News Is Free** (`http://www.newsisfree.com`)—News Is Free is a voluntary effort run by Mike Krus and Pino Calzo that provides a powerful and flexible portal for browsing, indexing, and publishing news headlines. In addition, `Newsisfree.com` offers additional tools for bloggers.

- **NewzCrawler** (`http://www.newzcrawler.com`)—NewzCrawler is a $25 product for Windows that gathers news content from each source channel and displays it in a scrolling list, News Balloon, or News Ticker. NewzCrawler features a Microsoft Outlook Express-like user interface and supports the Blogger API.

- **Peerkat** (`http://www.oreillynet.com/~rael/lang/python/peerkat/`)— Peerkat is a personal syndicated data aggregator that you download to your computer desktop.

Syndicating Your Blog with JavaScript

With JavaScript, it is possible to include a file in your blog's HTML template that will render another blog. You can do this because JavaScript's `document.write` method allows you to include text on a web page from a remote source. You can configure your blog so that other bloggers will be able to feature your posts if they so desire.

Why use JavaScript to syndicate your blog rather than RSS? Well, for one, maybe you're not yet comfortable with XML. For another, you might already be familiar with JavaScript from building other features into your blog. Or still another reason for syndicating your blog with JavaScript is that it's two projects in one. In other words, making your blog available for other bloggers to include in their blog means that it's also available in one of yours. Huh? Multiple blogs on one blog. That's all I'm saying. *Sheesh*.

Here's what my Blogger template might look like if I were to use JavaScript's `document.write` method:

```
document.write("<span class='genius_title'>genius<br></span>")
<Blogger>
<BlogDateHeader>
document.write("<span class='genius_dateheader'>
➥<$BlogDateHeaderDate$><br></span>")
</BlogDateHeader>
document.write("<span class='genius_body'>
➥<$BlogItemBody$></span><br>")
document.write("<span class='genius_footer'><span
➥class='genius_postedby'>posted by <$BlogItemAuthor$></span>
<span class='genius_timestamp'><$BlogItemDateTime$></span></span>")
</Blogger>
```

Using this template, I could create a blog that can be included on other blogs. You have to remember that the file must be named *something.js*. So when you are filling out your blog settings and Blogger asks you to name your blog, name it accordingly. In this example, mine would be named *genius.js*. All I need to do is offer this snippet to my readers:

```
<script language="Javascript"
SRC="http://www.bizstone.com/genius.js"></script>
```

Now other bloggers will be able to feature my posts on their blog—possibly as a module or sidebar.

Genius Tip

<span> Tag Trick

If you wrap all the unique elements in <span> tags with identifiable classes, each blogger choosing to republish your posts can use CSS to define the look of them to match their design.

If you decide to go this route, you'll need to be careful what you enter in your posts. Be sure to use ' instead of ", or you'll get a JavaScript error. For more information on syndicating your Blogger blog with JavaScript, see `http://publicmind.blogger.com`.

Getting the Word Out

The key to a high-traffic blog is having many other bloggers linking back to you. By syndicating your blog, you are increasing the number of ways people can find your work. After you've created your RSS file and displayed your XML button, it's just a matter of sitting back and watching your empire grow. Oh—and of course you'll have to continue to blog, or there will be nothing to syndicate!

Chapter 15

Sideblogs, Email Blogging, and Alternative Blogging Interfaces

Many bloggers seek different ways of blogging. This chapter shows you how you can use `includes` to display more than one blog on one web page, and then introduces you to a few alternative means of posting to your blog or sideblog.

Sideblogs

Normally, when people create blogs, they make them whole-page blogs, and they use whatever interfaces their blogging providers offer. However, sometimes bloggers find it necessary to add a sideblog to their home page or main blog. A *sideblog* is a smaller-style blog that is usually placed off to the side of a more prominent blog or tucked over on the side of a home page as a little "what's new" area. Figure 15.1 shows a real sideblog in action.

Figure 15.1

Matthew Haughey has built a sideblog to keep track of site news for his group blog, Metafilter.

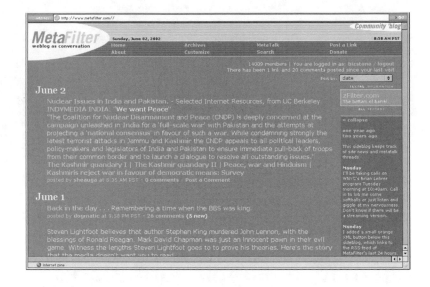

Creating a Sideblog at Blogger™

To create a Blogger-powered sideblog, you need to dig around a bit in your template and check into your server's capabilities.

Creating a sideblog is not too different from creating a standard blog at Blogger. To create a sideblog for your Blogger-powered blog, begin by creating a new blog. Here's the drill:

1. Log in to Blogger, and set up your new blog by clicking the Create a New Blog link in the right column.

2. Specify the information requested.

3. Click Settings to enter additional information. Let's use "`sideblog.html`" as the file name for this blog.

4. After you're all signed up and done entering settings, open the template for the new blog by clicking Template.

5. Then remove the `<html>`, `<head>`, and `<body>` tags, leaving only the Blogger code. It will look something akin to this:

```
<Blogger>
 <BlogDateHeader>
  <$BlogDateHeaderDate$>
 </BlogDateHeader>
 <$BlogItemBody$>
 <$BlogItemDateTime$>
</Blogger>
```

In terms of design, sideblog.html will be within your existing page, so it will use the body and CSS information provided by your main blog template. If you want the page to look different, you'll need to edit the template of sideblog.html until you've got it looking the way you want. Once you've done that, you're ready to add the `includes` to your template.

Genius Tip

Archiving Multiple Blogs
Archiving works just like commenting when it comes to multiple blogs. You can set up blog archives for your sideblog or any blogs you choose to display together on a page.
For more information, see Chapter 8, "Working with Blogger Archives."

About Includes

`Includes` exist on different servers and platforms. There are Server Side Includes, PHP, ASP, and Cold Fusion. The variety of `include` method you require depends on the platform your server is running as well as whether it has the functionality and setup to handle the `includes`. Ask your system administrator if you're not sure about this.

Adding the Sideblog to Your Existing Blog

To add the sideblog to your existing blog, open your main blog template and look for the location in the layout where you think a sideblog would work well. When you've decided on the right spot, all you have to do is type a bit of code. Remember that the code you use depends on your server's specifications, for example:

- Server Side Includes (SSI): `<!- -#include file="sideblog.html"- ->`

- PHP: `<?php include ('sideblog.html'); ?>`

- Active Server Pages (ASP): `<!--#include file="sideblog.html"-->`

- Cold Fusion (CF): `<cfinclude template="sideblog.html">`

After you've got your sideblog code in place, post and publish both of your blogs so that all the new files, as well as the changed files, are published to your server. Ask your system admin if you are unsure of the SSI format to use.

When you view your blog template, the `include` code will show up. Don't let this throw you—it will render properly on your site. Instead of that line of code, your readers will see the new sideblog dynamically included in your page. Your new multi-blog layout should look slick and integrated. And your fans will marvel at your amazing blog talent.

Different Extension Names for Different Servers

Because your server may not allow files with the standard .html extension to be parsed for `includes`, you may need to rename the main blog file name suffix to .shtml (for SSI), .php (for PHP), .asp (for ASP), or .cfm (for ColdFusion). Again, contact your server administrator if you are unsure.

Email Blogging

You can use email blogging to submit posts to your sideblog or regular blog. Email blogging is gaining popularity as it becomes a standard feature with many major blog providers. If you've set up a blog with Blogger, and you're a Blogger Pro user, you'll be able to email your posts straight to your blog. This is especially useful when you have a friend who is averse to technology and who you would like to contribute to your blog or you want an easy way to blog while you travel.

Blogger Pro's email-to-blog feature lets you write to a specific email address, and it shows up on the blog. Email blogging opens blogging up to a whole new crowd—anyone who knows how to email!

Tips for Email Blogging with Blogger Pro

To use Blogger Pro's mail-to-Blogger feature, you need to create a "secret" email address in your Blogger Pro settings. It's also helpful to note the following:

- **The Publish check box**—Leave the box unchecked if you want your email entries to be posted only to your Blogger account but not actually published to your blog. Check it to have the emails go straight into publication.

- **Your Email Subject**—The subject line of your email will show up as the title of your entry. If you do not have title tags in your template, no title will be displayed.

- **Privacy**—If you don't like the idea of other people gaining publishing access to your blog, don't include your email-to-blog address in the CC field of your email. You're better off putting it in the BCC (Blind Carbon Copy) field.

- **Attachments**—Anything you attach to your email will be ignored by Blogger.

- **HTML in Email**—You can include HTML tags in your email but actual HTML-formatted email won't work very well. It's best to just send plain-text posts.

Alternative Blogging Interfaces

Besides blogging via email, there are other ways of blogging you might find alluring. Sometimes you just want a change, other times you're looking for a feature not found with your blog provider software, or on some occasions you may need an alternative means to publish to your blog because of some kind of server malfunction on your provider's end. It can happen. This section shows you a sampling of alternative blogging interfaces—just in case of one of these situations crops up.

BlogApp

BlogApp (http://www.webentourage.com/blogapp.php) is a Mac OS X share-ware application for posting to your blog. It has a robust feature set:

- Spell Check
- Edit posts
- Contextual Menu support
- Multiple Undo's
- Drag and Drop text
- Manage Multiple Blogs
- Edit main template
- Edit archive template
- Instantly view blog after posting

- Reads text back to you out loud (Cool!)
- Compatible with many blog providers
- Tag insert buttons for HTML help

Figure 15.2 shows you what BlogApp looks like.

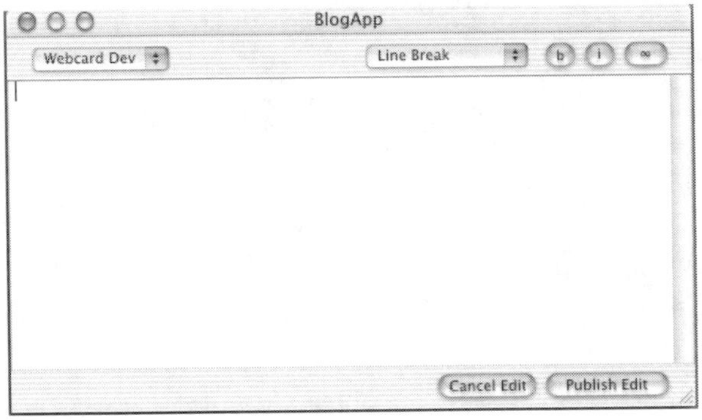

Figure 15.2

BlogApp makes me want to go out and buy a new iBook.

BlogBuddy

BlogBuddy (`http://blogbuddy.sourceforge.net/`) is like the PC version of BlogApp. It has similar features, including these:

- Posting of new entries
- Saving of blogId, username, and password
- Proxy settings
- Get list of available blogs
- System tray icon for quick posting

Other Blogging Interfaces

Other blogging interfaces include these:

- AvantBlog (`http://www.dentedreality.com.au/avantblog/`)—A simple wireless blogging interface for posting to a blog from a Palm or WinCE device via AvantGo, the default browser for Palm devices.
- Wicked Intellect's Flash interface for bloggers (`http://www.wickedintellect.com/?page=flash/xmlrpc/index`).

As blogging becomes more and more popular, we will see additional alternative blogging interfaces coming about. In an already convenient web publishing atmosphere, innovations for even more publishing options are on the rise. Good stuff.

Chapter 16

Beyond the Blog

After you've grown accustomed to the ease of blogging, you'll never go back to the old way of building sites. Storing your design templates and using web publishing software to add or change pages on your site is the way to go.

Content management was formerly reserved for big business, affordable only for enterprise-level clients who had thousands of dollars to burn on an easier way of maintaining their corporate sites. With the wide appeal of blogging, it has become obvious that consumers are looking for an easier way to manage their sites as well. And, as you'll see in this chapter, blogging providers are crossing over into whole-site management.

Template Management Systems: The Future of Site Management

The key to easy site management is a template management system—not unlike that of Blogger and other blogging providers, in terms of usability. Template management allows web designers to clearly separate web content from site design and then give non-technical users access to the site so that they can edit the content themselves.

This means that building, updating, and editing a site is similar to blogging. With a series of HTML-like tags, the web designer can customize the areas of the site that he or she wants content editors to be able to use. In addition to setting levels of editing capability and customizing the editing interface, the web site manager can give editors access to publish their changes directly to the web site.

Webmasters begin by choosing the sections of a site they want to give others the power to add, modify, update, and delete their own content. They then use a web-based HTML editor, or an HTML tool like Adobe GoLive, to create templates. Then the site manager decides where (or whether) the content is published.

Content editors should need to know only how to use an Internet browser in order to make updates or changes to the site. They can manage text, images, lists of articles, and other content all from a browser, whether they're at home or in the office. This is what site management will be like in the future.

Introducing...WebCrimson

WebCrimson was created by the same fine folks who built Xanga.com, one of the largest blogging software providers on the web. They knew that once people discovered blogging, they were going to want that ease of use for updating their whole site.

As a blogger, you've grown accustomed to the ease of publishing to your site with popular blog software, but now you want to be able to extend that usability beyond blogging. WebCrimson works in your browser to help you publish your weblog, webzine, web site—well, okay, anything that starts with "web." Users can build their page templates as well as update and FTP to their site in WebCrimson. Figure 16.1 shows the WebCrimson Demo with my site. Did I mention that this is all free? It's free to the general webmaster/blogging populace because the WebCrimson team mostly built this stuff for individual paying clients and they figured that since they already had it, and they're huge fans of the blogosphere, they might as well offer it for free.

Like Blogger, WebCrimson is designed to work with static sites. You operate within WebCrimson's, browser-based atmosphere, and all your work is shuttled over to your static site at the click of a button. And just as Blogger is suited for easy updating of a web page, WebCrimson is built to maintain an entire web site.

Bloggers already know that the easiest way to manage a site is to separate its design from its content. The way to do this is to turn each kind of page into a template so that updating the site doesn't involve any more design or formatting work—save that for the redesign.

Figure 16.1

WYSIWYG editing right in your browser.

Both Blogger and WebCrimson offer templating to separate design from content. However, a big differentiator is in the templating language: Blogger uses its proprietary Blogger tags, whereas WebCrimson uses the standard templating language XSLT. WebCrimson has even developed a tag converter that automatically converts Blogger tags to XSLT for people who want to make a quick switch.

WebCrimson's Standard Features

WebCrimson goes beyond blogging in that you are allowed to create almost any type of site. Here is a list of WebCrimson's standard features:

- WYSIWYG editing interface for updating and creating individual web pages and other content right inside your browser window.

- Automated templating technology for generating whole new areas of your site with a consistent look and feel including:

  - *Single entry templates*—Generate a set of web pages that each display a single entry from your WebCrimson database (for example, a single press release or essay).

  - *Index templates*—Generate a list of links to an existing set of Single Entry Pages (for example, a list of press release titles that automatically link to the full text of each press release).

  - *Blog templates*—Generate web pages that each display multiple entries from your content database (for example, multiple blog entries).

- Preconfigured data types for easy creation and management of content databases, including:
  - Press releases
  - Frequently Asked Questions
  - People (for example, team bios)
  - Job listings
  - Companies (for example, partner or portfolio companies)
  - Events (such as a schedule of appearances or conferences)
  - Blog entries
  - Articles and essays
  - Links (including other web sites and web resources)
  - Article links (for example, daily news summaries)
  - Photos
- Custom information architecture support, which is the ability to create custom information architectures (category sets) to classify data entries. For example:
  - Each individual category set may be used for multiple content databases, allowing cross-referencing of different data through shared categorization.
  - Each of your databases may use up to three different category sets, allowing individual data entries to be classified into multiple categories.
- Editorial controls, including the following:
  - Pre-set user permissions (for example, administrator, designer, and content editor)
  - Content approval queue, which is an optional setting that allows an administrator to review and approve any updates prior to their impacting the live site.
  - Customizable content publication dates

WebCrimson is blogging software that has matured. Traditional content management software solutions cost upwards of $10,000, while WebCrimson is free. It's a huge difference in cost—but amazingly, not all that much different in terms of offerings.

Fog Creek's CityDesk

You have other choices in addition to WebCrimson. One alternative is
CityDesk, created by software guru Joel Spolsky and the crew at Fog Creek
Software (see Figure 16.2). Unlike other content management systems, which
need to be installed on a web server, CityDesk is just a Windows program that
generates a site and transfers it to any web server automatically using FTP or
file copy.

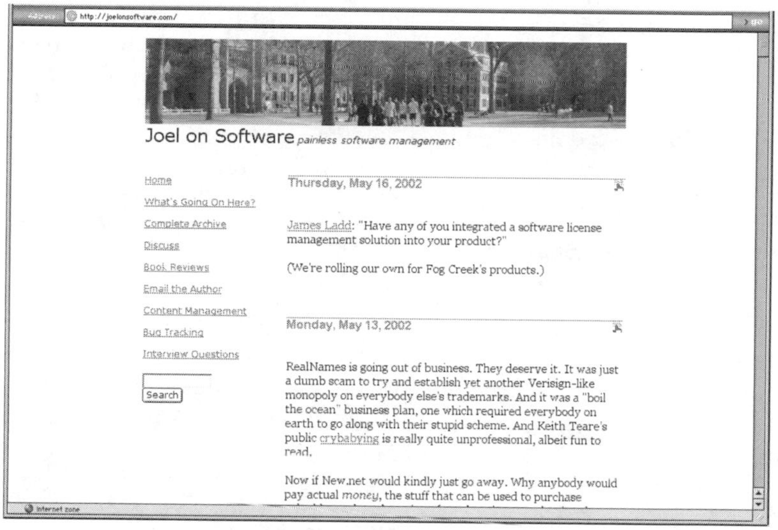

Figure 16.2

*Joel uses CityDesk to
publish his blog as
well as other pages on
his web site.*

Again with the Templates

Just like they do for blogging, templates make site editing easier. Like
WebCrimson, CityDesk applies templating technology to the entire site. This
means that every time you want to add an essay to your site, you simply
write it in CityDesk, and it is uploaded to your site with the same design as
your other essays—no fuss no muss.

It doesn't matter whether you're running a huge site with hundreds of contributors or a tiny site about knitting, CityDesk offers industrial-strength content management on the cheap and easy. Here is a list of CityDesk's features:

- **Automatically generate tables of contents**—Anytime you add a new
  essay or article, it is added to the appropriate table of contents, in the
  appropriate order. Create tables of contents based on folders, dates, or
  keywords. You can have as many sections as you like, each with their
  own contents, limited only by your imagination.

- **Anyone who can use a word processor can update the site**—CityDesk's built-in word processor includes a spell checker, word counter, find and replace, and formatting commands. Because the template is defined once, writers can't accidentally mess up the formatting of the site. And with one click, CityDesk figures out exactly what's changed, which files need to be regenerated, and uploads any changed files to a web server.

- **Powerful Content Management**—You can create multiple editions of your site for different audiences. Each edition can share as much or as little of the content as you need. You can even create editions that use a different set of templates, for example, a printer-friendly version of your site. Imagine issuing one command to republish your entire site in three languages, with four regional editions, with HTML, XML, and printer-friendly versions of each page, served off of a bunch of servers scattered around the world. You can even embargo stories so that they won't appear until a certain date.

Cost and System Requirements

CityDesk costs $79 for the Home Edition and goes up in price to $349 if you need it for professional use. They offer a free starter edition to try it out, and you can return it within 90 days if you don't like it. Because CityDesk is a Windows program, it has more requirements than a web-based solution like WebCrimson.

Hardware

These are the hardware requirements for CityDesk:

- A Pentium-class computer, running at 166 MHz or faster

- At least 64 MB of main memory (128 MB recommended)

- About 20 MB of free hard-drive space

- A screen capable of displaying High Color (16 bits) or more

Software

For CityDesk, you can use any of the following versions of Microsoft Windows:

- Microsoft Windows 95

- Microsoft Windows 98

- Microsoft Windows Me

- Microsoft Windows NT 4.0 (Workstation or Server)

- Microsoft Windows 2000 (Professional, Server, Advanced Server, Datacenter)

- Microsoft Windows XP (Home, Professional)

- Microsoft Internet Explorer 5.01 or later must be installed. I highly recommend Internet Explorer 5.5 or later. It does not need to be your default browser.

Internet

You'll also need a connection to the Internet if you want to upload files to a web server.

Crossover Blogging Providers

Radio Userland and MoveableType were both covered in Chapter 3, "Overview of the Major Blog Providers," because they are popular blogging applications. But they are different from other blogging applications because in addition to providing blogging, they provide whole-site management. It makes sense, and we may see more and more blog providers doing this.

Radio Userland

In terms of site management, Radio Userland works like CityDesk in that you download it to your desktop and work from there. And Radio Userland is Mac and Windows compatible, whereas CityDesk is only Windows-friendly. Because you already learned about the features of Radio Userland in Chapter 3, we don't need to list them all here. But it is worth mentioning that Radio automatically builds your site, organizes and archives your posts, and publishes your content without requiring that you have any knowledge of HTML, FTP, or graphic design. It is blog-like site editing for your whole site, packaged in a downloadable desktop application.

MovableType

MovableType is the beautiful application created by Ben and Mena Trott that powers many thousands of great-looking blogs. MovableType can power your whole site too, but it is different than CityDesk and Radio in that you don't download it to your desktop, but to a web server instead. This can be complex if you've never installed a CGI program, but if you can get a little help, it's worth it. (They'll help you do it for a small fee.) Figure 16.3 shows an example of a site that is powered by MovableType.

Figure 16.3

The Sew Wrong site is powered by MovableType.

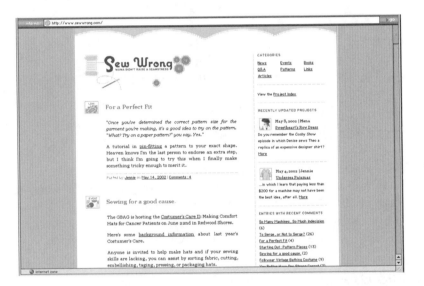

The Future of Blogging and Site Management

It's natural for bloggers to grow from maintaining one page, to working with archives, to wanting to spread their wings and manage additional pages for essays, articles, photos, or other projects. Blogging software is content management software, so it makes perfect sense that it is morphing into whole-site management. The blog has secured its position as the new home page, and as major blog providers (like Blogger, MovableType, Radio, and Xanga, Inc.) move into the site-management arena, bloggers will be able to publish more work with less hassle.

Chapter 17

Building a Blog-Related Application: Bloglet

There are key ingredients that go into building a web application for the blogging crowd. It's all about creating something bloggers want, building a useable site around it, having a public "presence," and pulling it all together into a site with a community element attached to it.

One of the reasons blogging is having such an impact is that many bloggers are extremely intelligent. Some of these extremely intelligent bloggers are also gifted programmers. When a blogger with a good idea can also code, magic happens. Monsur Hossain is one of these magicians.

Monsur's creation, Bloglet.com, is a web service aimed squarely at Bloggers—it fills a need in the blogosphere. Beyond that, Bloglet has all the ingredients of a successful blog application. Before we get into those ingredients, let's find out a little more about Monsur and how he created Bloglet.

A Chat with Monsur

Monsur contributed to the tech editing of this book, so it wasn't too hard to track him down. I've developed projects with Monsur in the past, and we sometimes hang out. So I already knew most of the stuff I asked him in this little fireside chat (without the fire). I must confess, though, that I didn't realize Monsur had a degree in Electrical Engineering. I think he can build robots.

BIZ: Where did you start your web programming career?

MH: At Amazon. I worked on developing shipping and warehouse software, as well as web programming for the "Your Account" section.

BIZ: What did you do before that?

MH: I received my Electrical Engineering degree at a time when the web was all the rage. So I decided to set aside my knowledge in semi-conductors in favor of web programming.

BIZ: And you started at Amazon? Nice.

MH: Learning how Amazon worked "behind the scenes" was an amazing experience. Once I even met Jeff Bezos at a company party.

BIZ: Did you ask for a raise?

MH: We chatted about his newly born son.

BIZ: How'd you end up "behind the scenes" of blogging?

MH: It was the allure of the web that took me to New York and Xanga.com. Xanga was my first exposure to blogs and the blogging community. My experience there taught me just what it takes to build a successful community on the web.

BIZ: So then you decided to create Bloglet?

MH: Yeah. The idea for Bloglet started while exploring the myriad of blogs out there. Each day I'd discover a new blog I wanted to read regularly. Pretty soon, the list of blogs I wanted to read was just too long. I needed a way to keep up-to-date on my favorite blogs without spending a day doing it.

BIZ: What is Bloglet?

MH: Bloglet is a service that allows you to send daily emails of your posts to anyone who subscribes to your site. So now instead of visiting every site you want to read, you can just have their content delivered to you in an email. It makes it much easier to keep updated on your favorite blogs.

BIZ: How does it work?

MH: Bloglet works through the XML-RPC interface, which allows two systems to basically "talk" to each other, regardless of what operating system or programming language they are using.

BIZ: C-3P0? Huh?

MH: XML-RPC is basically a standard format with which to send and receive messages across the web. It uses XML as the mode of communication; hence, the name XML Remote Procedure Call, or XML-RPC. Evan Williams (founder of Blogger.com) recently released an XML-RPC interface to Blogger.

BIZ: So this XML-RPC deal makes Bloglet possible?

MH: Yeah. There is a whole range of ways a programmer can interact with Blogger using XML-RPC. They can do things like retrieve and set a site's template, add or edit posts, or get recent posts. Programmers can use these functions to write their own services that interact with Blogger. The specific XML-RPC function that Bloglet uses gets the most recent posts from a site.

BIZ: Cool. So, Bloglet just interacts with Blogger on my behalf?

MH: This is exactly what Bloglet does. It uses Blogger's XML-RPC function to get the posts from a particular day. Then it sends these posts out to all subscribers. All you have to do is provide some basic information so that the program knows how to access your particular site.

BIZ: Yeah, but doesn't that lessen traffic?

MH: Not at all. Bloglet allows three formatting options for the email. You can either send the entire post in an email, send the first few characters of a post—you have control over how many characters—or just send a note to the subscriber saying that the site has been updated. Those options will provide just enough information to have your subscribers visit your site. In fact, I think Bloglet helps increase traffic, because the emails remind your readers that your site is being updated regularly, and they are more inclined to stop by for a visit.

BIZ: I see. You can send out a "teaser." But I would think people would shy away from signing up to too many blogs because of all the emails they'd get every day.

MH: The nice thing about Bloglet is that it only sends a single email to subscribers, containing all the updates from sites they are subscribed to.

BIZ: How long did it take you to build this subscription service?

MH: It took about two months to program Bloglet. Surprisingly, the actual code to get and send the emails, the meat of the program, wasn't that difficult. The majority of time was spent building the surrounding web site, making it usable and user friendly. This included stuff like building the web pages for users to administer their site and subscriptions (and making it quick and simple), building ways for users to quickly learn about Bloglet (Frequently Asked Questions and an About section), and building ways to let the user know there's an error with their site.

BIZ: Well, the work shows. Bloglet is really user-friendly.

MH: Thanks! I think one of the keys to Bloglet's success is its simplicity. It has all the power of an email subscription engine, but it only takes a few seconds to set up.

BIZ: What does "setting up" involve?

MH: If you want others to receive your blog posts in their email, all you have to do is create a Bloglet account, enter some data about your site, and then put the subscription box somewhere on your site. Then all your readers have to do is type their email address in the box, and they are automatically subscribed to your site.

BIZ: For all those techies out there, what did you build Bloglet with?

MH: The Bloglet site was written using ASP and ASP.NET. The backend uses C#. C# is new, but it has some great facilities for dealing with XML data.

BIZ: What else can Bloglet do?

MH: Since Bloglet uses XML-RPC, I can be very flexible with what I do with it. One of the cooler recent features was integrating Bloglet with Google's XML-RPC. Google recently released an XML-RPC interface to perform searches. Using Google's XML-RPC interface, I added a feature that searches Google for your site, and then reports how many results are returned and what the top 10 results are. This feature is great for bloggers who want to keep up on how their site is performing in the search engines.

BIZ: Google has XML-RPC too? Who else?

MH: Yeah, the Google XML-RPC interface created quite a buzz in the programming world. But many blog systems have been using it for a while. Shortly after Blogger released its XML-RPC interface, many other blog systems started doing the same. Through this interface, Bloglet was able to scale to many different systems. Bloglet currently supports Blogger, MovableType, Radio, WebCrimson, Nucleus, and Big Blog Tool. In fact, Bloglet can integrate with any system that uses XML-RPC.

BIZ: Is Bloglet going to support other blog providers?

MH: I'm always looking to expand to other systems as well. Hopefully one day you will be able to use Bloglet no matter what blog system you are on.

BIZ: What other plans do you have for Bloglet?

MH: The future of Bloglet is really open right now. It receives a good number of users every day, and I'd like to add a whole host of new features to make it better. I would like to add features to make Bloglet more flexible, and offer powerful new features for users who want a more robust email subscription engine, while still maintaining Bloglet's simplicity.

Bloglet: A Classic Blog Spin-Off Utility

Bloglet.com has all the elements of a great blog-enhancing service, and it is bound to have continued success. Monsur Hossain has ingeniously blended all the strategic elements that make a blog-related site useful, addictive, and memorable. Let's have a look at this little miracle.

Brand Recognition

Bloglet has a simple user interface that bloggers will recognize right away. Monsur has implemented a modular design that is common in the blogging arena. This approach allows for many elements to be displayed on a single page cleanly and without confusion (see Figure 17.1).

Figure 17.1

The Bloglet home page is easy for everyone.

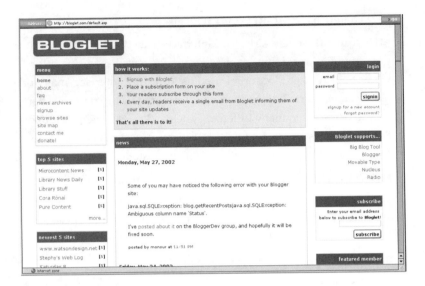

Mr. M. Hossain has also adopted the strategic use of minimal graphics on his site—really only one if you don't count the buttons near the bottom left. Even with this minimal approach, he has created strong brand recognition. Oh, and let's not forget the name, *"Bloglet."* It has the word *"blog"* in it—almost a necessity. Even better, it sounds like a cute little fun thing. Say it aloud, "Bloglet." Sounds like the name of a small, fluffy family companion. It also reminds me of *"bookmarklet,"* another kind of application in widespread use among bloggers.

The color of the main graphic is picked up in the title bars of the modules throughout the site to complete the brand. Bloglet is one of those sites that you can still see in your mind's eye when you are walking home from work. It is simple, yet memorable.

A Personal Touch

Successful pioneers in the blogosphere are careful to attach their voice to the project they are developing. The best way to do this, obviously, is with a blog. Monsur has installed a blog as the main feature on Bloglet.com. You can see it in Figure 17.2 (the news section). You may, of course, subscribe to this blog using Bloglet—an example of the product in action.

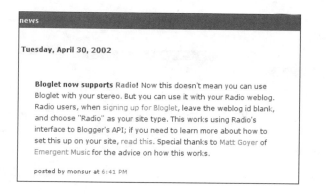

Figure 17.2

Monsur's entries are light and appreciative of fellow bloggers.

A blog on the home page does more than serve as an example of the product. Through the blog, Monsur is able to connect with the people who use his application, and they, in turn, are able to attach a persona to the service. Monsur himself becomes part of the brand.

It's important for small, one-man operations to develop this kind of relationship with "customers." This way, if anything goes wrong, people know that you are on the case. Beyond that, they see that there is someone behind the scenes working hard, and they are more likely to participate and/or help out if necessary. The blog warms up the whole operation and takes it in a direction away from the corporate machine-type of mentality. Bloggers respect grass-roots endeavors.

Community

Bloglet has modules and pages throughout the site that display data on various users. Figure 17.3 shows the modules that list the top five blogs, the newest five blogs, and featured member blogs. In addition, the "more…" link at the bottom of the modules calls a page where users can browse links by rank. Clicking the links brings you to the site, while clicking the [S] automatically subscribes you to the blog.

By aggregating Bloglet members into a navigable area and arranging them by popularity, the seeds of community begin to form. In addition, many bloggers will undoubtedly feel a compulsion to find some way of climbing the ranks.

Figure 17.3

*Bloglet brings blog-
gers together.*

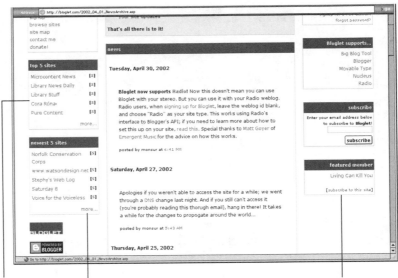

Top 5 Sites Module   Newest 5 Sites Module   Featured Member Module

Donations

Using popular payment systems from Amazon and PayPal (as discussed in
Chapter 7, "Blogging for Dollars"), Bloglet operates on a donation system (see
Figure 17.4). Essentially, the system is this: If you like it, send in a few bucks.
If you like it, but you don't have a few bucks, display a link on your blog. The
donation system can sometimes help defray some of the hosting and band-
width costs a product like Bloglet incurs.

There are other ways Monsur could make money with Bloglet as well.
Because his site is heavily trafficked, Monsur could set up a microadvertising
system, which is a method of advertising whereby users could pay around 10
dollars for 20,000 page views of their self-composed ad. And because Bloglet
sends out thousands of ads every day, Monsur also has potential to sell advertising space in the footer of those emails.

So even though Monsur created Bloglet out of pure interest in the blogging
community, he has methods of recompense he can pursue. I like it.

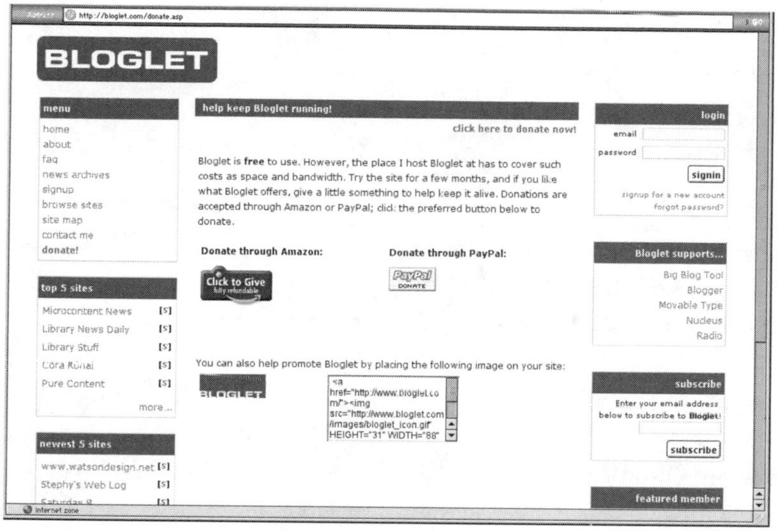

Figure 17.4

Bloglet accepts donations.

Usability

Bloglet has been engineered so that users are required to do the least amount of work possible to get what they want. This, coupled with intuitive design and strong brand recognition, makes for a good user experience. Figure 17.5 shows you how easy it is to sign up.

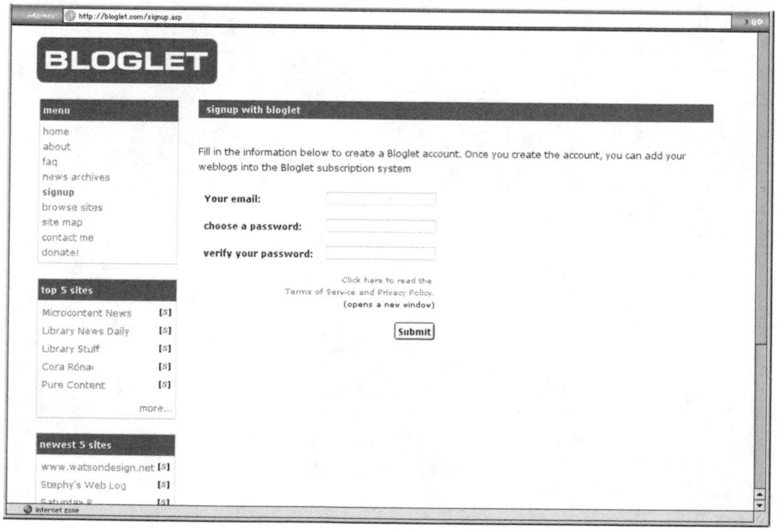

Figure 17.5

Signing up to Bloglet is painless.

You can use Bloglet by following these simple steps:

1 Signup with Bloglet.

2. Place a subscription form on your site.

3. Readers subscribe through this form.

4. Readers receive a daily email from Bloglet.

Bloglet is one of the easiest blog enhancements available. Once you sign up and pass along a little information about your blog, you just install Bloglet with a little cut and paste action, and you're good to go.

Installing the Bloglet Code

When I installed the Bloglet code, I also made a few modifications to get it to look the way I wanted. This is permissible as long as you keep the link back to Bloglet intact. The code itself is not at all daunting. Listing 17.1 shows what mine was, and Figure 17.6 shows what it looks like on my site.

Listing 17.1   An Example—My Bloglet code

```
<FORM METHOD="POST" ACTION="http://bloglet.com/subscribe.asp">
<INPUT TYPE="hidden" NAME="ID" VALUE="14">
Enter your email address below to subscribe to <B>Biz Stone,
➥Genius</B>!<BR><BR>
<INPUT TYPE="text" NAME="email" VALUE="" SIZE="20" MAXLENGTH="100">
<INPUT TYPE="submit" NAME="Submit" VALUE="subscribe"><BR>
<A HREF="http://www.bloglet.com/">powered by Bloglet</A>
</FORM>
```

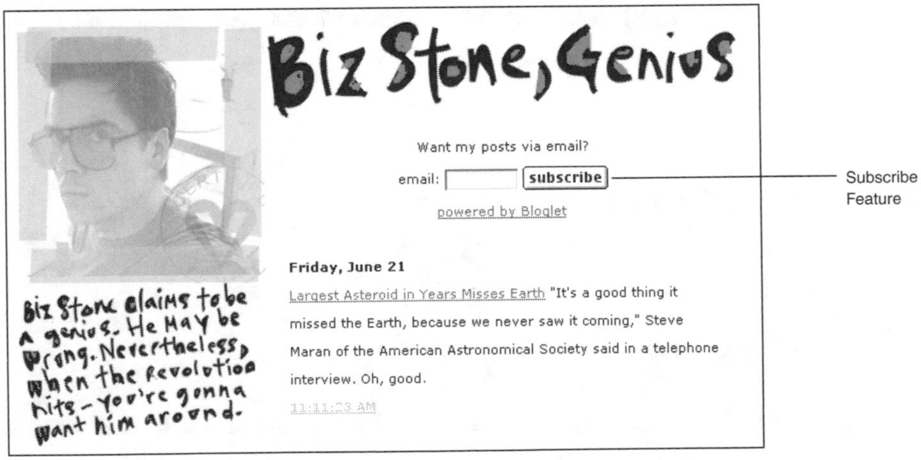

Figure 17.6

I put a subscribe feature on my site as soon as Bloglet launched.

Subscribe Feature

You can put your code anywhere within your blog template. It will display a text box with a submit button for your readers to enter their email address. If you do decide to alter the appearance, it is recommended that you follow these guidelines:

- <FORM METHOD="POST" ACTION="http://bloglet.com/subscribe.asp">—In order to have your subscriptions processed correctly the form must post to "http://bloglet.com/subscribe.asp".

- <INPUT TYPE="hidden" NAME="ID" VALUE="14">—This field must be somewhere in your form; otherwise, your readers won't be able to subscribe.

- <INPUT TYPE="hidden" NAME="redirect" VALUE="Redirect_Page">—This field is optional. Include this field to specify the page you want your readers to be redirected to once they successfully subscribe. If this field isn't specified, the reader is redirected to a default page.

You can get your code any time you need it by clicking on the appropriate icon in your account manager (see Figure 17.7). You'll need to be signed in to do this.

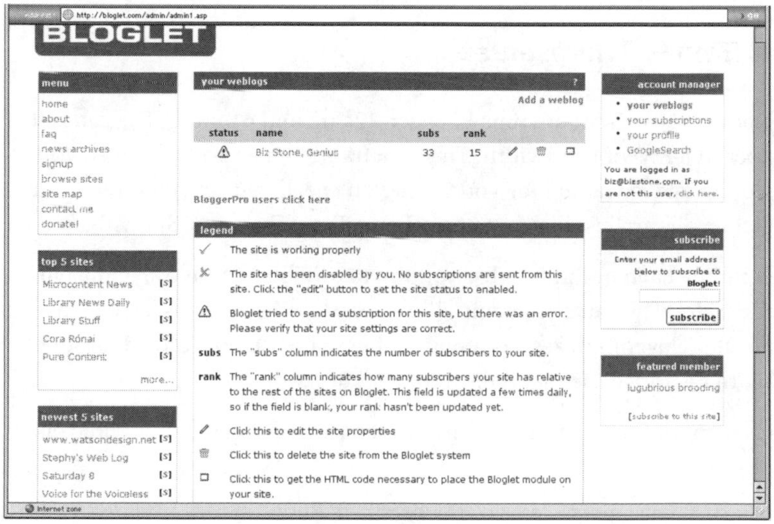

Figure 17.7

The Account Manager is your Bloglet "command central."

Requirements

After you sign up for Bloglet, all you have to do is place a simple subscription form on your site. Your readers subscribe to your blog by simply entering their email addresses in the form. To make use of the service, you need an existing blog that is managed either by Blogger, Radio Userland, Movable Type, Big Blog Tool, WebCrimson, or Nucleus. Once your account is created, you can add your blogs into the system.

> ### Usernames and Passwords at Bloglet
>
> Your username and password is used by Bloglet only to retrieve posts. Bloglet works through XML-RPC. For sites that support this interface, a username and password is required in order to validate a user. If you use the same username and password for everything you do online and if giving it out to applications like Bloglet makes you nervous, you should consider creating a username and password that you use only for blogging activities so that you can take advantage of Bloglet and other sites that work with blogs.

The Emails Themselves

Bloglet emails are sent anytime between 12a.m. and 6 a.m. EST because it's cheaper in terms of bandwidth. This timeframe is also good because your Bloglet update is waiting for you when you check your email in the morning. Bloglet emails are just like any normal email (see Figure 17.8).

Even if they have multiple subscriptions, subscribers receive a single email from Bloglet. This email contains all of a user's subscriptions, as well as a link to the site. This minimizes the amount of email received. At the bottom of the email, there's a tagline that links to Bloglet or its sponsors.

You can control what information your subscribers receive with three email modes:

- "Don't send post" lets your subscribers know you've updated your site without sending them the content of your post.

- "Send first ## characters of each post" sends your subscribers the first few characters of your post—you can control how many characters.

- "Send entire post" sends your subscribers the entire text of your post.

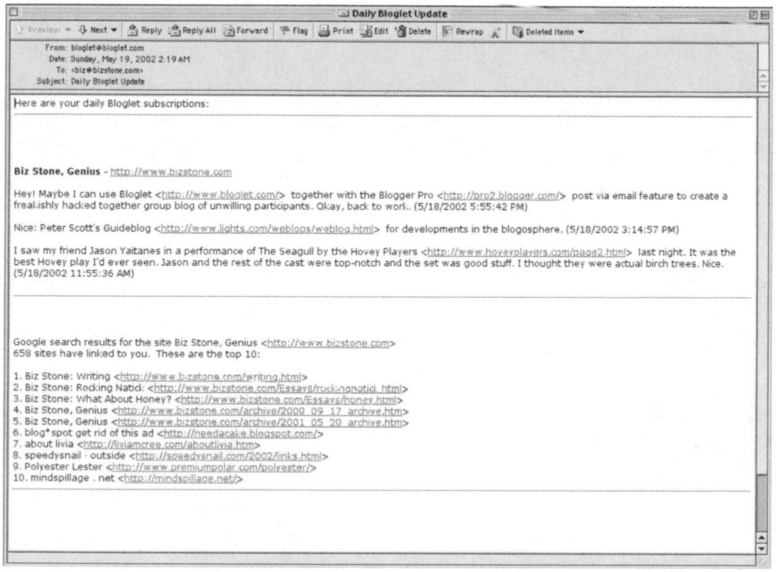

Figure 17.8

So I subscribed to my own blog. Sue me.

You can edit these options at any time through your email administrator (see Figure 17.9).

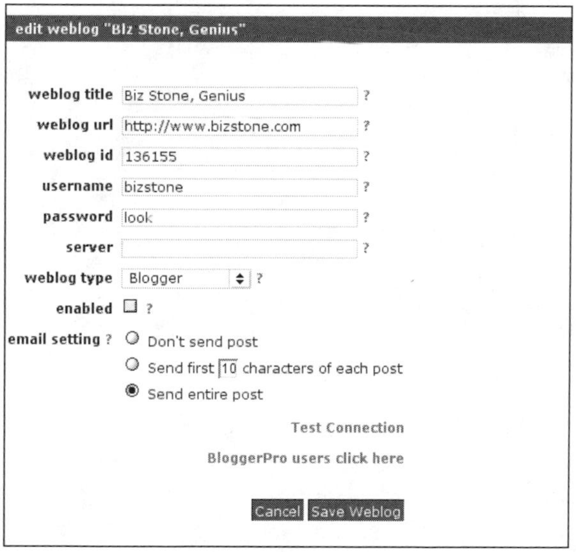

Figure 17.9

Control the amount of information your sub-scribers receive.

If you're one of those bloggers obsessed with how many people have sub-scribed to your blog, know this: Stats on Bloglet, including newest sites, top sites, subscribers and rank, are calculated at various intervals throughout the day. If you see a discrepancy in your stats, Monsur recommends that you check back at a later time. If you subscribe to your own site, these stats also are included in your daily Bloglet email.

Done Right

With Bloglet, Monsur has woven together the elements that make a successful blog spin-off project. Other projects that have done similarly well are the search and stat engines Blogdex and Daypop. Like Blogdex and Daypop, Bloglet has a bright future and an almost infinite number of ways to develop further.

Chapter 18

Blog Goodies

One of the greatest things about blogging is that there's always some cool new enhancement, add-on, feature, or other kind of goodie being developed. The number of techies, geeks, and programmers blogging ensures that new stuff is always being worked on. After you've been blogging for a while, you'll start digging around in some of this stuff. You'll see.

Genius Tip

Keeping Track of Blog Goodies
Peter Scott's Compendiumblog (`http://www.lights.com/weblogs/weblog.html`) and its associated collection of pages is where the curious blogger goes for the newest blog-related news and resources.

This chapter gives you a sampling of the kind of cool stuff you can find, and it ends with a bonus interview with…. (You have to read the whole chapter to find out who.)

Posting via AIM™

AOL Instant Messenger is a software application you can use while you're connected to the web to chat with friends who are also online. It's different from email in that the conversation is in "real time," meaning that you can have a kind of text-based conversation with links and graphics thrown in as an added bonus.

BloggerBot is a neat little application that works with AOL Instant Messenger™ to allow you to post to your blogger-powered blog as easily as you send an instant message. That's it. You send a message just like you would to a friend, and it is published to your blog (see Figure 18.1). Cool stuff.

Sending posts to your blog via AIM means you can blog in real time just as you would chat in real time. So if you were so inclined, you could post notes to your blog from a conference or class, chronicle a baseball game as you're watching it, or you could simply use AOL Instant Messenger as an alternative to signing in to Blogger.

Figure 18.1

I like posting with BloggerBot.

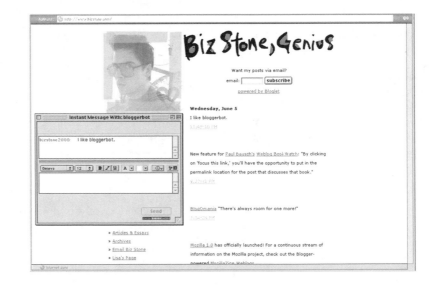

Using BloggerBot

To get BloggerBot to work for you, just follow these steps:

1. Add BloggerBot to your buddy list. If it isn't online, you can try the secondary screen name, BlogBot.

2. Type this command: **/register bloggerlogin bloggerpass**. bloggerlogin and bloggerpass are the login and password that you use to login to blogger.com.

3. Type **/list** to display all the blogs you can publish to. None will have a Y next to them, meaning that you don't currently have a default blog set.

4. Pick the blog you want to publish to, and note the id number of the blog.

5. Type **/default *blogidnumber*** where *blogidnumber* is the number you just noted.

6. Start posting. Every message you send to the bot is automatically posted and published to your blog. It's that easy.

You need to add BloggerBot to your buddy list only once. After that, repeat steps 2 through 6 each time you want to post to your blog via AIM.

AOL Instant Messenger Is Free

Whether you have AOL service or not, AOL Instant Messenger is a free download. To get AIM and start using it with Blogger (or to chat with friends online), just go to http://www.aim.com and download the version that's right for your computer setup.

Posting via Email

Posting via email means that you can blog from anywhere you have email access. If you have wireless email on your phone or palm-type device, you can blog about a book you just spotted while you're still in the bookstore, blog reminders to yourself throughout the day, or even blog notes in a class or conference.

Both Blogger Pro and Xanga Premium offer email-powered blogging. Once you've built your blog and set up email posting, you can blog from any email account. Xanga gives you a special number to put in your email's subject field, whereas Blogger Pro let's you choose a secret name like: bizstone.secretname@blogger.com for posting via email. Radio Userland also has an email blogging feature.

It's good to note that if anyone gets hold of this address, they can publish to your blog as you and possibly slander your good name. So when you make up your secret name, make it really sneaky—but not too sneaky or you might forget it. If you are running a group blog, each individual will choose his or her own secret email address for email posting.

Setting Up Email Blogging with Blogger Pro

To set up email blogging with Blogger Pro, just follow these steps:

1. Sign in.
2. Click "Settings."
3. Click the "Email" tab.
4. Choose a secret "Mail-to-Blogger" address.
5. Check "Publish" for easier email blogging.
6. Click "Save changes."

As an email blogger, it also behooves you to remember these things: The subject of the ignore email will be displayed as a title if you include `title` tags in your template; attachments and plain text messages work best.

Making It Legit

If you publish a blog, whether it's a solo project or a group gig, you qualify for an International Standard Serial Number (ISSN). That's right—you are a legitimate publication like any magazine or newspaper according to the National Serials Data Program, Library of Congress:

> "In the case of electronic serials—especially those available online, such as on the Internet—the most significant criterion is that the publication must be divided into parts or issues which carry unique, numerical designations by which the individual issues may be identified, checked in, etc. Electronic serials that are issued as individual articles meet this criterion as long as the articles carry a unique designation."[1]

1. *"Criteria for Assigning ISSN." ISSN for Electronic Serials. Available from the Internet:* `http://www.loc.gov/issn/e-serials.html`

Blogs are published to the Internet in unique individual posts, so they qualify. In many cases you can apply for your number over the web. If you'd like to be officially recognized as a periodical, here are the web addresses for registering in Canada and the United States for starters:

- Canada: `http://www.nlc-bnc.ca/6/13/`

- United States: `http://lcweb.loc.gov/issn/ISSN.html`

Why secure an ISSN for your blog? With an ISSN, your blog becomes a legitimate publication, just like any magazine. And the greater the number of bloggers registered, the more "seriously" the medium can be taken. Also, when you are registered with the Library of Congress, it is possible for people to find your work by asking a librarian to locate your blog in the ISSN database.

Meta Linker

Some say that the future of the web lies in reciprocal linking and the giant, organic, self-organizing system of information that is the semantic web. Meta Linker (`http://www.thinkblank.com/metalinker/`) is a blog goodie developed by the web pixies at ThinkBlank that works toward a smarter web. It's a secret blend of technology that helps keep track of debates and discussions within the blog community. Well, maybe it's not so secret, but the idea is that you might be blogging about a weird web site or a new gadget that others have also taken note of, and with Meta Linker, your readers are only a few clicks away from more information and discussion about your links.

The thinkers at ThinkBlank have come up with some JavaScript you can add to your blog. Once you've added it, Meta Linker uses Blogdex to "help bridge the gap between bloggers." In other words, every time you put a link in your blog, MetaLinker uses JavaScript to add another link right next to it (see Figure 18.2). The extra link will take your readers to a page that lists other bloggers who have mentioned the same link. In this manner, people get a few different commentaries on the same link.

Figure 18.2

The little [b] is Meta Linker in action.

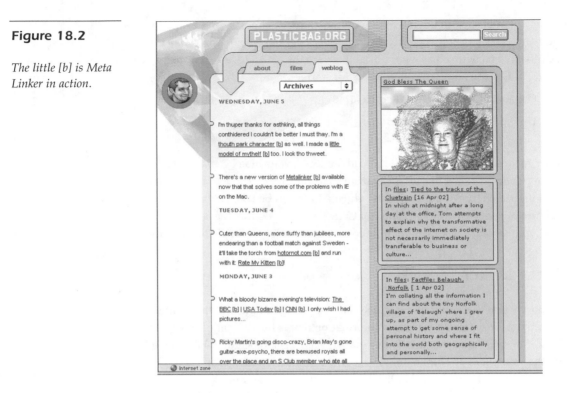

Installing Meta Linker

Meta Linker provides instructions for installing their service into your blog's template. Although it helps to know your way around JavaScript, it isn't necessary. Basically, you're just copying and pasting like so many other cool blog-enhancing goodies. Here are the steps you need to take:

1. The code in Listing 18.1 is to be saved in a file called *metalinker.js*.

Listing 18.1   Save this as "metalinker.js"

```
function tag_links(container, exclude_url, exclude_class,
pre_text, text, post_text, link_class, title){

        if (pre_text == null){pre_text = ' [';}
        if (text == null){text = 'b';}
        if (post_text == null){post_text = ']';}
        if (link_class == null){link_class = 'autolink';}
        if (title == null){title = 'metalink';}
```

```
var con_node = (container !=
➥null)?document.getElementById(container):document;
var a_nodes = con_node.getElementsByTagName('A');

var temp_nodes = new Array();
for(var i=0; i<a_nodes.length; i++){
    temp_nodes[temp_nodes.length] = a_nodes[i];
}

for(var i=0; i<temp_nodes.length; i++){
    var a_node = temp_nodes[i];

    //check if it's one we created
    if (a_node.className == 'autolink'){continue;}

    //check if tag is just an anchor
    if (a_node.href == ''){continue;}

    //check if tag is a link to exclude
    if ((exclude_url != null) && (exclude_url ==
    a_node.href.substr(0,exclude_url.length))){continue;}
    if ((exclude_class != null) && (exclude_class ==
    ➥a_node.className)){continue;}

    var new_div_node = document.createElement('SPAN');
    a_node.parentNode.replaceChild(new_div_node,a_node);

    var new_node = document.createElement('A');

    new_div_node.appendChild(a_node.cloneNode(true));
    new_div_node.appendChild(document.createTextNode
    ➥(pre_text));
    new_div_node.appendChild(new_node);
    new_div_node.appendChild(document.createTextNode
    ➥(post_text));

    new_node.className = link_class;
    new_node.href = "http://blogdex.media.mit.edu/
    ➥browseSource.asp?url=" + escape(a_node.href);
    new_node.target= "_blank";
    new_node.appendChild(document.createTextNode(text));
    ➥new_node.title = title;
    }
}
```

2. Then, insert the code in Listing 18.2, at the end of your blog template, before the closing body tag, </body>.

Listing 18.2   For the end of your blog template

```
<script language="javascript" type="text/javascript" src="met
►alinker.js"></script>
<script language="javascript" type="text/javascript">
<!--
tag_links();
//-->
</script>
```

MetaLinker also allows for some tweaking. For example, you can specify the way the link is presented. Or, if you don't want MetaLinker to operate on your archive pages, you can turn off meta-linking on those pages.

Blog BookWatch

Paul Bausch has created a blog goodie that searches blogs as they pass through the Recently Changed list at weblogs.com. This goodie is not something bloggers add to their site; rather, it's an application that works within the blogging community to deliver information that bloggers crave. Paul's program searches weblogs that pass through a "Recently Changed" list at weblogs.com looking for links to books at Amazon.com (see Figure 18.3).

Figure 18.3

Paul Bausch helps us keep an eye on the cool books.

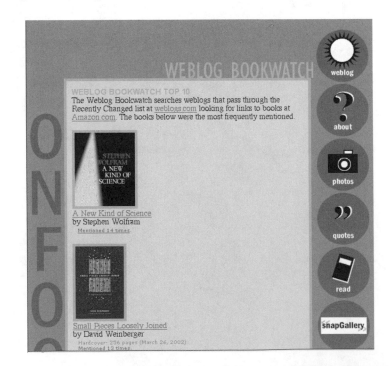

What is the Recently Changed list?

The Recently Changed list at weblogs.com is a list of links to blogs
that have recently been updated. To be a part of this list, your blog
provider must be equipped to "ping" weblogs.com whenever you
update your blog. Blogger offers a check box for this under the
Settings tab.

Popular blog search engine, Daypop, features a similar Amazon wish list-
tracking device (see Figure 18.4).

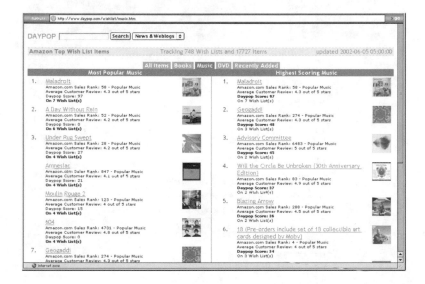

Figure 18.4

*Daypop tracks
Amazon wish list
items.*

Paul's Weblog Bookwatch (`http://www.onfocus.com/bookwatch/index.asp`)
and Daypop's Amazon Top Wish List Items (`http://www.daypop.com/wish-
list/`) are cool blog goodies because they keep a finger on the pulse of the
blogging community. They track what's hot on a daily basis, and they are
only the beginning of even cooler future web services that communicate with
blogs.

Displaying Playlists with BlogAmp

Winamp is a music player for Windows. BlogAmp is a free Winamp plugin that allows users to keep a list of the songs currently being played by the Winamp application. A list on your blog is updated via FTP in real time. In other words, you can create a module or sidebar on your blog that displays the title and file information for the last several songs you've listened to (see Figure 18.5).

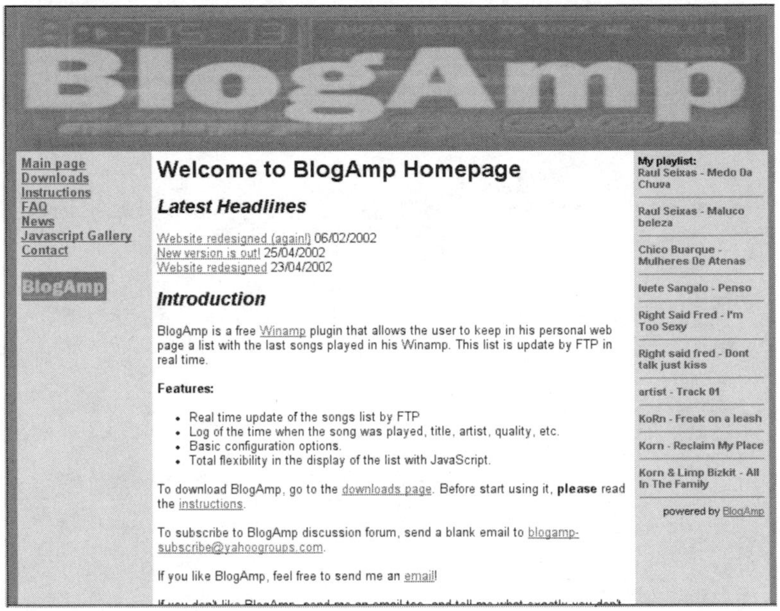

Figure 18.5

BlogAmp displays your Winamp music.

This is just another way bloggers share their interests with readers. It's all content.

Downloading and Installing BlogAmp

To use BlogAmp, you will need Winamp and access to an FTP server. Here are the steps that you should follow:

1. Install BlogAmp from the download page (`http://www.geocities.com/insanitydrops/blogamp/en/downloads.html`) and extract its contents into Winamp's plugins directory.

2. Start Winamp and configure preferences.

3. Insert code in your blog template.

Step by step instructions for installing BlogAmp can be found on its creator's home page (`http://www.geocities.com/insanitydrops/blogamp/en/instruc-tions.html`), along with the necessary code for copying and pasting.

NYC Bloggers

NYC Bloggers is an effort to bring the virtual and physical together to create a community site out of bloggers in New York's various boroughs. A map of the city, which is organized by subway stop, shows where the bloggers are (see Figure 18.6). Visitors can use the site to find out who's blogging in their neighborhood as well as discover new blogs to read. There's no code to paste into your template, you just fill out a form (`http://nycbloggers.com/form.asp`), and your blog is added to the map.

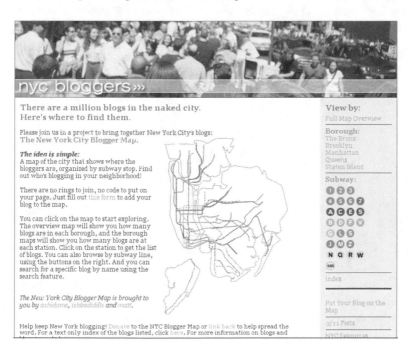

Figure 18.6

There are a million blogs in the naked city.

Users can explore the site by clicking on an area of the map. The overview shows how many blogs are in each borough, and the borough maps display how many blogs are at each station. Clicking on a station logo brings visitors to the list of blogs for that station. The site is browseable by subway line, and users can search for a specific blog by name. Other features include a store, a mailing list, a guestbook, NYC resources, and of course, an archive of posts from people who experienced and blogged about 9-11 (`http://nycbloggers.com/911.asp`).

Bonus Blog Goodie: Interview with Wil Wheaton

The Bloggies are publicly chosen awards given to blog writers. In 2002, actor Wil Wheaton dominated with six awards out of 30—including Best Merchandise of a Weblog, Best American Weblog, Best Tagline of a Weblog, Most Humorous Weblog, Best New Weblog, and Weblog of the Year.

Wil Wheaton

Wil Wheaton made a name for himself in Rob Reiner's film adaptation of Steven King's *Stand by Me* and later as a teenager in the TV series *Star Trek: The Next Generation*. Today, Wil continues to work in show business and has one of the most popular blogs on the web. More information about Wil's blog—specifically, his use of merchandising—is covered in Chapter 7, "Blogging for Dollars."

I chatted with Wil by email after his success to find out whether his blog has helped his acting career, why he chose the blog format in the first place, and how he really feels about Counselor Troi—among other things. (The stuff about Thai "streetwalkers," cheating at sports, and pornographic images was totally unsolicited.)

> **BIZ: So Wil, you decided you want a web site, and you wanted to build it yourself. What made you choose the blog format?**
>
> **WW:** I've always wanted to write, and I've always liked the idea of dynamic content. It also gave me a chance to clear up all the misconceptions about me and show the world that the person behind Wesley Crusher is even more annoying than the guy on screen. Oh, and sexier. Much, much sexier.
>
> **BIZ: I'm not so sure you got that across, but you did sweep at the Bloggies. Congrats on that.**
>
> **WW:** Thanks. Recognition for my work is always nice, but that was very unexpected.
>
> **BIZ: Did you know a little HTML before you set out? How much web-building experience did you have before you created your blog?**
>
> **WW:** None. I taught myself in about six weeks—by studying really hard and learning from my mistakes. I also had some help from some very skilled and patient people.
>
> **BIZ: Setting a good example for the kids. Nice, I like that.**
>
> **WW:** It's too bad that you can't cheat on web design, like you can cheat at sports.
>
> **BIZ: Okay, forget the part about the kids. Wow, you started from scratch. But why build it all yourself? Why not just use Blog*Spot or some other easy blog host?**
>
> **WW:** My friends who own Logjamming.com do all sorts of awesome stuff for five bucks a month, so I didn't need to host with anyone else. I understand that I've brought them lots of business, so if I ever go with them to Bangkok, the hookers are on them. You think Blog*Spot would buy you a hooker? Not in a million years, baby.
>
> **BIZ: I wouldn't know. You'd have to email Jason Shellen about that. But getting away from hookers, what have you taught yourself? What programming languages?**

WW: I only know enough PHP to do `includes`. But I'm learning more scripting so that I can do cool stuff on my web site. I use Dreamweaver to do all the basic markup; then I clean everything up in Notepad.

BIZ: Do you think your blog has helped your acting career?

WW: Yeah.

BIZ: Really? In what way?

WW: I think it's reminded people that I was still acting, still writing, and it's shown the industry that people still care about what I'm doing. I mean, I'm getting 250,000 hits a day. Without a single pornographic image. Take that, William Shatner!

BIZ: Cool, so the industry responded to your blog. Wow, 250,000 hits a day? You must have thought about trying to make a few bucks. How much money have you generated?

WW: None, really. I haven't sold any ads, because I hate advertising. I suppose I could make some money if I wanted to, but that's not why I'm doing this. I make enough to cover the costs by selling T-shirts and stuff in my store—with whatever's left being split evenly between the "take my wife out to dinner" and "buy Wil a PS2" funds. I've recently put up a tip jar thingy, and the regular readers of my site seem to think it's a cool thing.

BIZ: But what about hosting TextAds?

WW: Hey, I just said that I hate advertising.

BIZ: Yeah, but...

WW: Are you even listening to me?

BIZ: Okay, no ads. I'll change the subject. One of your Bloggies was for Most Humorous Weblog. Say something funny.

WW: No. You're not the boss of me.

BIZ: Fine. What blogging software did you try? What did you end up with, and will you stick with it?

WW: I started with Blogger, which I really liked, but didn't like having content sort of "out of my control." Then I used Greymatter, which I absolutely loved, but my server couldn't handle the massive CGI load it created. Now, I'm using Movable Type, which I really like, and I am very, very happy with. I'm on version 1.4 right now, and 2.0

is supposed to be out next week. If it does all the stuff they say it will do, I'll probably stick with it forever. Or at least until my 15 minutes run out. Then I'll keep my blog on the backside of Jack Daniel's labels.

BIZ: I'll be reading it daily. What was the biggest problem you had to overcome? What produced the most profanity?

WW: The whole f***ing thing, man. I hate computers, and I really hate the Internet.

BIZ: I see.

WW: Wait, I didn't mean that. I love computers! I love the Internet. I can change. Give me another chance! I feel like a battered user sometimes.

BIZ: So, are your Star Trek X co-stars going to ask you to build them blogs?

WW: I doubt they'd ask me. They've all got professional webmasters who could kick my ass in a coding contest.

BIZ: Whose blog would you bookmark?

WW: I bet they'd all be cool to read in their own ways. But I'd only read Marina's if she'd go on and on about how much she regrets not having sex with me when I turned 18.

BIZ: Do you think that blogs are going to replace the traditional home page?

WW: Yes. I think it's happening already. I also think that blogs are rapidly changing the way information moves across the net—thanks to sites like Daypop, Fark, and blogdex.

BIZ: So blogs are changing the Internet and publishing in general?

WW: It's another step in the evolution of communications, like the printing press, or fortune cookies.

Part IV

Appendix

Appendix A

Blog Web Links

The blog universe is ever-expanding. People are jumping in and out of the flow on an almost daily basis. Although it can be difficult to pin down resources in a book like this, it's still worth it to have a big list to keep handy.

I discover new and interesting blog-related endeavors almost every time I surf around. Bloggers are quick to develop their ideas on the web and seem to have boundless energy to do so. Without further ado, let's look at some of the blog extras that are out there. You'll want to fire up your web connection before you start. Also, please visit http://www.bizstone.com for a link to this directory.

Awards

Everybody likes to get a gold star every now and then. The Blog awards in Table A.1 are a positive, encouraging way to promote blogging and bind the community together. Awards can range from quirky, "one-man" shows to bigger, more orchestrated endeavors like the Bloggies.

Table A.1   Blog Awards

Title	URL	Description
5 fish blog awards	`http://www.fishrush.` `com/links/blog.htm`	Figure Blogging is one of the more obscure blog-related activities. It is a physical approach to blogging and has more to do with how the bloggers approach their chair before they sit down to begin blogging than what they actually write or post to their blog or web site.
The Anti-Bloggies	`http://www.` `antibloggies.com/`	The Anti-Bloggies are an awards ceremony spun off from another awards event called Bloggies.

The Bloggies	`http://www.fairvue.`
	`com/?feature=awards`
	`2002`
		The Bloggies™ are publicly chosen awards given in 30 categories to blog writers and those related to blogs.

The Third Annual Medley Medals	`http://www.uncorked.`
	`org/medley/2001/`
	`medals2001.html`
		These are my awards, and they're just for fun; I can change the rules whenever I want.

Scripting News Awards for 2001	`http://www.scripting.` `com/awards/2001`	These are my favorite blogs, by category. They are all great blogs.

Commenting Systems

Adding reader comments to your blog is a great way to encourage conversation. Reader contributions can help make your blog more valuable than the sum of its parts. When it comes time to build reader commenting into your blog, start your homework with the addresses shown in Table A.2. Many commenting systems launch and later close their doors when they have reached maximum capacity, but these URLs will help give you an idea of what you're looking for and point you to a solution that's good for you.

Table A.2   Commenting Systems

Title	URL	Description
Aspcomments	http://www.sneaker. org/projects/ aspcomments.shtml	Simple to set up if you already have ASP support on your web server.
BlogBack	http://www.tecknik. net/blogback/	BlogBack allows visitors to comment on your blog posts for free, without the need to host the service yourself. You don't need special web hosting. You don't need to have elite programming knowledge. You just need a blog.
blogKomm	http://www.blogkomm.com/	BlogKomm for (blogger) blogs allows the reader to place comments on your posts, but comments appear within your blog, below the posts, without any popups. Comments are stored in a text-file on your web server.
CgiComments	http://www.knurdle.com/ commenting.php	CgiComments is a Perl-based commenting system for use with blogs.

continues

Table A.2 continued

Title	URL	Description
Reblogger	`http://jsoft.ca/ reblogger.php`	Allows readers of blogs managed by Blogger to post comments on a post. Features a post counter, which indicates how many comments have been made on a certain post.
Xcomments	`http://www.groovetheory. net/xcomments/`	Xcomments is an XML-based commenting system written by Josh, of groovetheory.net. Its intended use is as a companion to blogger. As you delve into the code, however, you will find that the Xcomments system can be use for many purposes.
YACCS	`http://rateyourmusic. com/yaccs/`	If you use Blogger, then YACCS does all the work for you! But even if you don't use Blogger, adding YACCS requires you to add only two lines to your template/layout. To use YACCS, you don't need a host that supports scripting, and you don't have to know anything about programming. YACCS has currently reached maximum capacity but is an excellent example of an easy-to-add commenting system.

no new users since (handwritten annotation)

Community

Community means shared interests. Bloggers tend to form pockets of interest on the web like it's going out of style. The communities listed in Table A.3 can range from ultra simple (girls who blog) to more specific and wacky (Naked

Bloggers), but they are still groups of bloggers who have found one another through some common interest.

Table A.3   Community Blogs

Title	URL	Description
24 Hour Blogathon	`http://www.frykitty.com/blogathon/thon.html`	Blogging for charity.
BlogCon 2002	`http://www.blogcon.com/`	A bunch of bloggers decided that it'd be a fun thing for everyone to actually meet and just hang out.
The Blogger Code	`http://www.leatheregg.com/bloggercode/`	A survey to generate descriptive codes for blogs.
Blogger Insider	`http://www.realityremixed.com/bloggerinsider/`	A get-to-know-your-fellow-blogger project.
Bloggo!	`http://www.notsosoft.com/blog/bloggo.shtml`	A bingo-like game with blog clichés.
Blogster Network	`http://www.blogster.net/`	A collection of resources for bloggers.
Blogstickers	`http://www.blogstickers.com/`	A kind of community museum for stickers that you put on your blog.
Burn, Baby, Burn!	`http://www.encorswish.com/burnbabyburn.htm`	CD swap for bloggers.
Link and Think	`http://www.linkandthink.org/`	Bloggers linking to resources about HIV/AIDS or publishing personal stories about how the AIDS pandemic has affected them. Created in observation of World AIDS Day.
The Peer-to-Peer Review Project	`http://acutecut.com/p2p.html`	Bloggers review blogs.

continues

Table A.3   continued

Title	URL	Description
The WhyILog	`http://www.stormpages.com/totalchaos/whyilog.html`	Group blog where people explain why they keep blogs.
Asianlog	`http://m.webring.com/hub?ring=dotty`	Asian bloggers.
Aussie blogs	`http://nav.webring.org/cgi-bin/navcgi?ring=aussieblogs;list`	Throw another blog on the barbie.
BlogCanada Webring	`http://www.pithlog.com/webring.php`	Canadian bloggers.
Bloggers With Content - The 1%	`http://t.webring.com/hub?ring=onepercent`	For blogs with (mostly) original content.
Bloggers with Webcams	`http://nav.webring.org/cgi-bin/navcgi?ring=blogcams;list`	Bloggers with webcams.
BLOG/GIRLS	`http://f.webring.com/hub?ring=bloggirls`	Girls addicted to bloggers.
Blogphiles	`http://www.ringsurf.com/netring?ring=blogphiles;action=list`	For people who love their blogs.
Blogs By Women	`http://bonni.net/blogsbywomen/`	I am woman; read my blog.
Blogsters	`http://nav.webring.org/cgi-bin/navcgi?ring=digitalblog;list`	A web ring for Blogger blogs.
BLOG The Brunei Way	`http://t.webring.com/hub?ring=blogthebruneiway`	Bloggers from Brunei.
Blog This!	`http://u.webring.com/hub?ring=blogthis`	General Blogger/Pitas web ring.
Boylogs	`http://nav.webring.org/cgi-bin/navcgi?ring=boylogs;list`	Boys that blog.

Title	URL	Description
Christian Bloggers	`http://o.webring.com/` `hub?ring=jesusblog`	Christians who blog.
CollegeBlog Webring	`http://nav.webring.org` `/cgi-bin/navcgi?ring=` `collegeblog;list`	A web ring of college bloggers.
everything/ nothing	`http://o.webring.com/` `hub?ring=eenn`	Web ring for the E/N community.
greyLOGS/ greyJOURNALS	`http://grey.` `glory-box.com/`	For users of the Greymatter blog software.
Lord of the Rings Blog Clique	`http://q.webring.com/` `hub?ring=` `lordoftheringsbl`	For LOTR fans who blog.
Naked Bloggers	`http://www.ringsurf.` `com/netring?ring=` `nakedb;action=list`	People who have blogged naked—at least once.
No Animals Were Hurt In The Creation Of This Weblog	`http://e.webring.com/` `hub?ring=` `noanimalswerehur`	Compassionate bloggers.
NYU Blogs	`http://www.angelfire.` `com/ny/newyorkmetsfan/` `nyublogs.html`	Bloggers who attend New York University.
Scarleteen blogs	`http://n.webring.` `com/hub?ring=` `scarleteenblogs`	For registered users of scarleteen.com who blog.
Southern Bloggers	`http://nav.webring.` `org/cgi-bin/navcgi?` `ring=southernblogs;` `list`	Y'all come back now.
SpiritCircle	`http://v.webring.com/` `hub?ring=spiritcircle`	Bloggers who discuss spirituality and the like.
UW web bloggers	`http://p.webring.com/` `hub?ring=uwwebbloggers`	For bloggers from the University of Waterloo.
Verbosity	`http://www.skittish.` `org/verb.html`	For people who blog often.

continues

Table A.3   continued

Title	URL	Description
The Webloggers Webring	`http://www.jish.nu/webloggers/`	The original web ring for bloggers.
Weblogging Women	`http://d.webring.com/hub?ring=webloggingwomen`	For women with blogs or journals.
WedBlog	`http://u.webring.com/hub?ring=wedblog`	Engaged or newlywed couples blogging their marital bliss.

Directories

There are so many blogs that it can be difficult to figure out which ones you might like to investigate. Directories can help put the right blogs in the right place. Take a tour through some of the blog directories in Table A.4 if you're looking for a specific topic-based blog.

Table A.4   Blog Directories

Title	URL	Description
Bloggando	`http://www.bloggando.com/`	Italian blog directory.
Diary Registry	`http://www.diarist.net/registry/`	Good resource for finding online journals and diaries.
GBLOGS	`http://gblogs.threadnaught.net/`	A directory of blogs in the United Kingdom.
Get Linked	`http://fried-spaghetti.com/links/`	A database for blog and journal links.
Google	`http://directory.google.com/Top/Computers/Internet/On_the_Web/Weblogs/`	Google's directory of blogs.
Library weblogs	`http://www.libdex.com/weblogs.html`	Blogs for or by librarians.
Open Directory - web logs	`http://dmoz.org/Computers/Internet/On_the_Web/Web_Logs/`	Sorted by subject. Features a tools section.

Title	URL	Description
The Pepys Project	`http://pepys. akacooties.com/`	Blogs from around the world, indexed by geographical area.
Pitas.com	`http://pitas.com/ members/list. phtml?entries=50`	Latest updated Pitas sites.
[P O P B L O G]	`http://www. popblog.com/`	Directory of blogs on pop culture.
Yahoo	`http://dir.yahoo.com/ Social_Science/ Communications/Writing/ Journals_and_Diaries/ Online_Journals_and_ Diaries/Web_Logs/`	A listing of personal blogs.
Xenoblogs	`http://www.fawny. org/xenoblogs/`	Blogs from outside the USA.

Discussion

Similar to communities, mailing lists and discussions focused on the topic of blogs and blogging bring people together in the exchange of information. Table A.5 lists some of these resources. Mailing lists are great for keeping up with what's going on with a certain group—just don't join too many, or you could end up checking email six hours a day!

Table A.5   Blog Discussions

Title	URL	Description
antville2000	`http://groups.yahoo. com/group/antville2000`	Antville blog tool mailing-list.
Bbtsupport	`http://groups.yahoo. com/group/bbtsupport/`	Support list for users of Big Blog Tool.
bloggerDev	`http://groups.yahoo. com/group/bloggerDev/`	Discussion of the Blogger API.
Bloglodyte	`http://groups.yahoo. com/group/bloglodyte/`	General blog discussion.

continues

Table A.5   continued

Title	URL	Description
Blogtech	http://groups.yahoo.com/group/blogtech	Technical discussion of blog-related software.
CO-Bloggers	http://groups.yahoo.com/group/CO-Bloggers	Mailing list for Colorado bloggers.
Dutch-weblogs	http://www.egroups.com/group/dutch-weblogs/	Mailing list for Dutch bloggers. (All in Dutch.)
K-Logs	http://groups.yahoo.com/group/klogs	Blogs as knowledge management.
Pinoyblogs	http://groups.yahoo.com/group/pinoyblogs/	Filipino bloggers unite!
Swabbers	http://groups.yahoo.com/group/swabbers	Social bloggers around the San Francisco Bay.
The Weblogger User Group	http://webloggerinterestgroup.manilasites.com	Blog group in Silicon Valley.
weblogs-com	http://groups.yahoo.com/group/weblogs-com/	Developers working with the weblogs.com API.
Weblogs-Reborn	http://www.egroups.com/group/Weblogs_reborn	A place for bloggers to congregate and discuss.
weblogs-social-baltimore	http://groups.yahoo.com/group/weblogs-social-baltimore/	Social list for Baltimore-area bloggers.
weblogs-social-dc	http://groups.yahoo.com/group/weblogs-social-dc/	Social list for Washington DC area bloggers.
Weblogs2	http://www.egroups.com/group/weblogs2	Another place for bloggers to congregate and discuss.
Xanga	http://groups.yahoo.com/group/xanga/	Mailing list for Xanga users.

Blog Browsing

Like directories, blog browsing sites make it easier to find blogs you might like to check out. Sites in Table A.6 like BlogHop (which includes a rating system for blogs) are great when you just want to surf some blogs.

Table A.6   Blog Browsing

Title	URL	Description
B.L.O.G.G.E.R.N.Y.M.	`Http://web-therapy.com/bloggernym/`	Feel like part of the in-crowd by generating meaningless cryptic acronyms.
BlogHop	`http://www.bloghop.com/`	Your friendly neighborhood blog portal.
BlogView	`http://www.foreword.com/blogview/`	An interface to webcams run by bloggers.
ForumZilla	`http://forumzilla.mozdev.org/`	XUL application to read some blogs in a newsreader-like format
ISSN for Weblogs	`http://www.fawny.org/issn.html`	How to apply for an International Standard Serial Number for your blog.
Social Network Explorer	`http://blogdex.media.mit.edu/socnet/index.asp?ego=larkfarm.com`	Blogdex tool to discover the network of links between blogs.
Some Weblog	`http://zymm.com/raster/misc/someweblog.html`	The output of a Perl script that chooses one blog from the Weblog Monitor list to display each day.

Posting APIs and Tools

Bloggerdom is like a playground for tech-savvy developer types. When they get an idea in their head, there's no stopping them. Table A.7 has links to some cool tools that various blog aficionados have whipped up to make life a little more interesting.

Table A.7   Tools That Work with Blogging Applications

Title	URL	Description
Blog	`http://www.iternum.net/ developer/webservices/ blog/index.jsp`	Works with Blogger.
blogBuddy	`http://blogbuddy. sourceforge.net/`	Windows front-end to Blogger.
Bloggenmoz	`http://bloggenmoz. antville.org/topics/ download`	Blogger API support for Mozilla Composer.
Blogger-2-LiveJournal	`http://www.tswoam.co. uk/index.php?n_go=14`	CGI-based XML-RPC server that allows using Blogger API calls to post to LiveJournal.
Blogger API	`http://plant.blogger. com/api/`	Details of the XML-RPC interface to Blogger.
BloggerBot	`http://www.fibiger.org/ bloggerbot/`	AIM client for Blogger.
bloggerCOM	`http://software.caetano. com/bloggercom/`	COM interface to the Blogger API.
blogger.el	`http://mah.everybody. org/hacks/emacs/blogger. el.txt`	EMACS module to post using the Blogger API.
BlogScript	`http://www.webentourage. com/`	Mac OS X.1 tool for easy posting to Blogger-powered blogs.
fyuze	`http://fyuze.com/`	News aggregator that allows using the blogger API to port items to a blog (free account required).

Title	URL	Description
jabber-blog-it	`http://www.langreiter.com/space/jabber-blog-it`	An interface from a jabber instant messaging bot to the Blogger XML-RPC API. If you don't understand that, you don't need it.
MetaWeblog API	`http://www.xmlrpc.com/metaWeblogApi`	Userland extensions to the Blogger API.
PHPbloggerAPI	`http://www.dentedreality.com.au/bloggerapi/`	PHP implementation of the Blogger API.
Wasabii	`http://www.wasabii.org/root/`	Vendor-independent blogging API.
XML-RPC for Flash5	`http://www.wickedintellect.com/?page=flash/xmlrpc/index`	A Flash interface to Blogger.
Yet Another Weblog API Proposal	`http://weblogapi.antville.org/`	From the creators of Antville.

Blogging Software

An overview of the major blog providers is covered in Chapter 3, but the variety of software grows almost daily, and there might be a perfect fit for your needs out there. Check out some of the powerful, home-grown, and industrial-strength blogging software in Table A.8 to get an idea of what's available.

Table A.8 Some Blog Software

Title	URL	Description
Antville	`http://www.antville.org/`	Free open-source blog site.
AvantBlog	`http://www.dentedreality.com.au/avantblog/`	AvantGo interface to allow blogging from Palm and PocketPC devices.
b2	`http://www.cafelog.com`	A classy news/blog tool.

continues

Table A.8   continued

Title	URL	Description
BigBlogTool	`http://www.bigblogtool.com`	A feature-rich commercial blogging service that costs $13/year.
Blog	`http://cyberian.tripod.com/Blog.htm`	Windows-based blogging program that provides its own editing and FTP upload capabilities.
Blogger	`http://www.blogger.com/`	A popular blogging provider with many free and paid services.
Blogger Pro	`http://pro.blogger.com/`	Subscription-based version of Blogger with substantial extra features.
BlogMax	`http://billstclair.com/blogmax/index.html`	A blogging package for Emacs.
BlogWorks	`http://www.blogworks.com/`	Free ASP-based blogging application.
blos.xom	`http://www.oreillynet.com/~rael/lang/perl/blosxom/`	Lightweight Perl CGI blogging script for Mac OS X.
Blog Oriented Publishing (BOP)	`http://sourceforge.net/projects/bop/` `http://bop.sourceforge.net/`	An open-source database-backed system written in Perl. Still in early alpha and looking for contributors.
CONTENjecT Publisher	`http://www.port41.com/Publisher.jsp`	Server-side solution that uses JScript to insert blog items into your site.
Drupal	`http://www.drupal.org/`	Another Slashdot-style system released under GPL.
Facto	`http://www.facto.org/factosystem.asp`	The software behind Factovision, based on ASP and Microsoft Access.

Title	URL	Description

GeekLog	`http://sourceforge.net/`
	`projects/geeklog`
	`http://geeklog.`
	`sourceforge.net/`
		The software used by the Security Geeks web site. Focus on "performance, privacy, and security."

gir.blo.gs	`http://gir.blo.gs/`	A rough clone of Blogger.
GreyMatter	`http://noahgrey.com/` `greysoft/`	Perl-based blog tool with many advanced options including comments, karma voting, and more.
GrokSoup	`http://www.groksoup.com/`	Online blog creation tool that will provide server space. Lists sites in its directory.
Horizon	`http://3e.org/horizon/beth/`	PHP source for Just a Log. `source.php`
LiveJournal	`http://www.livejournal.com/`	Open-source journal software with free hosting.
MKDoc	`http://www.mkdoc.com/`	Apache/MySQL/Perl package with built-in standards compliance and metadata support.
Monaural Jerk	`http://www.monauraljerk.` `com/`	PHP/MySQL system for maintaining a journal or blog.
More Like This	`http://www.whump.com/` `moreLikeThis/how.html`	A blog that makes its custom PHP and MySQL code available as a gnuzipped tar archive.
Movable Type	`http://www.movabletype.org/`	Perl-based blog content management system.
NewsBruiser	`http://crummy.com/devel/` `newsbruiser/`	A blog management system written in Python.
NewsPro	`http://www.amphibianweb.` `com/newspro/`	A CGI/Perl script for maintaining an updated news page, suitable for a blog.

continues

Table A.8   continued

Title	URL	Description
Onclave	http://www.onclave.org/	An online tool and home for collaborative blogs.
Open Journal	http://www.grohol.com/ downloads/oj/	Server-based Perl script for maintaining a blog or diary.
PHP-Nuke	http://www.phpnuke.org/	PHP/MySQL/Apache based SlashDot-style system.
PHPSlash	http://www.phpslash.org/	Another open-source SlashDot-style blog, this one using PHP as its core scripting language.
PhpWebLog	http://www.phpweblog.org/	Another PHP/XML based SlashDot clone.
PikiePikie	http://pikie.darktech.org/ cgi/pikie?WebLog	Blog tool derived from WikiWiki ideas.
Pitas	http://www.pitas.com/	Online blog creation tool that will provide server space.
PithCode	http://www.pithlog.com/ pith_code.php	Blog system used by Pith and Vinegar blog; PHP and MySQL.
Pivot	http://www.mijnkopthee.nl/ pivot/	Free PHP-based blog tool.
Pmachine	http://www.pmachine.com/	PHP/MySQL system with many features beyond blog maintenance, including mailing lists and dynamic content management.
Radio Userland	http://radio.userland.com/	A powerful desktop blogging tool with features galore.
Siteframe	http://siteframe.org/	Lightweight content-management system based on PHP and MySQL.

Title	URL	Description
SlashCode	http://www.slashcode.com/	Open-source archive of the code behind SlashDot. Version 1.0 released 3/30/2000.
Slogger	http://www25.brinkster.com/dazzle/#slogger	Blog system in ASP.
SquishDot	http://squishdot.org/	Create a SlashDot-style blog (open-source, works with Zope). You'll need some Linux/UNIX savvy to get this one up and running. (MIA 11/00)
Squishy FORUMS	http://www.surrealization.com/	ASP.NET/C# blogging system.
Supasite	http://php.techno-weenie.com/	Content management system in PHP4/MySQL.
Thatware	http://www.thatware.org/	Another slash-style engine, PHP3 and MySQL- based.
Tinderbox	http://www.eastgate.com/Tinderbox/	"Personal content management assistant," commercial software for Macintosh.
Upsaid	http://www.upsaid.com/	Blog tool with comments, guest book, hit counters, and other features built in.
WebCrimson	http://www.webcrimson.com/	Industrial strength independent publishing tool with full-featured blog capabilities.
we::blog	http://www.danchan.com/weblog/	Blogging system with built-in comments and syndication.

continues

Table A.8 continued

Title	URL	Description
xanga.com	http://www.xanga.com/	Blog provider with numerous features that make blogging easy and a strong, welcoming community.
Yet Another Weblog News System	http://freshmeat.net/ projects/yawns/	Slash clone in Perl, designed to be 100% XHTML 1.0 Strict compliant.

Searching

Besides directories and browsing sites, search engines are the most obvious way to find what you are looking for. The search engines in Table A.9 are blog-specific.

Table A.9 Blog Search

Title	URL	Description
Blogdex	http://blogdex.media. mit.edu/	Not a search engine, exactly, but a project that uses the timeliness of blogs to find important and interesting content on the web.
Daypop	http://www.daypop.com	A Google-inspired search engine that focuses on news sites and blogs.
BlogHop	http://www.bloghop.com/	Allows searching and rating of blogs.
Blogtracker	http://www.dansanderson. com/blogtracker/	Lets you see when your favorite blogs have been last updated so that you can read the freshest blog entries.

Title	URL	Description
eatonweb portal	`http://portal.eatonweb.com/`	Started in early 1999 when there were less than 50 known blogs.
blogSearch	`http://markpasc.org/code/blogSearch/`	Search tool for Radio Userland.

Statistics

Because blogs have a way of digging up the web and finding the good parts, sites that seek out blogs and use their cumulative filtering power to present information that is currently popular are very useful. The sites in Table A.10 are great for seeking out "what's hot" on the web on a daily basis.

Table A.10   Statistical Projects

Title	URL	Description
Blogdex	`http://blogdex.media.mit.edu/`	Popular links determined by "crawling" blogs.
Daypop Top 40	`http://www.daypop.com/top.htm`	Most popular links in the blogging community.

Templates

Want to have a cool blog design? Want someone else to do it for you? The sites in Table A.11 point you toward some blog templates you can use as is or tweak to suit your needs. It's great when someone else does all the work.

Table A.11   Finding Templates for Your Blog

Title	URL	Description
Blog Bits	`http://tandq.com/blogbits/`	Templates for Blogger and Greymatter.
Blog Templates	`http://countryangelsgraphics.com/blog.html`	An assortment of Blogger and Greymatter templates from Country Angels Graphics.

continues

Table A.11 continued

Title	URL	Description
B8 Graphics	`http://www.b8graphics.com/blogplates.htm`	A collection of blog templates from B8 graphics for $15 each.
Point of Focus	`http://www.pointoffocus.com/Graphics/focusblogger.html`	Linkware blog templates for Blogger-powered blogs.
BlogDesigns	`http://www.blogdesigns.com/`	Brandi McHargue, Nicole Brown, Kandee Wright, and Crystal Yocum provide an "escape from bland" with a collection of linkware blog templates.
Blogger Template	`http://www.glish.com/css/blogger/`	Contest-winning CSS templates from glish.com.
Blogger Template Contest	`http://www.blogger.com/special/template_contest/winners.pyra`	Results of the contest and free templates.
Blogplates	`http://www.blogplates.net/`	A web ring of blog templates featuring tutorials.
Miz Graphics	`http://www.mizjenna.com/~mizgraphics/`	A collection of photo graphic blog templates.
EyeForBeauty	`http://www.eyeforbeauty.com/Linkware/journaltemp.html`	An extensive collection of interesting blog templates.
Blog Skins	`http://www.blogskins.com`	A site dedicated to sharing templates for Blogger users.

Text Advertising

Text advertising grew out of the blog community as a way to generate a little revenue and spread the word about blogs. Who makes the money and who spends the money depends on who is hosting ads and who is buying ad space. Table A.12 points you toward both text ad hosting services and sites selling text ads. Most of these services use online payment processing, such as that provided by Paypal.com, to make things easier.

Table A.12   Text Advertising

Title	URL	Description
Ad Farm	`http://adfarm.org/`	Advertise your site or blog in a dozen different places for $10. You can also monitor your ad's progress to see which locations are generating the best response, and make adjustments.
BlogSnob	`http://blogsnob.idya.net/`	An experimental service for members of the blogging community. It enables you to tell everyone Out There about your blog, through simple text-based ads (it's free, too).
Daypop	`http://www.daypop.com/adcenter`	Place an ad on this blog search engine: $2 for 1,000 impressions.
Flazoom.com	`http://www.flazoom.com/textads.shtml`	Text ads are priced at $2 per 1,000 impressions, with a minimum of 5,000 impressions.
Google AdWords	`https://adwords.google.com/AdWords/Welcome.html`	Current rates are $15, $12, $10 per 1,000 ads shown.
AdWords Select	`https://adwords.google.com/select/`	Google's "cost-per-click" program based on AdWords.
idya Adsystem	`http://adsystem.idya.net/`	Implement your own text ad system.
kuro5hin	`http://www.kuro5hin.org/`	Minimum purchase price: $12.
Linbo.com	`http://www.linbo.com/refer.cgi?id=912`	Free text link exchange network for bloggers.

continues

Table A.12   continued

Title	URL	Description
Mcsweetie.com	`http://www.mcsweetie.com/`	Free text ads for blogs. No reciprocal link required.
MetaFilter TextAds	`http://www.metafilter.com/ textads.mefi`	Non-invasive, non-annoying, low-cost way to get your site in front of thousands of people, to announce new projects, or boost traffic to your sites.
OliverWillis.Com	`http://chaosn.com/ advertise/`	Ads start at $2 per 1,000 ads.
pyRads	`http://www.pyrads.com/`	A service for purchasing, managing, and serving microadvertising on web sites from the makers of Blogger.
Rini.org	`http://www.rini.org/`	$10.00 for a minimum of 2,500 impressions.
skip ads	`http://w.skipintro.org/ads/`	Text advertising per le masse (in Italian).
Textad Exchange	`http://www.kalsey.com/ textad/`	Exchange micro ads with other sites. Ads use simple cut and paste HTML and Java-script code. Customizations are done with CSS.
TextAds	`http://textads. sourceforge.net/`	Open-source program that allows webmasters to offer self-serve text-based advertising to their web site users.
TextAds	`http://www.textads.nl/`	Self-service text advertising network in Dutch.
textads.biz	`http://www.textads.biz/`	A flat 10% of revenue generated from the ads is taken by the host.
TextAds.de	`http://www.textads.de/`	German text ad site.

Index

Q-R

VOICES THAT MATTER

HOW TO CONTACT US

VISIT OUR WEB SITE

WWW.NEWRIDERS.COM

On our web site, you'll find information about our other books, authors, tables of contents, and book errata. You will also find information about book registration and how to purchase our books, both domestically and internationally.

EMAIL US

Contact us at: **nrfeedback@newriders.com**

- If you have comments or questions about this book
- To report errors that you have found in this book
- If you have a book proposal to submit or are interested in writing for New Riders
- If you are an expert in a computer topic or technology and are interested in being a technical editor who reviews manuscripts for technical accuracy

Contact us at: **nreducation@newriders.com**

- If you are an instructor from an educational institution who wants to preview New Riders books for classroom use. Email should include your name, title, school, department, address, phone number, office days/hours, text in use, and enrollment, along with your request for desk/examination copies and/or additional information.

Contact us at: **nrmedia@newriders.com**

- If you are a member of the media who is interested in reviewing copies of New Riders books. Send your name, mailing address, and email address, along with the name of the publication or web site you work for.

BULK PURCHASES/CORPORATE SALES

The publisher offers discounts on this book when ordered in quantity for bulk purchases and special sales. For sales within the U.S., please contact: Corporate and Government Sales (800) 382-3419 or **corpsales@pearsontechgroup.com**. Outside of the U.S., please contact: International Sales (317) 581-3793 or **international@pearsontechgroup.com**.

WRITE TO US

New Riders Publishing
201 W. 103rd St.
Indianapolis, IN 46290-1097

CALL/FAX US

Toll-free (800) 571-5840
If outside U.S. (317) 581-3500
Ask for New Riders
FAX: (317) 581-4663

New Riders

WWW.NEWRIDERS.COM

Solutions from experts you know and trust.

www.informit.com

OPERATING SYSTEMS

WEB DEVELOPMENT

PROGRAMMING

NETWORKING

CERTIFICATION

AND MORE...

**Expert Access.
Free Content.**

New Riders has partnered with **InformIT.com** to bring technical information to your desktop. Drawing on New Riders authors and reviewers to provide additional information on topics you're interested in, **InformIT.com** has free, in-depth information you won't find anywhere else.

- **Master the skills you need, when you need them**

- **Call on resources from some of the best minds in the industry**

- **Get answers when you need them, using InformIT's comprehensive library or live experts online**

- **Go above and beyond what you find in New Riders books, extending your knowledge**

As an **InformIT** partner, **New Riders** has shared the wisdom and knowledge of our authors with you online. Visit **InformIT.com** to see what you're missing.

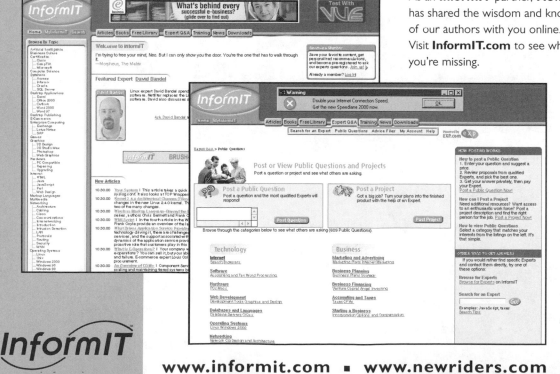

Colophon

The cover was created with Adobe Photoshop and QuarkXPress. Many people are said to believe that Biz Stone does not exist; that he is, in fact, a mythical being like Sasquatch. Steve Snider proved them all wrong when he photographed Biz for the cover of this book. The image was brought into Photoshop as a layer at 25% opacity with a Multiply Layer effect applied. The background is a four-color red (100% Magenta and 100% Yellow). The typeface used on the cover is Helvetica Inserat. Also included on the cover is a selection from Biz's own blog, www.bizstone.com. (It should also be noted that the cover does not employ "scratch n' sniff" technology, as it would not be appropriate.)

This book was written and edited in Microsoft Word, and laid out in QuarkXPress. The font used for the body text is Bembo and Mono. It was printed on 50# Husky Offset Smooth paper at VonHoffmann Inc. in Owensville, Missouri. Prepress consisted of PostScript computer-to-plate technology (filmless process). The cover was printed at Moore Langen Printing in Terre Haute, Indiana, on 12 pt., coated on one side.